AFTER THE PROTESTS ARE HEARD

RELIGION AND SOCIAL TRANSFORMATION
General Editors: Anthony B. Pinn and Stacey M. Floyd-Thomas

After the Protests Are Heard

Enacting Civic Engagement and
Social Transformation

Sharon D. Welch

NEW YORK UNIVERSITY PRESS
New York

NEW YORK UNIVERSITY PRESS
New York
www.nyupress.org

References to Internet websites (URLs) were accurate at the time of writing. Neither the author nor New York University Press is responsible for URLs that may have expired or changed since the manuscript was prepared.

Select portions of this book were published in a previous version in "In Praise of Imperfect Commitment," in *The Oxford Handbook of Professional Economic Ethics*, edited by George DeMartino and Deirdre McCloskey. Reproduced by permission of Oxford University Press, www.oup.com. Copyright 2016.

Select portions of this book were published in a previous version in "Machiavellian Dilemma," in *Tikkun Magazine*, May/June 2010, www.tikkun.com. Copyright 2010. Reproduced by permission.

Select portions of this book were published in a previous version in "Aesthetic Pragmatism and a Third Wave of Radical Politics," in *Ain't I a Womanist Too?*, edited by Monica Coleman. Fortress Press. Copyright 2013.

Select portions of this book were published in a previous version in "Audacity, Virtuosity and Wonder," in *A People So Bold*, edited by John Gibb Millspaugh. Boston: Skinner Books. Copyright 2010.

Library of Congress Cataloging-in-Publication Data
Names: Welch, Sharon D., author.
Title: After the protests are heard : enacting civic engagement
and social transformation / Sharon D. Welch.
Description: New York : New York University Press, [2019] |
Series: Religion and social transformation |
Includes bibliographical references and index.
Identifiers: LCCN 2018012215| ISBN 9781479883646 (cl : alk. paper) |
ISBN 9781479857906 (pb : alk. paper)
Subjects: LCSH: Social justice. | Social change. | Political participation. | Democracy.
Classification: LCC HM671 .W46 2019 | DDC 303.3/72—dc23
LC record available at https://lccn.loc.gov/2018012215

New York University Press books are printed on acid-free paper, and their binding materials are chosen for strength and durability. We strive to use environmentally responsible suppliers and materials to the greatest extent possible in publishing our books.

Manufactured in the United States of America

10 9 8 7 6 5 4 3 2 1

Also available as an ebook

For Zoë, Hannah, Meg, and HK, my companions
on the journey

CONTENTS

Introduction

The Soul of Democracy

There are moments in history when there are major breakthroughs in the power of social movements. Large numbers of people recognize the depth of injustice, see possibilities of beauty and integrity heretofore unknown, and find new forms of coming together to bring about change. We are living in such a time.

We also live in a time of genuine threat—rising authoritarianism, racism, and xenophobia, increasing environmental degradation, morally unconscionable income and wealth disparities, a dangerously militarized police force, and a criminal justice system that disproportionately targets people who are African American, Native American, and Latinx. Moreover, we are confronting ongoing threats of war and terrorism, escalating Islamophobia, and a national political system that is largely ineffective, paralyzed by increasingly high levels of division and polarization.

We are in a struggle for the very soul of democracy, and all that we hold dear—interdependence, reason, compassion, respect for all human beings, and stewardship of the natural world that sustains us—is under direct, unabashed assault. The words of the sociologist and writer Michael Eric Dyson in *Tears We Cannot Stop: A Sermon to White America* are telling: "We have, in the span of a few years, elected the nation's first black president and placed in the Oval Office the scariest racial demagogue in a generation. . . . The remarkable progress we seemed to make with the former has brought out the peril of the latter."[1]

This book is meant for those who are concerned about dangers to our democracy and to our social health as a nation. It is for those who desire to work for social justice, and to respond to essential protests by enacting progressive change. In this book, we will take up three essential challenges. First, we will confront head on why expansive social change has been followed by increases in violence and authoritarianism. Second, we will examine how we as a nation might more fully acknowledge the brutal costs of racism and the historical drivers of racial injustice. And, third, once aware of these dynamics, we will examine how people of all races can take up our roles in containing such violence in the present and preventing its resurgence in the future. This book focuses directly on the ethical challenges faced by those people who have a measure of social and economic power—those who have found themselves in positions to shape political, economic, and educational policies and practices. We can use our power responsibly and collaboratively to work for a genuinely inclusive democracy. We can confront both the scope of white violence and the depth of our dependence upon Americans of all races for the very ideals of a democracy that fully expresses the values of liberty and justice for all.

First, let us address in more detail the scope and depth of the threat that we are facing at this juncture in history. Many people throughout the world were profoundly heartened by the election and then reelection of President Barack Obama in 2008 and 2012. Though there were media reports and musings by pundits and citizens about the inauguration of a "post-racial" society, the signs of ongoing racism were all too clear—the relentless Republican obstruction of his leadership and the explicitly racist and demeaning personal attacks on both him and on First Lady Michelle Obama. Many continued to point to the ongoing serious problems of structural racism in our nation, as manifest in mass incarceration, educational and income inequality, and the debilitating social and political effects of implicit bias.

As political philosopher Iris Marion Young has argued, it seemed that we were in a time in history in which injustice was perpetuated primarily through systems rather than through systems and individual hatred and fear.[2] The explicit racism, sexism, and hatred of the Trump campaign in 2016 appeared to represent the death throes of white supremacy, not its possible birth pangs. I certainly did not expect to see the return of explicit racial hatred on a large scale—the resurgence of the Ku Klux Klan, of neo-Nazis, and of campaigns on college campuses nationwide for a white identity politics that explicitly advocates for white supremacy. Nor did I expect to see blatant denials of the scope and depth of the racist violence of the past.

Perversely, what eases my shock at the rise of authoritarianism and explicit racism is the realization that it did not rise in spite of the best efforts of all progressives to contain it. In fact, it is my contention that it rose for just the opposite reason. Many of us, as whites, did not work with our fellow African American, Latinx, Native American, and Asian American citizens to do what was needed to stop its resurgence now and to prevent its rise in the future.

In the face of these rising threats, my stance—and the motivating premise of this book—is not despair but awakening. It can be that bad again. There can be lynchings, hate crimes, and other forms of white violence against people of color. White activists who are committed to racial justice were not doing enough to stop the rise of explicit racism and hatred, and we can and must and will do more. While we decried the devastating impact of structural racism and implicit bias, many of us thought that there was a threshold below which we would not go. That we have gone below it is for many of us a challenge to our basic under-standings of human nature, of the relationship between good and evil, and the multiple dimensions of social change.

There are tasks that we have not taken up that are essential in sustain-ing a fully inclusive and expansive democracy, and there are tasks that we have pursued, but not as completely, not with as much creativity and persistence as is necessary. This book offers insight into how to expand what we know works to create justice, and on how to enter into new areas of research and experimentation in an effort to contain the worst cruelty and folly of humankind.

Here is our challenge. How do we learn from what is going well how to respond, with courage, creativity, and persistence, to genuine threats and growing dangers? How do those who have achieved positions of institutional power—in corporations, on university campuses, within religious organizations, and beyond—take up the task of transforming those institutions' structures and practices to foster justice and equal-ity? How do we challenge assaults on the fundamental rights of an in-formed and equal citizenry, and on the essential principles of checks and balances between the various branches of government? The first step is simple—looking with both a critical and an appreciative eye at the many manifestations of constructive civic engagement that grace our world. What are the ethical values, the tactics, and the strategies that enable people to live out their highest values? The second step is more difficult. How do we apply these lessons, how do we honor these constructive efforts, as we engage on the ground with challenges that are seemingly intractable?

In the pages that follow we will take up both tasks, exploring examples of constructive civic engagement and gleaning insights for models they may offer for our own work for social justice. We will also examine the ethical challenges of such work and evolving theories of what enables constructive social change.

Both the grave challenges and inspiring opportunities that confront us are equally real. In addition to rising threats of hatred and violence, we are also currently immersed in a constructive wave of political engagement in which people throughout the world are working together to address basic issues of environmental risk and social inequality. This is a third wave of progressive political engagement that is increasingly influential, and it is only possible because of the ongoing power of the first two waves of progressive politics.

The first wave of progressive politics was the forceful denunciation of manifold forms of social injustice—slavery, the oppression of workers, and the secondary status of women—all systems of social control defended for millennia as divinely ordained or as part of the natural order of things. These struggles for social justice were augmented by a second wave of activism, the work of identity politics, the resolute claim for the complex identities and full humanity of people with disabilities; those who are gay, lesbian, bisexual, and transgender; and ethnic, racial, and religious minorities—all deprived of cultural respect and full political participation. Within these two ongoing waves of political activism, people are exposing and denouncing with power and courage the five forms of oppression identified by the political philosopher Iris Marion Young: exploitation, marginalization, powerlessness, cultural imperialism, and violence.[3]

I find it ironic that I began my career as an activist and academic as an outsider calling for social change—declaring that the nuclear arms race was a test of faith, seeing the political and ethical challenges of what many of us perceived as the increased likelihood of nuclear war and the possible end of all life on the planet.

Today, I am an insider. From my perspective inside academic halls of power, I see us as experiencing another test of faith. This time, it is not one of refusing to see danger. This time it is the inability to see real and rising danger, and to see as well equally real progress and profound opportunities. While the critical work of denouncing social injustice and striving for the full recognition of human rights for all peoples goes on, these tasks now occur within a third wave of pragmatic political activism. Once we recognize that a situation is unjust, once we know who should be included, how then do we work together to go about actually enacting change?

Like many activists, I know firsthand the appeal of speaking truth to power: the inspiration and sense of identity evoked by clarion denunciations of injustice and faithful witness to ideals of justice and peace. As first a director of women's studies, department chair, and then provost, I have confronted personally and collectively another reality—one as stark but more ambiguous—the painful discovery that to care passionately about injustice does not mean that we, the "revolutionary vanguard," are equally skilled in the task of coordinating and managing human and natural resources justly, creatively, and in a way that lasts for the future. As we take up the task of using power truthfully, we recognize that the work is not done when the protests are heard. Rather it is here, it is now, that another, equally difficult type of work begins.

This book focuses on the enactment of progressive politics. How do we translate the recognition that a situation is unjust into tangible political change, creative forms of civic engagement, and more just social institutions? This book offers examples of the work for social justice that is being done on the ground in such arenas as criminal justice reform, environmental sustainability, and economic life. It explores the work of corporations that pay attention to social justice, not just profit, and of universities that engage with communities to solve shared social challenges. It offers concrete examples of how the work in enacting social change is being accomplished by insiders who have both the power and responsibility to enact fundamental institutional change. It showcases how various individuals, corporations, and other entities are embracing opportunities to transform institutional practices and structures to foster justice and equality. And it also addresses the ethical challenges and political responsibilities of those managers and owners who are instituting such just economic practices.

This constructive work of responding to protests by implementing new policies and creating new social structures requires an ethic of risk. As we embrace the artistry of multiracial and cross-cultural partnership and leadership to enhance the common good, we know that unpredictable and unforeseen consequences are the norm. We must create cultures of honest accountability and generative critique, learning as much from our unpredictable mistakes as from our catalytic successes. This work extends, therefore, the argument that I made in *The Feminist Ethic of Risk.*[4] I wrote that book early in my career from the perspective of an outsider demanding social change. This book is written from the point of view of insiders who have both the power and the responsibility to respond to protests by enacting fundamental institutional change. Its goal is to help scholars, students, and activists who are focused on enhancing progressive social change, and who are in need of models for how to bring their desires for such change into reality. It illuminates a range of work already being enacted for social justice with the aim of helping readers to explore how they too can bring about, sustain, inspire, and support such work.

In order to fully live out the promise of constructive political and social change, it is important that we also fully acknowledge a fourth wave of catalytic social engagement. To engage in the other three waves of political engagement with genuine accountability and the utmost creativity requires that we see, name, and contain our constitutive and intrinsic forms of evil.

It is here that we have much to learn from the work of Carol Lee Sanchez. Sanchez is of Pueblo and Lebanese descent, raised in the Laguna Pueblo, and an author, artist, and retired professor of American Indian studies. In her writing and in her teaching, Sanchez shared with us the fundamental insight that the indigenous respect for the natural order is not simply natural, and, in fact, is just the opposite. Reverence for the natural world is learned from hard-won lessons of what had gone wrong when there was a lack of respect for both the natural and the social order. Respect is maintained only through two ongoing social processes—telling the stories of environmental degradation and social inequity, and checking the tendencies to repeat those patterns through specific rituals. In her teaching and writing, Sanchez did not share with us the rituals that were used by the people of the Laguna Pueblo, but encouraged us to tell our own stories of disruption and to create our own rituals of respect and belonging, our own recognition of the necessity and power of the Beauty Way.[5]

We find the same wisdom offered by Robin Wall Kimmerer. Kimmerer is a botanist and a member of the Potawatomi Nation. We will explore what she calls the "original instructions," the challenge to shape our lives as individuals and as a society by seeing the responsibilities and gifts that come with our place in the natural order.[6] In addition, however, to seeing our gifts, and learning to use them in responsible ways, Kimmerer challenges us to see and check our constitutive evil. She tells the story of the Windigo, a person driven by greediness with a heart as cold as ice, only focused on his or her own needs. Once focused only on one's own needs, the longing for more becomes both insatiable and ruthless, even leading one to experience pleasure in taking from others and causing pain to others.[7]

Kimmerer provides a compelling account of the way in which the Windigo shapes the lives of so many of us, not only indigenous peoples. She sees the Windigo at the core of rapacious globalization and exploitative and extractive capitalism. The wisdom here is pointed. We can see this greed and violence and contain it in others, and we must see it and contain it in ourselves:

> Gratitude for all the earth has given us lends us courage to turn and face the Windigo that stalks us, to refuse to participate in an economy that destroys the beloved earth to line the pockets of the greedy, to demand an economy that is aligned with life, not stacked against it. It's easy to write that, harder to do.[8]

While we can find antidotes to the Windigo, we cannot destroy the ongoing threat of isolation and insatiable greed. The Windigo remains as a recurring temptation that can lead us away from a respectful grounding in the social and natural plenitude that could sustain us.[9]

Now, here is the crucial lesson. What are our other forms of evil and injustice? For those of us who are white, what are the forms of evil that prevented us from seeing the humanity of the indigenous peoples of the

Americas, the humanity and dignity of the African people we so readily and cruelly enslaved, that led us to the exploitation of both the natural world and of the human resources of those people of all races who were seen primarily as labor to be used, rather than as fellow human beings to respect?

It is clear that we too, have been and are shaped by the Windigo spirit of greed and domination. Our task, then, is threefold—first, how do we honestly tell the histories of this exploitation? Second, how do we identify other forms of intrinsic evil that have shaped our collective lives and limited our moral imagination? Third, how can we learn to check all of our Windigos earlier rather than later?

Here is the challenge. I have not found the political science that demonstrates empirically the constitutive weaknesses of white liberals who are committed to constructive social change. What I have to offer are hypotheses for further research, and invite you to join me in this process. These are hypotheses based in my lifelong work as an activist that will be explored in more detail in each of the following chapters.

The first danger is obvious—the consumerist Windigo. Although liberals and progressives are rightly critical of the social and environmental costs of extractive capitalism and exploitative consumerism, it takes ongoing effort to shape our lives by "belonging, rather than belongings."[10]

A second moral danger is clear, and is demonstrated in the research on liberalism. We may be tempted to choose excessive forms of individualism, of isolated self-assertion, rather than finding our freedom and creativity in collaboration and mutual respect.

A third danger is manifest in much of our organizing and political activism. All too often progressive and liberal activists turn the strengths of successful nonviolent resistance movements into weaknesses. We defeat ourselves by fighting over strategies and tactics, rather than finding ways to create resonances between varied and multifaceted forms of political and communal engagement.

A fourth danger is remaining unaware of our own capacity for error and partiality. We can be morally pure but strategically inept, and when that happens we lose.

A fifth danger is our failure to take on the multiple expressions of racism and checking these in our personal, civic, and professional lives. We must confront both the ongoing dangers of implicit bias and structural racism as well as the resurgence of violent and virulent racism by white Americans against people who are African American, Latinx, Asian American, Muslim, and Native American. Both threats require deliberate and sustained attention, analysis, and activism.

A sixth danger, closely related to the fifth, is the utopian expectation of definitive revolutionary change, or linear and assured progress. We can become complacent about the solidity of hard-fought social gains. When this happens, we fail to be vigilant guardians of an expansive democracy that genuinely embodies liberty and justice for all.

A seventh danger is just the opposite of the sixth. When total change is not possible, we can be discouraged from creatively working with partial successes. How do we avoid reforms that divert us from the work of expansive social justice? How do we use partial victories as the catalysts for more work for justice? How do we avoid both the complacency of mere reform and the illusion of definitive revolutionary change?

Let us return to the words of Michael Eric Dyson: *To replace racial demagoguery with expansive and inclusive democracy requires that we remain vigilant in our work for justice.* When we no longer expect linear assured progress or passively endure pendulum swings between authoritarianism and progressivism, we can become responsible makers of history, resolutely nurturing our best and creatively containing our worst.

Given the profound political and ethical challenges and opportunities of our time, this book is one of mourning, rage, and critique, and it is also one of profound gratitude for all those who are living for justice as citizens, activists, neighbors, parents, workers, managers, owners, and investors. The stories offered in this book provide examples of the critical work being done in an effort to create generative interdependence: a community that fully values diversity and connection, that nurtures creativity and scientific rigor, and that embodies responsibility for others and the freedom to find new and better ways of living out, and creating, expansive human communities of connection, respect, and cooperation.

In this book, we will explore the worlds of social enterprise, impact investing, and other attempts to create economic systems that are environmentally sound and economically just. We will study the way in which universities and colleges are educating students to be critical participants in creating a truly just and sustainable social order. In each of these instances, activists are working from positions of power within institutions to transform institutional practices and structures to foster justice and equality. Their work, "after the protests are heard," aims at actually enacting social change once injustices are brought to light. These institutional insiders are living out a shift in honor codes—principles by which members of societies hold themselves and others in particular regard. They are responding to rallying cries against injustice by instituting changes in policy and practice, and in so doing are helping to foster a convergence of ideas within our society around right, just, and appropriate forms of constructive civic engagement.

At the core of democracy is respect for the rights of all, and, what is of equal importance, a recognition of the limits of all. We are all partial, fallible, and capable of the misuse or abuse of power to serve the needs of the few rather than the good of the many. We need checks and balances to address the possible misuse of power; we need multiple voices and perspectives to address the partiality of our knowledge and the mistakes in our reasoning.

In 2016, Thomas Mann and Norman Ornstein issued an updated version of their insightful and definitive 2012 analysis of the forces leading to the erosion of the democratic process in the United States. Our electoral system and our governing institutions are paralyzed by increasing polarization and division. In that book, and in the follow-up volume written with E. J. Dionne Jr., *One Nation after Trump: A Guide for the Perplexed, the Disillusioned, the Desperate, and the Not-Yet-Deported*, they provide an essential guide to what it takes to "bring democracy to life."[11] The tasks are multiple; the tasks are all of equal importance: ending gerrymandering and voter suppression, removing the dysfunctional role of money in politics, changing the Electoral College system, honoring our governmental system of checks and balances, and finding ways to deliberate across differences in service of the larger common good. All of these tasks are necessary "to reclaim the dignity of public life and the honor of democratic politics."[12]

The unravelling of democracy has occurred over decades. It will take time and ongoing vigilance to restore an electoral system and processes of governance that fully embody generative interdependence. There are many places in our society where the soul of democracy is being expressed, and places where it is under fundamental assault. We can amplify the energy of the former and use it to transform and contain the latter.

* * *

Note to the reader: This book incorporates a number of examples of professionals involved in institutional and social change. These vignettes were written by Lynda Sutherland, and are based on interviews, some conducted by Sutherland alone, and some by myself and Sutherland. Her contributions will be indicated each time with an endnote.

1

A Declaration of Interdependence

The Science of Democracy

To appreciate the many challenges of social justice work, we must first understand the specific situation in which it is happening. Our context is one of growing threats, resilient critique, and deeply rooted alternative forms of inclusive and expansive social life. We are now experiencing a rise of authoritarianism in the United States that is as dangerous as the anticommunism of the McCarthy era of the 1950s, potentially as deadly as the eradication of basic political and human rights for African Americans after the Reconstruction period following the Civil War. We are also witnessing a resurgence in authoritarianism not seen in Europe since the rise of fascism in the 1930s.

Within the world of political science there is a well-established analysis of what activates authoritarianism. This analysis is both challenging in what it discloses and profoundly evocative in what it fails to see.

First—what it discloses. According to many political scientists there is a significant proportion of the human population that remains authoritarian. There is also a larger subset of the population whose authoritarianism is episodic, not constitutive, and is evoked under conditions of normative threat and extensive social change.[1]

Authoritarians perceive the world as a threatening place, and value community based on hierarchy, order, and sameness. They seek and respect leaders who are "simple, powerful and punitive."[2] Authoritarians also take deep satisfaction in violence against those perceived as threatening and inferior. The political scientists Marc Hetherington and Jonathan Weiler provide a stark summary of the core characteristics of authoritarianism, describing it "as a social attitude, composed of three clusters—submission, conventionalism, and aggression." Equally salient to authoritarianism is "a tendency toward intolerance predicated upon one's need for social conformity and, consequently, aggression toward those perceived as threatening the status quo." And, a fundamental driver of this aggression and intolerance is "a need for order" and a lack of "tolerance for ambiguity."[3]

According to these political scientists, there is a strong tendency toward authoritarianism, nationally and internationally, that is activated at times of perceived threat and extensive social change.[4] While this seems to be a salient characteristic of human communities worldwide, in the United States authoritarianism has long been expressed in virulent racist attitudes and physical attacks against people who are African Americans and Latinx, and it is now being manifest also in attacks on Muslim citizens and refugees.[5]

Political scientist Karen Stenner argues that authoritarians are characterized by a desire for group cohesion, and that the "attitudinal and behavioral consequences of authoritarianism" are "racial, political, and moral intolerance," all enforced through punitive measures.[6] She also states that there is a basic divide between a desire for group cohesion and individual autonomy and freedom.[7] She describes these political options as a divide between authoritarianism and libertarianism, and her prognosis for a genuinely democratic society is grim. She goes so far as to conclude that the pace of social change must be curtailed and that democracy itself has to be limited in order to survive, and she challenges us, therefore, to forego the "religion of democracy for the science of democracy."[8] Given this intrinsic disconnect between democratic aspirations and human longings and desires, Stenner claims that democracy has to be limited in both the pace and scope of social change.

> If there are inherent predispositions to intolerance of difference, if citizens so predisposed pop up in *all* societies, and if those predispositions are actually activated by the experience of living in a vibrant democracy, then freedom feeds fear that undermines freedom, and democracy is its own undoing. The overall lesson is clear: when it comes to democracy, less is often more, or at least more secure. We can do all the moralizing we like about how we want our ideal democratic citizens to be. But democracy is most secure, and tolerance is maximized, when we design systems to accommodate how people actually are. Because some people will never live comfortably in a modern liberal democracy.[9]

If Stenner is right, gains in civil rights, equality for women, people who are LGBTQIA (lesbian, gay, bisexual, transgender, queer, intersex and asexual), and those with disabilities, as well as increasing racial, cultural, and religious diversity, will inevitably produce authoritarianism. Stenner is not alone in seeing a disturbing connection between social progress and social regression. Other researchers agree, finding that there is a tension between the desire for social order and the expansion of freedom. For example, the journalist Amanda Taub claims that "the forces activating American authoritarians seem likely to only grow stronger. Norms around gender, sexuality, and race will continue evolving. Movements like Black Lives Matter will continue chipping away at the country's legacy of institutionalized discrimination, pursuing the kind of social change and reordering of society that authoritarians find so threatening."[10]

While this political science is clear in its diagnosis of what activates the resurgence of authoritarianism, its findings are also fundamentally flawed and intrinsically limited, and here is our hope, here is our task. There are two significant defects in the current research on authoritarianism. The first is intrinsic to the ways in which our basic political values are measured. Authoritarianism is measured not by political beliefs, but by childrearing values that are then correlated with specific political positions. Before we proceed further, I ask you to join me in an experiment. What are four childrearing values that you think are most important? After you consider these, let us turn to the choices that are posed in the existing research.

The study used by Karen Stenner sets the following values in opposition to each other, and asks people to choose one over another.[11]

Obeying one's parents	Thinking for oneself
Respecting elders	Following one's conscience
Following the rules	Exercising good judgment
Being well-mannered	Being responsible for one's own actions
Being neat and clean	Being interested in how and why things happen

This is a second scale, utilized by Marc Hetherington and Jonathan Weiler:[12]

Respect for elders	Independence
Obedience	Self-reliance
Good manners	Curiosity
Well behaved	Considerate

Do you notice anything missing in both sets of choices? Are there other values that you hold central?

I have asked this question of audiences throughout the United States, and the answers are clear. What is missing? Kindness, cooperation, a commitment to justice and fairness, empathy, compassion, service to and with others, delight in helping people and in helping others grow. Moreover, values in both Stenner's and Hetherington and Weiler's scales that are set in opposition actually sustain and evoke each other. For example, being well mannered because we are considerate, or respecting our elders because they nurtured our independence.

Let me be clear. The fundamental flaw is not in the correlation of childrearing values and political beliefs. The flaw is in the limited range of childrearing values that are offered by these political scientists for consideration. Neither of these widely used scales names options that may well correlate with other views of social pluralism, individual freedom and individual responsibility, and group cohesion.

The measures used by Stenner, for example, incorporate nothing about our attitudes toward others. The choice is that of cohesive community based on obedience and uniformity or progress grounded in individual freedom and creativity. There is nothing about individual creativity expressed in helping others, or in working with others for common goals. The more current research by Hetherington and Weiler is slightly better in this regard. One of their measures does entail attitudes toward others—consideration. They pose it, however, as the opposite of being well behaved, rather than imagining that the motivation for good behavior is consideration of others.

Stenner sees people as existing on a spectrum of authoritarianism and libertarianism, seeking either cohesive community or emancipated individualism. Missing from this dichotomy is what many of us honor and uphold: the desire for generative interdependence, a community that fully values diversity and connection, that nurtures creativity and scientific rigor, that embodies responsibility for others and the freedom to find new and better ways of living out, and creating, expansive human communities of connection, respect, and cooperation.

The second flaw in this research is that the data is not broken down by race. This is significant because we find in much of the work of people who are African American, Latinx, and Native American a very different view of social order. Here we find traditions in which the choice is not cohesive community or diversity, not coherent communities or emancipated individualism. The real choice is that of a cohesive order based on creativity and collective problem solving or a cohesive community based on hierarchy, violence, control, and sameness.[13]

Even Stenner's qualitative research shows the flaws of her own and her colleagues' quantitative measures. In interviews with people who measured as most libertarian, interviewers found them to be deeply connected with others, appreciating "their friends, neighbors, their social lives," and "courteous and respectful of others."[14] It is clear that these people do not care only about themselves. They are genuinely interested in others, eager to learn from them and to explore new ideas with them.[15] This is not just a libertarian pursuit of individual freedom and a disregard for community. It is, rather, a different way of being in deep community.

What we who are liberal and progressive embody at our best is a beloved community of generative interdependence. There are alternatives to either emancipated individualism or authoritarian community based on fear, exclusion, domination, and control. At this moment in history we can and are combatting authoritarianism and exercising countervailing power. We are living for justice and saying no to hatred: no in our votes; no in our laws; no in our policies.

And yet it is vital to remember that our no to hatred, fear, and violence is grounded in a deep, generative, and expansive yes: a yes to difference; a yes to the richness of diversity, to the gift of reason, to the joy of cooperation, to the deep soul satisfaction of compassion.

As Cory Booker, U.S. senator from New Jersey, stated at the Democratic National Convention in 2016, we have not just a declaration of independence, but one of interdependence. Community cohesion can be based on the exclusion of outsiders, on clear rules, lack of change, and obedience to authoritarian leaders who are simple, punitive, and powerful. But cohesion can also have a radically different shape. You may also know the saying that my mother had above her desk: "There are only two gifts that we can give our children, roots and wings."

What is missing in much of the literature on authoritarianism is a recognition that what fuels interdependent creativity and expansive civic engagement is not emancipated individualism but openness to the new grounded in the solidity of the same. The "same" is generative connections between adults and youth, and community practices of resilience, acknowledging and learning from both mistakes and successes.

Current research on the moral foundations of conservatism and of liberalism is addressing just this lack. Yet, once again, this research is both valuable for what it measures and evocative in what it fails to see.

First, what it measures. The psychologists Jeffrey S. Sinn and Matthew W. Hayes criticize the Moral Foundations Theory developed by psychologists Jesse Graham, Jonathan Haidt, and Brian Nosek. Sinn and Hayes argue that MFT "misconstrues both morality and ideology." They summarize the conclusions of Moral Foundations Theory as follows:

> Moral Foundations Theory (MFT) attempts to explain all moral motivation and the differences between liberals and conservatives with five moral foundations. According to MFT, liberals rely primarily on two 'individualizing" foundations (Harm/Care and Fairness/Reciprocity), whereas conservatives rely on these plus three additional "binding" foundations (Authority/Respect, Ingroup/Loyalty, and Purity/Sanctity.)[16]

Sinn and Hayes argue that Moral Foundations Theory is a mischaracterization of both liberalism and conservatism. Rather than seeing liberalism as primarily a concern with individualism, they have found

> [t]hat the moral commitments of liberalism are much broader, endorsing nature, reason, and diversity as moral sources (Taylor 1992). Further, we believe liberalism entails a broader sociality as well and even motivates the setting of limits on individuals to serve the common good.[17]

In their studies, they found that liberals are more likely than conservatives to subsume individual concerns for a larger collective good. They find, therefore, a richer understanding of liberalism than that measured by either Karen Stenner or by Jonathan Haidt. Sinn and Hayes find that the choice is not community or individualism, but a conservative closed community based on hierarchy and exclusion or a liberal community based on respect, curiosity, and responsibility.

> [L]iberals are not anti-community but rather prefer a broader, less provincial form of community. In fact, liberals appear ready to restrict individualism on a number of issues (i.e. gun ownership, housing choice, car choice, and private property rights) for broader social goals, thus undermining MFT's depiction of liberalism as mere individualism.[18]

Sinn and Hayes argue that Moral Foundations Theory misses both the strengths of liberalism and the intrinsic dangers of the type of binding community valued within conservatism. Their studies show that the choice of "binding" community was also "correlated with fear and hostility towards outgroups, a result disputing the purely prosocial, selfishness-suppression logic of the 'binding' label."[19] Within conservatism we do not merely find cohesive communities based on order and respect. Far from it. Cohesion is based on devaluing and dominating others. Sinn and Hayes find at the core of conservatism "an intragroup or defensive ethnocentrism, emphasizing ethnic devotion, collective security, and cohesion" and "intergroup ethnocentrism stressing superiority, exploitation, and group-based dominance."[20]

Sinn and Hayes also see strengths in liberalism not recognized by these other psychologists. They claim that liberalism is best understood not as an individualizing motivation, but as universalizing motivation, one that "resists within-group exploitation" and "alpha-domination" and favors instead "broader, more inclusive communities." They see the Enlightenment expanding this sense of morality, one in which reasoning is valued, the natural order is respected, and diversity is seen, not as a threat, but as a moral good.[21]

The research of Sinn and Hayes is extremely valuable in laying out the challenges before us. Yet, again, it is equally evocative in what is left out. Sinn and Hayes point out the constitutive risks of conservatism, but, while acknowledging that liberalism "may cause other problems," they do not specify what those problems might be.[22]

What are the fundamental dangers and constitutive limitations and risks of liberalism and generative interdependence? As stated earlier, what are our "Windigos," our fundamental failings? One of our challenges is learning how to more effectively convey the power of generative interdependence and live it out more thoroughly in our businesses, our schools, our parenting, and our civic lives. Then, how do we honestly recognize, and reckon with, the constitutive and ongoing forms of human cruelty and folly of those liberals and progressives committed to an expansive and just democratic order?[23] Another of our basic challenges lies in working with different ways of implementing shared values, and fully recognizing that ideological purity does not necessarily lead to tactical success.

The current research in political science is compelling, but it is incomplete. I have yet to find rigorous studies of the intrinsic limitations of liberalism, progressivism, and generative interdependence. I believe that there can be a deeper science, not a religion, of democracy that enables us not just to maintain, but even to expand, the pace and scope of inclusive democratic practices. For example, Van Jones, the founder of Green for All, an organization "that promotes green jobs for disadvantaged communities," calls us to an American Dream that includes economic and social equity, environmental sustainability, and racial justice.

> We want to build a green economy strong enough to lift people out of poverty. . . . We want to ensure that those communities that were locked out of the last century's pollution-based economy will be locked in to the new clean and green economy. We know that we don't have any throwaway species or resources, and we know that we can't have any throwaway children or neighborhoods either. All of creation is precious and sacred. And we are all in this together.[24]

This dream of "a cross-race and cross-class partnership," a "Green New Deal," does not have to be invented. It is real. It is practiced in the multiple efforts of social enterprises, in B corporations, in engagement scholarship, and in criminal justice reform. It can be taken to all communities, rural and suburban, as well as urban.[25] The challenge for liberals is clear: in our focus on what is wrong, we are frequently not as evocative in sharing what may be right. The dream that is offered by Jones is grounded in actual economic practices. With its commitment to racial justice, it also builds on what is so crucial for the creation of sustainable and inclusive communities in the United States, acknowledging the role of racist exploitation in past and current forms of economic and political life.

What is missing in much of the literature on what fuels deep community is an openness to the new, grounded in the solidity of the same. One dimension of the "solidity of the same" is honesty: not honesty as only pointing out the flaws of others, but honesty as recognizing and acknowledging our mistakes, our own complicity and agency in structures and systems of injustice. There can be an honest reckoning with the evils of the past and present. We can acknowledge the ways in which many groups have done grave harm to others and will do so again without a social contract of ongoing checks to human capacities for exploitation and violence. Here let us look at the writer Ta-Nehisi Coates's compelling critique of the American Dream.

In his elegiac text, *Between the World and Me*, written as a letter to his 15-year-old son, Ta-Nehisi Coates describes the power of the white American Dream—a vision of the social good that denies the history and present of racist exploitation that has been crucial to economically sustain that Dream. In short, it is a dream that is not honest.

> This is the foundation of the Dream—its adherents must not just believe in it but believe that it is just, believe that their possession of the Dream is the natural result of grit, honor, and good works. There is some passing acknowledgment of the bad old days, which, by the way, were not so bad as to have any ongoing effect on our present. The mettle that it takes to look away from the horror of our prison system, from police forces transformed into armies, from the long war against the black body, is not forged overnight. This is the practiced habit of jabbing out one's eyes and forgetting the work of one's hands. To acknowledge these horrors means turning away from the brightly rendered version of your country as it has always declared itself and turning toward something murkier and unknown. It is still too difficult for most Americans to do this. But that is your work. It must be, if only to preserve the sanctity of your mind.[26]

Not only is it a Dream that is not honest, it is Dream that resolutely and repeatedly denies the magnitude of the violence and systemic and structural exploitation of slavery, segregation, and mass incarceration.

The forgetting is habit, is yet another necessary component of the Dream. They have forgotten the scale of theft that enriched them in slavery; the terror that allowed them, for a century, to pilfer the vote; the segregationist policy that gave them their suburbs.

Perhaps that was, is, the hope of the movement: to awaken the Dreamers, to rouse them to the facts of what their need to be white, to talk like they are white, to think that they are white, which is to think that they are beyond the design flaws of humanity, has done to the world.[27]

Ta Nehisi-Coates's alternatives for Black Americans are to acknowledge their own flaws and to resist the white Dream: "I would not have you descend into your own dream. I would have you be a conscious citizen of this terrible and beautiful world."[28]

Coates's challenge to white Americans is also clear. He tells his son:

> But do not struggle for the Dreamers. Hope for them. Pray for them, if you are so moved. But do not pin your struggle on their conversion. The Dreamers will have to learn to struggle themselves, to understand that the field for their Dream, the stage where they have painted themselves white, is the deathbed of us all. The Dream is the same habit that endangers the planet, the same habit that sees our bodies stowed away in prisons and ghettos.[29]

This book is meant to enable readers to take on this challenge with honesty and creativity, aware of the particularity of our experiences as members of different racial and social groups, and as members of different economic classes. First, we must be honest, acknowledging the scale of racist exploitation and its ongoing impact. Will we learn from the past and present structures of white exploitation and violence? Will we learn how to check these practices in the present? In later chapters, we will explore what it takes to do just that, drawing on the work of Daniel Kahneman, Albert Bandura, Carol Lee Sanchez, Leslie Marmon Silko, and studies of administrative evil.

The check to ongoing and future exploitation (and incremental reforms that do not go far enough) is not the purity of our ideals and the rigor of our critiques but the resilience of our communities—our abilities to learn from and with each other, to work with each other, to see and learn from unintended mistakes and unexpected success. Here we have an ongoing immersion in an ethic of risk. While we cannot predict the results of our actions, we can know them: we can examine the impact of our actions and refine, revise, and correct policies and procedures in an ongoing commitment to justice and flourishing.

There will be mistakes, there will be further injustice, and there will also be unexpected gains. We cannot know in advance the impact of our work for social justice, but we can be vigilant, open, and creative and sustain practices that enable ongoing struggle. Here I concur with the struggle centered approaches of the humanist theologian Anthony Pinn and the social ethicist Miguel De La Torre. Pinn's definition of "struggle centered approaches" to work for justice is evocative and compelling:

> Struggle centered approaches recognize we may never destroy systems of injustice in ways that can constitute what we mean typically by "freedom," "liberation" or "justice." Rather than measuring "success" in light of destruction of the elemental nature of this troubled system, it is more useful to see in struggle our success. In our ability to foster greater awareness, to expose injustice, we find something of our agency, of our humanity, and of our fundamental worth and value. And we capture this sense of ourselves and ourselves in relationship to others all the while knowing that the system will adjust and we will have to continue to struggle. We should understand "liberation" not as an outcome but rather as a process, a process of perpetual rebellion against injustice.[30]

Like Pinn, I celebrate the fact that we can work for social justice without an expectation of triumph, of fundamentally changing human nature, but with a wide-eyed, openhearted engagement with the worst as well as the best in who we are now as human beings. Like De La Torre, I affirm the meaningfulness of this work: "Even in the absence of any assurance of future success, the work toward justice continues for its own sake."[31]

While we live in a time of increasing crisis and loss, this is also a time in which people are taking direct action to build a world of social equity and environmental sustainability. In so doing, they are creating alternatives to authoritarianism and excessive individualism. They are creating cohesive communities based on bonds of respect and practices of generative and accountable civic engagement. In the following chapters we will explore specific examples of the emerging movement of catalytic social engagement as manifest in the world of social entrepreneurship—growing numbers of co-ops, small- and medium-scale social enterprises, and corporations with a commitment to social equity and environmental sustainability. This movement is also manifest in the work of nonprofits that are increasingly attending to rigorous measurements of impact and efficacy in their work for social justice and environmental flourishing. It is manifest in the work of engagement scholarship, public and private universities committed to the co-creation of knowledge that is culturally responsive, scientifically sound, and directed to enhancing the common good. It is also exemplified in people denouncing an unjust, racially discriminatory, and ineffective criminal justice system, coming together to both stop police violence against people of color and to enact substantive criminal justice reform.

In *Blessed Unrest*, the environmentalist and entrepreneur Paul Hawken makes a startling claim: "We are in the midst of the largest social movement in all of human history." Hawken states that throughout the world there are "tens of millions of people dedicated to change" who are expressing that commitment through their work in nonprofits focused on "ecological sustainability and social justice."[32] He claims that these organizations have "three basic roots: environmental activism, social justice initiatives, and indigenous cultures' resistance to globalization. These nonprofits have common goals, learn from the communities with which they work, and pay increased attention to measuring in appropriate and self-critical ways the actual impact of their attempts to sustain the common good."[33]

I wager that you are either a participant in this movement yourself, know of others who are, or both! This movement is not protest. It is not prophetic critique. It is not charity. This movement is people living justly, working where we are and with what we have to build relationships and institutions that embody social equity and environmental sustainability.

Shared Concerns

Let me tell you some stories about manifestations of these shared concerns in unlikely places. Late winter and early spring 2011–2012 were quite intense in Chicago. With the city scheduled to host the NATO (North Atlantic Treaty Organization) and G8 (Group of Eight) summits, there were extensive preparations for both events from multiple social locations, from the groups affiliated with the Chicagoland Chamber of Commerce to the Chicago Council on Global Relations to the Occupy movement. I attended many of the meetings of the Chamber and the Council, settings in which the 1%–10% were talking to one another about issues of economic and political volatility. What I witnessed was both surprising and heartening in terms of the long-term dynamics of sustainable social change.

On March 23, 2012, Robert Rubin, cochairman of the Council on Foreign Relations and former secretary of the United States Department of the Treasury from 1995 to 1999, spoke on "The Economic Outlook and Policy Challenges for the United States and Europe." Rubin begin his career in finance in 1966 at Goldman, Sachs and Company, and was co-senior partner and copresident from 1990 to 1992. His tone was somber, direct, and measured. He claimed that the outlook for the U.S. economy was the most complex and uncertain of his lifetime, and asserted that anyone who claimed to understand the economy most certainly did not. He described a crisis facing the outlook for the United States and Europe in stark terms. Economic inequality and insecurity are a social, moral, and economic issue. Current levels of income distribution in the United States are a real threat to social cohesion. He went on to claim that we know of strategies that might address these moral and economic threats, but we are stymied by our current political system, paralyzed by the 60-vote rule in the Senate and the pernicious influence of the *Citizens United* decision in allowing unrestricted political expenditures by corporations. The strategies that he advocated were clear—more and smarter financial regulations and a robust investment in education to bring the poor into the economic mainstream.

On April 23, 2012, Martin Wolf, the associate editor and chief economics commentator for the *Financial Times*, also spoke on the struggle for a new world economy to a packed meeting of the Chicago Council on Global Affairs. Wolf was a member of the United Kingdom's Independent Commission on Banking and a senior economist at the World Bank's division of international trade, and he has advised governments and international organizations on trade and economic integration. He was recognized as one of *Foreign Policy*'s "Top 100 Global Thinkers" in 2009, 2010, and 2011. As you might guess from these credentials, his ideas carry weight with the 1%!

Wolf's remarks that evening to a packed gathering were stark, uncompromising, and a shocking departure from conventional wisdom. He reminded us that between 2007 and 2012 Europe, Japan, the United States, and Canada had experienced zero economic growth, and warned that economic stagnation is likely to continue, while there was impressive economic growth in Brazil, Russia, India, and China, growth that is likely to continue. As a result, he claimed that there is a significant shift in economic and political power. We no longer have a world economy designed and managed by the West for our interests. His conclusion was clear: "One-sixth of the world's population doesn't get to run the world forever. Sorry, chums, that's the way it is!"

While Wolf offered no comprehensive solutions, one simple and foundational, albeit partial, solution was raised, the fact that the top 1% in the United States is woefully undertaxed. This point was met by this group of wealthy individuals and members of the professional managerial class, not with outrage, but with resounding applause.

Angel Gurría, secretary general of the Organization for Economic Co-operation and Development, is another voice for change. On March 9, 2012, Gurría spoke on "Combating Global Headwinds: The OECD Perspective." The OECD grew out of the Marshall Plan of 1947. It was founded in its current form in 1961, and has 34 member countries. Gurría was introduced as the leader who had changed the OECD from a rich men's club to a reformers' club. His charge to the assembled business and governmental leaders was straightforward: "Go Social, Go Green." He claimed that the member countries of the OECD cannot wait for universal compliance with fundamental economic and political change but can, and must, begin to act now to improve the well-being of their citizens in an environmentally sustainable manner. Go Social— redress income inequality and provide opportunity and education. Go Green—act now to implement green growth strategies or face the costly consequences of irreversible damage to the environment.

On September 17, 2011, 5,000 people began demonstrations and occupations in New York City to protest unconscionable wealth and income disparities, and the deleterious effects of money in democratic politics.

The protests quickly spread from New York to Toronto to Sydney, reaching 951 cities in 82 countries.[34] Although the Occupy movement was only active on a large scale for four months, as the journalist Charles Blow pointed out, its language regarding the disparity between the 99% and the 1% vividly expressed the concerns of large numbers of people throughout the world over growing income and wealth inequality.[35] These concerns for economic justice were and are expressed in grassroots organizing efforts throughout the world. Conferences held in May 2015 in Chicago and New York demonstrated that there are glimmers of concern and concrete manifestations of change in other sectors of society as well.

In Chicago, people met to explore the role of cities in addressing basic issues of how to create both environmental sustainability and equitable jobs, how to implement inclusive and transformative education in the public schools, how to provide comprehensive health care and adequate food and water, how to address issues of urban violence, and how to both use technology and data collection for urban planning and protect individual privacy. The description of the forum on "Designing Environmentally Sustainable Cities" incorporates concerns with both economic growth and environmental justice:

> As growing hubs for people, commerce, industry, and transportation, global cities are leading contributors to stresses on the environment. According to UN Habitat, cities cover less than two percent of the earth's surface but produce 60 percent of all greenhouse gas emissions and consume 78 percent of the world's energy. Yet global cities have the capacity to identify solutions for sustainable development. How do cities ensure quality of life, open spaces, and healthy communities? What new technologies should cities adopt for more energy efficient infrastructure? How will buildings be designed so that they are responsive to their surroundings? How can unused land or obsolete infrastructure be repurposed? What efficient transportation options exist that move people away from cars, congestion, traffic, and pollution?[36]

An accompanying session continued the focus on "reimagining urban infrastructure," adding to the concerns of environmental sustainability those of social equity: "How are global city leaders, the private sector, and civic communities collaborating to invest in developments and urban renewal that benefit and enhance the standard of living of all communities?"[37] This panel included people with expertise in urban planning as well as the artist and community activist Theaster Gates. Gates is internationally known as a practitioner of relational aesthetics, with projects in Chicago, St. Louis, and Omaha. Gates's goal is certainly audacious—"to strengthen neighborhoods by creating spatial equity and investing in creative entrepreneurs and local artists to spark local economies." Gates describes all dimensions of this project as a work of art— "identifying talented people in the community, [working with them], empowering them, figuring out how they can help to maintain and enlarge a community of innovation, enterprise and security." As he states, these multiple efforts are all necessary for the creation of an "ecology of opportunity."[38]

Urban planning can focus on select communities and exacerbate social and economic inequality and divisions, or it can focus on all communities, bringing the same standards of excellence to neighborhoods that have been marginalized and ignored.[39]

One of the opening day panels on cities and the global economy addressed forthrightly not only pressing environmental and social challenges but the need for new forms of community engagement to address those challenges. The panel included Ajay Banga, president and chief executive officer (CEO), MasterCard; Helen Clark, administrator, United Nations Development Programme, and former prime minister of New Zealand; Henry M. Paulson Jr., founder and chairman, Paulson Institute, and the former secretary of the U.S. Treasury; Robert E. Rubin, cochairman, Council on Foreign Relations, and the former secretary of the U.S. Treasury. All shared the goal expressed succinctly by Paulson of a green economy, for both equitable job creation and sustainable environmental protection. While Rubin argued that only national policies could address those needs, the other panelists disagreed. While they agreed that such action would be desirable, they saw it as unlikely in the near future. Given the paralysis in the United States at the national and, in many cases, at the state level as well, they argued for new forms of cooperation between businesses, civic groups, and city governments to address directly the risk to the ecosystem of the environmental footprint of cities and redress the severe wage gap that is poisonous ethically, politically, and economically.

While the goals were clear, all also agreed that the means of obtaining what may seem like opposing objectives, that is, combating poverty through inclusive economic growth and implementing environmental sustainability, required rigorous and creative urban planning, and extensive experimentation to move to a just and inclusive green economy.

The upshot of the three days was described concisely by one of the sponsoring organizations, the Chicago Council on Global Affairs:

> Global cities drive political, social, and economic policies and solve critical world challenges. Leaders in the major pillars of urban life—business innovators, education visionaries, cultural luminaries, civic pioneers—discussed how they can collaborate to improve their cities, and the world. Sessions addressed global cities as world economic drivers, the importance of art education, the foreign policy of cities, sustainability, security . . . the list goes on. Big issues. Big ideas.[40]

These "big issues and big ideas" were also explored in a similar forum on the future of cities that took place in New York on May 28–30, 2015. Like the Chicago Forum, key issues of environmental sustainability, social inclusion, and data and privacy were explored. In addressing these issues, social inclusion was at the forefront. How are those who are often invisible made part of processes of social change?[41]

The speakers at IDEA CITY included political leaders like Julian Castro and activists like Micah White. Micah White was a co-creator of Occupy Wall Street. Julian Castro was secretary of the U.S. Department of Housing and Urban Development under President Obama, and during his three terms as mayor of San Antonio, Texas, was known for socially equitable urban development. One panel, "Make No Little Plans, Part 2. Policy and the Invisible City," drew on the wisdom of Chicago's 19th-century urban planner, Daniel Burnham. Burnham is noted for a city design that provided access to the lakefront and green spaces for all citizens of the city, and not just the wealthy few. While his views did assume that what was beneficial for the wealthy would also serve the interests of the poor, according to the historian Carl Smith, Burnham created a plan for the city that "speaks with surprising directness of the city's need and right to place limits on speculators and landowners." The plan "implicitly condemned the excesses of capitalism" and argued that the lakefront "by right belongs to the people." In the New York forum, panelists took up Burnham's challenge:

> In light of the entreaty made by Daniel Burnham (author of Chicago's seminal modern master plan) to "make no little plans," how will urbanists, architects, and activists think about creating a habitat that anticipates drastic future change, overcrowding, and climate change? What are the guiding principles in an architecture that is preventative? This discussion will analyze both the extraordinary challenges of designing for unpredictable conditions, accelerated change, and the new opportunities that arise when one takes radical change into account.[42]

The convergence of the May New York and Chicago conferences on cities and social change is not an anomaly. It reflects both the power of protest movements and the recognition by some of those in power that fundamental change in our economic lives is ethically, politically, and even economically necessary.

Shared Solutions: Community Economies

J. K. Gibson-Graham (Katherine Gibson, Australian National University in Canberra, and Julie Graham, University of Massachusetts, Amherst, who wrote as a single persona from 1992 until Graham's death in 2010) have described a new political imaginary. They analyze, nurture, and celebrate the reality, opportunities, and challenges of community economies. People all over the world are finding ways of shaping their economic lives to recognize the power of interdependence, not a "common being" but a "being in common." J. K. Gibson-Graham describe the ways in which people embody interdependence in such economic practices as employee buyouts in the United States, worker takeovers in the wake of economic crisis in Argentina, the antisweatshop movement, shareholder movements "that promote ethical investments and police the enforcement of corporate environmental and social responsibility," the living wage movement, efforts to institute a universal basic income, and social entrepreneurship. These are all part of a community economy "that performs economy in new ways."[43]

J. K. Gibson-Graham build on the insights of queer theory and political and feminist theory and organizing, emphasizing that shared questions often lead to different answers. Just as there is no one way to be a feminist, there is no single way to perform economic relations justly. There are, however, salient questions, choices to be made in each situation. Here the economy becomes the product of ethical decision making, different ways of answering the same questions:

> . . . what is necessary to personal and social survival:
> . . . how social surplus is appropriated and distributed
> . . . what and how social surplus is to be distributed and consumed, and,
> . . . how a commons is produced and sustained.[44]

In making these choices, J. K. Gibson-Graham make a claim as startling as that of there being no preferred model of economic justice: *it is as difficult for workers to live within community economies as it is for owners.* For all of us, the challenge of new forms of subjectivity, sociality, and interdependence are "best shaped by practical curiosity as opposed to moral certainty about alternatives to capitalism."[45]

This form of practical curiosity and attention to the power of interdependence is not limited to the world of the academy or to grassroots organizing, but is increasingly widespread in the world of business.

Social Enterprise and Entrepreneurship

In 1998, Gregory Dees, a professor at Duke University's Fuqua School of Business, wrote a definitive essay describing the emergence of social entrepreneurship, innovative leaders who combine "the passion of a social mission with . . . business-like discipline, innovation, and determination."[46] Dees was the Rubenstein Senior Fellow in Social Entrepreneurship with Duke's Innovation and Entrepreneurship Initiative and the founding faculty director of the Center for the Advancement of Social Entrepreneurship at Duke's Fuqua School of Business. In 2007, the Aspen Institute and the international organization Ashoka presented him with their first lifetime achievement award in social entrepreneurship education.[47]

Entrepreneurial approaches to social problems emerge from two factors—a recognition of the failures of many efforts by governmental agencies, nonprofit organizations, and social activists to redress issues of social and environmental risk, and the imperative of moving beyond mere critique of the failings of other institutions to the embrace of the challenge of actually creating more effective ways of meeting our needs for not only survival but for flourishing.

Following the insights of Dees, social entrepreneurs see themselves as creating new institutions to redress seemingly intractable social and environmental problems. From the Social Enterprise Alliance website we find this clear description of the genesis and goals of social enterprise:

> It appears that the world's problems are outstripping our ability to address them, but what may be more accurate is simply that traditional institutions are no longer sufficient.
>
> Social enterprise is emerging as the "missing middle" sector between the traditional worlds of government, nonprofits and business. It addresses social concerns,
>
> More efficiently than government, which no longer has the mandate or resources to solve every social problem;
>
> More sustainably and creatively than the nonprofit sector, which faces declining funding streams and increased demands for innovation, proof of what works and collaboration; and
>
> More generously than business, which is mandated to place pre-eminence on shareholder returns, but is also realizing it can't succeed in a decaying world.[48]

These concerns for social equity and environmental sustainability are not limited to small enterprises. There are increasing numbers of for-profit enterprises that share the same goals and are equally committed to using the power of business to creatively and sustainably address basic social needs and solve daunting social problems. These entities have a triple bottom line—people, planet, profit. To meet those goals of being sustainable and accountable agents of social change, rigorous external evaluation is required. Certified Benefit Corporations, or B Corps, are businesses that achieve at least a minimum score on the B Impact Assessment, which measures a company's social and environmental impact.[49] Benefit corporations are legally structured to put social mission first, and also have third party certification of the ways in which they meet their goals of treating employees justly (for example, paying a living wage, and not just a minimum wage), meeting social needs directly through their goods and services, and exercising environmental responsibility.[50]

As of January 2018 there were 2,358 certified B corporations in over 50 countries. To qualify as a B corporation a firm "must have an explicit social or environmental mission, and a legally binding fiduciary responsibility to take into account the interests of workers, the community, and the environment as well as its shareholders."[51]

The B corps declaration of interdependence is well worth pondering:

We envision a global economy that uses business as a force for good.

This economy is comprised of a new type of corporation—the B Corporation—which is purpose-driven and creates benefits for all stakeholders, not just shareholders.

As B Corporations and leaders of this emerging economy, we believe:
That we must be the change we seek in the world.
That all business ought to be conducted as if people and place mattered.
That, through their products, practices, and profits, businesses should aspire to do no harm and benefit all.
To do so requires that we act with the understanding that we are each dependent upon one another and thus responsible for each other and future generations.[52]

These social goals are indeed promising, and the attention to making sure that they are achieved is ongoing. Built into the work of this form of socially responsible capitalism is a full awareness of the Windigo, of the ways in which business can be short-sighted and socially and environmentally destructive, and an equally full awareness that the way to create a different form of responsible capitalism requires not only critique, but new values and regular monitoring of practices that bring those values to life.

Impact-Driven Nonprofits

In *Blessed Unrest*, Paul Hawken describes the ways in which these same concerns with interdependence are changing the work of nonprofits in fundamental ways to ensure actions that are more accountable and effective. An example of a nonprofit that includes equal attention to critique, vision, and implementation can be seen in the current work of the Unitarian Universalist Service Committee. In its 2012 annual report, UUSC's president and CEO William Schulz laid out three elements of constructive social activism:

> First, engagement. We're eager to use the people power at our disposal to optimize our effectiveness. Our members, most of whom are associated with Unitarian Universalist congregations, are natural born activists. They're itching to get their hands dirty, be it on their computer keyboards taking online actions or by building an eco-village in Haiti.
>
> Second, innovation. Wherever we go in the world, we ask ourselves, "who's been forgotten and who is doing the most creative, groundbreaking work to transform and empower those forgotten populations." By finding the most innovative, entrepreneurial approaches to problems and crises . . . we encourage new solutions to old quandaries; we engage with communities of women or ethnic minorities, too often marginalized in their societies.
>
> Third, impact. . . . we're experimenting with different approaches to measuring impact because we know that at the end of the day the only thing that really counts is how many lives we've actually changed.[53]

Although this movement to build just and creative businesses and institutions is vast, its effects considerable, and its numbers steadily increasing, it is unrecognized and unnamed, even by many of its participants. Hawken asks a basic question, "If it is so large, why isn't this movement more visible?" The reasons are simple—"the movement doesn't fit neatly into any category in modern society, and what can't be visualized, can't be named."[54] He puts this vast social change in the context of other movements that have fundamentally reshaped human society: "The Industrial Revolution went unnamed for more than a century, in part because its development did not fit conventional categories, but also because no one could define what is taking place, even though it was evident everywhere." Hawken names another distinction that makes it hard to identify this movement—"what unifies it is ideas, not ideologies. . . . ideas question and liberate, ideologies justify and dictate."[55]

Let's step back. We are in the midst of a burgeoning social movement with no single leader, with no shared vision of how best to identify and respond to dire social and environmental ills. What we do have, however, is a forthright commitment to move beyond protest to direct action.

Here is a story that illustrates what drives social enterprise. Michal Bachmann, cofounder of the Impact Hub in Zurich, interviewed Jonathan Robinson, a cofounder of Impact Hubs worldwide. Robinson and others were part of the antiglobalization movement that became active at the beginning of the 21st century.

> "There was a huge amount of criticism of the current economic models but almost no attention to different modes of progress," says Jonathan Robinson. . . . "We asked ourselves, What if half of that energy went into imagining and demonstrating some real alternatives?" The problem, as Robinson saw it, was not a lack of aspiration or inspiration. "Everyone has ideas for making the world a better place, . . . but where does one go to make that happen?"[56]

Robinson worked with others to create spaces where people who are committed to social entrepreneurship can share office space, share community, and learn from each other's successes and failures. As of 2016, there were 80 Impact Hubs with 15,000 members throughout the United States, South America, Europe, Africa, and Asia.[57]

Ethical Challenges: Ethical Opportunities

As people move, like Robinson, from thinking about how the world could be better to working together to make it better, there are new ethical challenges and opportunities. This is a burgeoning social movement in which people throughout the world are working together to address basic issues of environmental risk and social inequality. These forms of constructive activism are primarily pragmatic and nonideological, transcending polarizing political divisions in the implementation of just, sustainable, and creative social and economic policies. Rather than demanding that others change, they are changing themselves and the institutions they manage and own. They are creating businesses that pay workers fairly, that give as much attention to environmental sustainability as they do to long-term profitability.

They are exercising the artistry of cross-cultural and multiracial partnership and leadership, and creating hiring and management practices that draw on the wisdom of people from many racial and cultural groups, while checking on a routine and continuing basis the limiting factors of implicit bias and structural injustice.

They are living out an ethic of risk, implementing new policies, and creating new social structures to enhance the common good, and knowing, as they do so, that unpredictable and unforeseen consequences are the norm. They create, therefore, cultures of honest accountability and generative critique, learning as much from their mistakes as from their successes.

The move from knowing what *should* be done to getting it done is as great a shift ethically and philosophically as is the move from *is* to *ought*. For here, as we move from *ought* to *how*, we encounter a paradox. Not only does work for constructive, institutional forms of justice take significant amounts of time, but there are also intrinsic differences between prophetic critique, prophetic vision, and democratic leadership. We may critique alone, and we may even envision alone, but to implement that vision, to build on that critique, requires the cooperation of other people—other people to actually carry out the work on a daily basis, and other people to judge, refine, and critique new systems and processes. And, as you may have noticed, other people tend to have different ideas—not only different ideas of how to meet shared goals, but possibly better ideas about the most fitting, concrete ways to administer health care, or to support ecologically sustainable forms of energy production.

Pragmatists encourage us to seek the best in any given situation. The reality, however, is that there are multiple and mutually exclusive "bests," and we cannot implement all plausible solutions at a given time. How, then, do we work creatively with profound and seemingly irreconcilable differences in policy, strategy, and tactics among those who share the same social critique and are moved by the same hopes for justice?

Key Insights for Progressive Action

As we immerse ourselves in the complexity of institutional change, we encounter a defining paradox, a fundamental lack of parity between the moral certainty of our denunciation of existing forms of injustice and our ethically reasonable uncertainty about the justice and feasibility of our cherished alternatives. To engage in this work with courage, creativity, and persistence, it is essential that we tell the truth. Without true stories of ambiguity, creativity, failure, and risk, without nondualistic accounts of imperfect humans struggling to live justly and well, we will lack the moral imagination to recognize and respond to what is so powerfully right. And what is so powerfully right is the creative embrace of risk, failure, growth, and resilience in the pursuit of human and environmental flourishing.

Constructive social and civic engagement emerges in conjunction with protest and prophetic witness. In these pages we will explore both the theory and practice of direct institutional change. As we move from the work of minority critique to vital collective action, there are fundamental challenges of democratic leadership in the work of institutional change that we need to recognize and understand. Such leadership can be even more effective as it is grounded in the science and history of social change. In the past few years, scholars in the fields of history, sociology, philosophy, public policy, and the cognitive sciences have been changing our understandings of the complexity and multiple dimensions of successful social movements. Self-critical social engagement requires a thorough understanding of these dynamics and of what motivates human behavior for good and for ill. To quote William Schulz, "effective social activists must (1) be aware of the multiple dimensions of social change; (2) be clear about where a particular initiative fits into the trajectory of social change; (3) and thereby be able to contribute to the creation of effective strategies for the implementation of just social policies."[58]

In our work for social justice, criminal justice reform, environmental sustainability, and economic equity, the shift from critique to constructive resolution is profound. The tactics and strategies that have worked, and continue to work, for the first two forms of political activism—denouncing what is unjust and naming who should be included—are insufficient for the third form of constructive social engagement. In this movement, new and different strategies of constructive community engagement are being developed and tested. This shift poses a profound challenge for activists and community organizers, and for liberation theologians and social ethicists. I write as a social ethicist who works with other social ethicists and liberation theologians who have long explored the ethical and theological imperative of exposing and denouncing injustice. We now need to pay as much attention to the daunting challenges of building just institutions and implementing environmentally sound and socially equitable economic practices. In so doing, the basic methods of analysis of liberation theology and social ethics continue, but with a focus on a different set of problems.

From liberation theology this volume highlights three core methods of engagement and analysis:

(1) Beginning with action and then moving to reflection and enhanced action (orthopraxis);
(2) Giving primary attention to the experience, agency, and insights of those who are marginalized, exploited, and excluded;
(3) Acknowledging our own social and political location.

From social ethics this volume focuses on the structures that determine what is normative, and the systems that are necessary to live out the imperatives of economic and environmental justice; it draws on the social sciences for an analysis of what is occurring in human lives and for an analysis of what shapes and influences patterns of human behavior.[59]

In this book, I am taking up the challenge of expanding the prophetic imagination that is described so well by the professor of philosophy and religion Johnny Bernard Hill and by the theologian Peter Heltzel and the faith-based activist Alexia Salvatierra. In his book *Prophetic Rage*, Hill describes the challenge that we have of transforming "our prophetic rage into positive, constructive programs and policies that can build the beloved communities in our cities, states, and nations."[60] He calls for a "new world economy" and challenges people from all social classes to match "radical love with prophetic protest":

The intellectual and activist, politician and preacher, banker and borrower alike, must engage in the kind of passionate and self-sacrificial response to nihilism and human suffering that has characterized moments of social crisis throughout history.[61]

In their book on faith-based activism, Heltzel and Salvatierra describe a prophetic imagination that "calls us to a collective worldview rooted in the love of neighbor and aflame with the passion to build a beloved community."[62] Heltzel and Salvatierra invite and challenge people of all social classes to take up this work, and, in so doing, recognize that everyone's work for justice includes not just critique of others, but awareness of our own potential failings: "Neither the rich nor the poor can escape this innate temptation to oppress others."[63]

They also point to the need for an expansion of the prophetic imagination from a critique of what is wrong and a vision of what is right:

> A vision is not a plan. This sounds simple, but anyone who has done any organizing work knows that the translation of mystical vision into an effective prophetic plan is hard work. In order to create change, we have to move from the identification of our common dream to a strategic focus on immediate issues with clear objectives.[64]

Like Hill, Heltzel and Salvatierra call people of all classes to this work, and describe the need for religious ethical guidance for the poor and oppressed, for the powerful, and for the essential work of the poor and the powerful working together in empowering and accountable solidarity.[65]

The significance of the movement for constructive social engagement is both quantitative and qualitative. It is unprecedented in scope and size, and is as significant a shift, as innovative, new, and creative in what establishes social justice as the invention of nonviolence, of civil disobedience, of protest itself as organized and systematic challenges to unjust social structures. At the core of this movement is a basic change in how we live out our values of social justice, not witnessing for them, not pressuring others to follow them, but, rather, following them ourselves in the businesses we create and the institutions we lead.

Van Jones described this shift well: "Our organization needed to go beyond fighting against the things we did not want. We also needed to start working toward a future that we did want. . . . Along the way, I found my true calling—working with the private sector and policy leaders to spread the benefits of eco-friendly business opportunities into struggling communities."[66]

As we, like Jones, move from protest to solutions, we encounter a series of generative paradoxes:

> There is a fundamental lack of parity between the moral certainty of our denunciation of existing forms of injustice and our ethically reasonable uncertainty about the justice and feasibility of our cherished alternatives. We may want the same thing, but for different reasons and may have the same reasons, but want different things.
>
> Finding what enables people to thrive in ways that are equitable and ecologically sustainable is more a matter of critical experimentation and risk-taking than it is a matter of moral and theological certainty.
>
> The measure of our success is not the perfection of our efforts but our honesty, accountability, resilience, and audacity in the face of unintended consequences and ongoing challenges.
>
> There is no moral safe harbor, no course of action guaranteed to be free of risk, loss, and negative side effects.
>
> The primary issue is not the clarity of our ideals but the sustainability, efficiency, and efficacy of our solutions.

This book showcases the lives and work of people living for justice. In these pages we will explore the story of social entrepreneurship and impact-driven nonprofits. We will examine the forms of education that are teaching people how to live with both global awareness and cultural sensitivity, and examine universities and communities working together to redress social and environmental injustices. We will also see the ways in which these attempts to live justly and well may be grounded in the wisdom of indigenous traditions of gratitude and reciprocity. In addition, we will explore the types of creative protest movements that both challenge the costs of injustice and lay the foundations for inclusive and expansive flourishing.

This is not the ethic of the savior who solves problems for others. It is not the purity of prophetic witness and critique. It is the dance of reciprocity and belonging, acknowledging and expecting failure and learning as much from mistakes as from times of healing and transformation.

In the next chapter we will turn to the study of strategic nonviolence, and the fundamental characteristics of successful movements of protest and transformation. As we explore more of the science of democracy, in this case the political science of successful social movements, we will encounter a profound challenge. Resistance movements against injustice that are the most successful have within them the seeds of living justly. They are simultaneously a resolute "no" to authoritarianism and oppression and an invigorating "yes" to generative interdependence.

2

"The Lightning of Possible Storms"

Theories of Social Change

In an interview conducted in 1980, the French philosopher Michel Foucault gave this poetic invocation of radical social critique:

> I can't help but dream about a kind of criticism that would try not to judge but to bring an oeuvre, a book, a sentence, an idea to life; it would light fires, watch the grass grow, listen to the wind, and catch the sea foam in the breeze and scatter it. It would multiply not judgments but signs of existence; it would summon them, drag them from their sleep. Perhaps it would invent them sometimes—all the better. All the better. Criticism that hands down sentences sends me to sleep; I'd like a criticism of scintillating leaps of the imagination. It would not be sovereign or dressed in red. It would bear the lightning of possible storms.[1]

This chapter explores the forms of catalytic social engagement that "bear the lightning of possible storms": the insights that produce such engagement; the values that sustain it; and the measures by which we gauge its success.

To take up this constructive task requires an expansion of the prophetic imagination. Once we recognize that a situation is unjust, once we grant the imperative of including the voices and experiences of all peoples, how then do we work together to build just and creative institutions? A twofold form of social engagement, with as much attention to implementation and impact as to critique or vision, is possible because of nuanced histories of successful social movements and of contemporary developments in the behavioral sciences. To paraphrase the insights of the economists Esther Duflo and Abhijit Banerjee, "Ideologies, whether of the right or left, are no match for studies of what actually motivates and enables people to act in ways that support the common good."[2]

Once motivated and enabled to act, ideologies are also no match for studies of which are the most effective actions in achieving specific forms of social change. One of the first insights is simple: catalytic social engagement requires attention to two dimensions of just living: first, exposing and dismantling systems of injustice, and second, including all stakeholders and building just social structures and forms of economic life. Here, too, is another key question—how do we expose and dismantle in a way consonant with the goals of inclusion and building?

At this junction in history radical critique and dismantling structures of injustice are as needed as ever. While our situation is undoubtedly dire, there are also new resources that have not yet been thoroughly integrated into the work of social activists. In this chapter we will explore the work of historians and social scientists whose scholarship can help us to develop new strategies for more fully embodying generative interdependence in all aspects of our collective lives.

Strategic Nonviolence

We begin with the groundbreaking work of the political scientists Erica Chenoweth and Maria J. Stephan. In 2011 Chenoweth and Stephan published *Why Civil Resistance Works: The Strategic Logic of Nonviolent Conflict*.[3] In this book, they share the results of their analysis of "323 violent and nonviolent resistance campaigns between 1900 and 2006."[4] These were campaigns for regime change, against occupation, and for secession. Their findings are surprising, heartening, and challenging. They found that nonviolent resistance movements were far more likely to be successful than violent resistance campaigns. In fact, they found that "between 1900 and 2006, nonviolent resistance campaigns were nearly twice as likely to achieve full or partial success as their violent counterparts."[5] The successful nonviolent movements that they studied are diverse geographically and temporally, ranging from the 1931 resistance in Chile to the Carlos Ibáñez regime, the People Power movement in the Philippines against the Ferdinand Marcos regime from 1983 to 1986, and the "Singing Revolution" in Estonia in 1989 against the communist regime. They also analyze the failed antiapartheid campaign in South Africa from 1952 to 1961, and then the successful antiapartheid campaign from 1984 to 1994.[6]

In addition to discovering the fact that nonviolence has been more effective than violent resistance in achieving fundamental social change, Chenoweth and Stephan also examine *why* nonviolence has been more effective than violence. Before we examine the factors that have led to success in the past, and may lead to success in the future, let us return to the work of Robin Wall Kimmerer, and take up the analysis of Chenoweth and Stephan in the spirit of the indigenous wisdom of "original instructions."

Kimmerer begins *Braiding Sweetgrass* by sharing the lessons of the Skywoman story. These stories are "shared by the original peoples throughout the Great Lakes," and how they are offered is as challenging to white, nonindigenous peoples as what they offer:

> These are not "instructions" like commandments, though, or rules; rather, they are like a compass: they provide an orientation but not a map. The work of living is creating that map for yourself. How to follow the Original Instructions will be different for each of us and different for every era.[7]

In this spirit of both humility and experimentation, let us turn to the analyses of Chenoweth and Stephan of past struggles for social justice. How might we use these lessons, not as commandments or rules, but as a compass for our work for social justice in the present? What are the implications of this research for our ongoing work in challenging white supremacy and the multiple forms of racism, combatting the erosion of democratic institutions and checks and balances, defying the erosion of human rights for immigrants, refugees, women, and people who are LGBTQIA, and stopping the spread of exploitative and extractive capitalism?

Chenoweth and Stephan build on prior well-known and influential studies of nonviolence by the political scientist Gene Sharp, and by Peter Ackerman and Jack DuVall, the founders of the International Center on Nonviolent Conflict.[8] Chenoweth and Stephan add a key dimension to this earlier scholarship. Ackerman and DuVall identify the principles common to successful nonviolent social movements. Chenoweth and Stephan empirically test which principles are most salient in the success or failure of nonviolent and violent social movements. While Sharp's massive work on nonviolence has been widely studied and applied in nonviolent social movements throughout the world, most recently by activists in Serbia and in the Arab Spring, it had not yet been tested empirically.[9]

I worked with Sharp during the nuclear weapons freeze campaign, and was inspired by his pragmatic approach to nonviolent strategies. He argued that we should use these strategies not just because they are moral but because they are also effective. Even the most repressive regime requires the consent of the governed, and that consent can be withdrawn nonviolently in strategic and effective ways. According to Sharp, a people may not be able to overthrow a tyrant directly, but they can withhold obedience and thereby remove the tyrant's sources of power. He challenged us to see and accept our power—our ability to refuse to cooperate in the maintenance and operation of unjust economic and political systems.[10]

Chenoweth and Stephan show us what happens when social movements do just that—see and use their power to expose and dismantle systems of injustice. Nonviolent movements are more successful than violent campaigns because they attract more participants and thereby obtain a wider range of support of people from across the social, political, and economic spectrum. Nonviolent campaigns have a membership that is both numerically larger and more ideologically and culturally diverse than violent campaigns. Having a "more diverse membership" leads to the following factors that are all equally important in the success of nonviolent campaigns. Nonviolent campaigns

(1) produce "higher levels of civic disruption";
(2) are "more likely . . . to win meaningful support in the international community";
(3) are "more adept at developing tactical innovations";
(4) are "better at evading and remaining resilient in the face of regime repression";
(5) and, finally, with nonviolent campaigns, "regime repression . . . is more likely to backfire."[11]

The implications of this empirical study of the key factors in successful forms of nonviolent resistance are clear. Should there be mass gatherings taking place at key events such as national holidays, and prior to and after significant elections? Should there be widely dispersed smaller demonstrations, not only in large cities but in small communities throughout a nation? Should the tenor of these demonstrations be that of somber vigils, die-ins, and expressions of grief and mourning? Should they be jubilant celebrations of collective power and humorous and irreverent critiques of repressive power structures and of people in power? Should they be defiant expressions of resistance and rage?

The answer to these choices is clear—yes, a resounding and enthusiastic yes! All of these forms of protest are powerful and even more powerful when all are used at different times and by different groups.

Another series of questions: Should activists do more than participate in demonstrations? Should there be boycotts, strikes, walkouts, letter writing and phone campaigns to elected officials and prospective voters, one on one conversations with prospective voters, elected officials, business, and civic leaders? Should there be letters to the editors, petitions, declarations, wearing buttons and T-shirts to express shared goals, and teach-ins at community gatherings and in educational institutions?

Again, the answer is simple and the implications profound. Yes, all of these tactics are partial and insufficient in themselves, yet all can be used and combined to create fundamental social change.

* * *

What leads to the failure of nonviolent campaigns is not regime resistance. On the contrary, regime resistance often breeds resilience, and such resistance even backfires, leading to more, not less, support from a wider array of the people. What, then, leads to the failure of nonviolent campaigns? Chenoweth and Stephan found that one in four nonviolent campaigns failed and that the causes of that failure are straightforward—lack of persistence, loss of unity, and the inability to employ new and different tactics.[12] What often leads to the loss of unity is seeing as a weakness what can be our strength: multiple actors with different ways of pursuing a common goal.

The lessons here for activists are clear. Nonviolent social movements have a "participatory advantage" over violent social movements, and that advantage is "both qualitative and quantitative." Not only are more people involved, but there is a greater range of actions. Note the paradox here—key strengths are often the cause of debilitating infighting. Here we see the destructive power of our third Windigo, paralyzing infighting over strategy and tactics. Too often we try to get mass numbers of participants, but insist on limiting the number of actions to those that we personally find most compelling. Rather than welcoming multiple strategies, all too often we seek to impose our preferred strategy. Rather than encouraging both low-risk and high-risk activities, we often push people to move from low to high risk, rather than seeing the need for a wide range of activities.

Ideological and tactical rigidity, not repression, also leads to the failures of strategic nonviolence. While we must have an overarching shared goal, how can we learn how to embrace the fact that people may share the same goal, but for different reasons, and support the same goal, yet live it out in different dimensions of our civic, personal, and professional lives?

Ideological purity limits the number of participants. Tactical rigidity limits the quantity and quality of participation. Chenoweth and Stephan are clear—in the face of repression, tactical innovation and the creation of new strategies are essential. Further, multiple strategies enable the movement to attract the sympathy of more pillars of support of the oppressive and unjust regime. Some of those pillars may be reached by demonstrations and vigils, others by boycotts, and still others by phone calls, letter-writing campaigns, and conversations at townhall meetings.

This is the key insight from Chenoweth and Stephan. Strategic nonviolence fails most often through its internal conflicts and lack of creativity rather than through its external repression. In fact, external repression can actually backfire and make us stronger. What draws us apart is when we fight each other, and do not find ways of working together, seeing our multiple gifts as a weakness, rather than a strength. Here I am profoundly grateful to Robin Wall Kimmerer and the wisdom of indigenous traditions. Remember what she wrote about the "original instructions." These are not strict rules, or rigid guidelines, but rather a compass, an invitation to each of us to be aware of our gifts, and be aware of the responsibilities that come with these gifts. We can live out the call to justice in our daily lives and in extremis, taking extraordinary measures. In both forms of action, it is vital that we honor our different gifts and do not assume that there is only one gift that will either maintain a healthy way of life or effectively challenge injustice.

When we embrace quantitative excellence and foster tactical and innovative creativity, we move to a different way of holding the prophetic imagination. Rather than the prophetic imagination being primarily a critique of the limitations of other activists (if only they would do it our way the unjust social system would fail), it challenges us to enter into a logic of prophetic invitation. That is to say—I see this need: we see this need. We have these gifts. Now, how can we work together to express these gifts more fully? How can we use our leverage points to build justice?

We are called to be bold. We are called to take risks. We are called to resist and build on our strengths in responsible and creative ways. Chenoweth and Stephan are clear: "[J]ust because a campaign is nonviolent does not guarantee its success. Just as on a battlefield, poorly managed campaigns are more likely to fail. Campaigns that constantly update their information, adapt to conditions, and outmaneuver the adversary are more likely to succeed than campaigns that expect to succeed merely by virtue of their causes and methods."[13] Moral virtue alone does not lead to success. We may be morally right and strategically inept, right in our critique of injustice and wrong in our use of specific tactics. We may persist with tactics that worked in the past, but lack resonance in another time and place.

There is, however, one matter of heated debate among activists where the political science is only partially clear. While it is demonstrable that nonviolent campaigns are more successful, is there a role for violent elements in the campaign? Does a more radical and violent fringe element lead to greater success, or to failure? Here Chenoweth and Stephan are blunt. The data is inconclusive. In some incidences, a violent fringe element leads to the entire social movement being discredited and losing support. In others, the repressive regime chooses to negotiate with the nonviolent campaign as a way of disempowering the violent fringe. Chenoweth and Stephan find that "there is no consensus among social scientists about the conditions under which radical flanks either harm or help a social movement." While it is thus not clear whether a radical, violent fringe helps or hurts a movement for social change, one thing is certain. If there is violence it needs to remain on the margins, rather than becoming central to a campaign.[14]

As activists learn from the history of successful movements for social change, there is another lesson that is of as much importance as the need for mass participation and diverse forms of noncooperation. In addition to providing widespread resistance to injustice, successful campaigns create alternative democratic and peaceful forms of collective political, economic, and cultural life. In fact, when violent campaigns do succeed—for example, the Russian Revolution (1917), Chinese Revolution (1946–1950), Algerian Revolution (1954–1962), Cuban Revolution (1953–1959), and Vietnamese Revolution (1959–1975)—they are characterized by many of the same factors that lead to the success of nonviolent movements: large numbers of participants, a wide range of activities, and the creation of alternative and peaceful forms of governance and community. Chenoweth and Stephan claim that it may well be that the cause of their success is their similarity to the strongest and most innovative nonviolent campaigns.

> [I]t is clear that many of the features common to successful nonviolent campaigns occurred in these revolutions, especially diverse, mass mobilization, which led to loyalty shifts within the ruling regimes' economic and military elites. [They also succeeded] in building a strong base of popular support while creating parallel administrative, political, social, and economic structures. [This suggests] that the nonviolent components of successful armed campaigns are as significant—or possibly even more significant—than the military component.[15]

There is a final lesson that can be drawn from history that provides a compass for our ongoing resistance. Nonviolent campaigns are more likely to be followed by the creation of democratic institutions.[16] It is vital that there be a resonance between all dimensions of social change—exposing and dismantling unjust systems, including all stakeholders, and building inclusive and democratic institutions: "[M]ass participation in nonviolent political change, we suggest, encourages the development of democratic skills and fosters expectations of accountable governance, both of which are less likely when transitions are driven by opposition violence."[17]

The lessons of history are clear. Nonviolent campaigns are more likely to lead to expanding forms of freedom and democratic forms of governance. What, however, is required to make that possible? What is our work after the protests are heard?

In June 2011, at the Unitarian Universalist General Assembly, William Schulz, drawing upon his experience as executive director of Amnesty International USA and president and CEO of the Unitarian Universalist Service Committee, described five fundamental steps in systemic social change. Four of those can be seen in the work of Chenoweth and Stephan. The fifth, however, is different and describes the ongoing challenges that we face after our nonviolent campaigns succeed.

> First, most successful movements—at least at their outsets—have identifiable adversaries. It can be a person—LBJ or Bull Connor; it can be a government—the apartheid South African government; it can be a corporation—General Motors in the case of seat belts; Philip Morris in the case of tobacco. . . . most successful movements . . . find some entity or entities that personify the problem.[18]

The second step in social change is more challenging:

> finding a common message with which to address that adversary . . . and finding a message that will broaden that initial base of support and win sympathy from people who were initially indifferent or skeptical about the movement.[19]

The third step is creating "multitiered strategies for translating goals into reality (education, legislative change, litigation)." The fourth is "exercising public pressure to bring about change," and the fifth is creating a new sense of honor, persuading "people with power that the social change we seek is ultimately in their best interest."[20]

Schulz explores further the implications of the fifth characteristic of social movements, why it is so important, and why it is so very difficult. First, where we often fall short:

> [S]caring people with power doesn't last unless those people can be persuaded that the social change we seek is ultimately in their best interest

also. And here too progressives fall short. We fail to place our short-term goals in a larger context. We're good at getting our adversaries' attention; occasionally good at scaring them into doing the right thing; but not so good at re-framing issues so that decision-makers can see that ultimately persecuting undocumented workers or decimating budgets in lieu of reasonable tax hikes are not in the long-term interests of anybody.[21]

Second, he describes the power for good that may be unleashed when we do succeed with this fifth task:

> The reason progressive movements have always generated resistance, sometimes violent resistance, is because they have known how to threaten the avatars of power. But the reason they have been successful is because they have eventually convinced those avatars that they too want to live in a new world.[22]

What are the core ethical and political challenges of the next stage in social movements; what must be addressed when those in power decide that "we want to live in a new world" and begin to bring that new world into being?

As we take up this task it is helpful to explore one of the crucial insights of the liberation theologian Gustavo Gutiérrez. Gutiérrez, born in Peru in 1928, is a Dominican priest and theologian. In 1973, in what became a classic text, Gustavo Gutiérrez described the power of liberation theology. His statement was concise and compelling: the theology of liberation frees the oppressed from their exploitation and marginalization and frees the oppressor from their isolation, alienation, and arrogance.[23]

Let us now explore what it means to live out a theology of liberation from the point of view of the oppressor who genuinely sees the cost of systemic injustice, sees their/our role in perpetuating that system, and commits to using their/our power in solidarity with the oppressed and in the service of equitable human flourishing.

Protests are an essential ingredient in social change, yet liberation theologians and social ethicists fail when we focus solely on the theological and ethical imperative of prophetic critique and do not provide leadership for responding to that critique with power, creativity, and ongoing self-critical accountability. What are protests for? Once protests are heard, how do we grapple with the ethical and political challenges of establishing structural and systemic justice to replace structures and systems of injustice? What happens when the holders of power see the legitimacy of social critique and choose to be accountable and creative agents of social change? The work of bringing a social vision to life requires far more than good intentions and a compelling critique of the costs of injustice. It requires as well a constructive, creative pragmatism that is being expressed throughout the world in new approaches to environmental sustainability, health care reform, economic justice, criminal justice reform, and the transformation of urban spaces.

Sustainable policy development and implementation requires an ethic of clarity, persistence, and discipline in the face of ambiguity, failure, and unintended consequences. It is useful to bring this constructive and catalytic work for social justice into direct conversation with current scholarship in the sciences of what enables social change. This multidisciplinary scholarship is vast and growing, and its implications are far-reaching. As the behavioral scientist Brian Wansink states, "The 20th century saw great gains in sanitation and public health. The 21st century could be as great a period for behavior change."[24]

Honor Codes—Kwame Anthony Appiah

The philosopher Kwame Anthony Appiah explores what happens when those in power are successfully challenged and choose to live more justly. In *The Honor Code: How Moral Revolutions Happen*, Appiah charts the transformation of "private sentiment" into public norm in the abolition of dueling in England, foot binding in China, and slavery and the slave trade in England, and examines what may well be leading to a similar shift now in the honor killing of women in Pakistan, Afghanistan, India, and Turkey. In each case he finds that moral critiques were not enough. In fact, each practice had been discredited by religiously and philosophically based moral critiques decades before the practices came to be seen not just as wrong, but as unseemly.

Appiah focuses on the shift from widely held "moral sentiments" to substantial changes in "moral behavior." He contends that these changes can take place fairly rapidly, and can be a fundamental break in what was previously seen as honorable and acceptable behavior: "[A]t the end of a moral revolution, as at the end of a scientific revolution, things look new. Looking back, even over a single generation, people ask, 'What were we thinking? How did we do *that* for all those years?'"[25]

In looking at the three examples of the abolition of dueling, foot binding, and slavery, Appiah finds significant commonalities that may help us to hone our efforts for ongoing shifts in honor codes. One of the most salient lessons that he draws from his examination of these shifts is that they *were not primarily motivated by new and persuasive moral critiques*: "Whatever happened when these immoral practices ceased, it wasn't, so it seemed to me, that people were bowled over by new moral arguments. Dueling was always murderous and irrational; footbinding was always painfully crippling; slavery was always an assault on the humanity of the slave."[26]

What led to changes in behavior is that influential groups in society decided that these practices were not just immoral, but were an affront to what it meant for them to be worthy of respect and what it meant for them to live with honor. Let us look more closely at the abolition of slavery and the slave trade in England, and the crucial role played by the sense of identity held by two classes that were growing in economic and political power in British society, workers and members of the middle class. Appiah highlights the key role played here by the increasingly powerful English working class: "in finding their own honor as working people, the English working classes in the mid-nineteenth century allied themselves against the culture of slavery, which associated freedom (and whiteness) with honor and slavery (and blackness) with dishonor."[27]

Appiah is clear that the discredited systems were themselves once seen as a manifestation of a particular form of honor: "[P]lantation slavery in the Atlantic world was not just an economic institution—a source of labor—but also an honor system, in which manual labor was assigned to a dishonored race, and the honor of white people, even those of the very lowest social standing, was enhanced by their identity as members of a race that could not legally be enslaved." Appiah makes an important point about the abolition of slavery. While there have been key shifts, this is a transition that is still ongoing: "labor and African descent had to be dissociated from dishonor. (This last process is still underway)."[28]

Now—what can we learn from the shifts that led to the abolition of slavery to what is still needed in the present? It was important that slavery was seen to be morally wrong, to be a fundamental violation of the humanity and dignity of those who were enslaved, and, for those who were religious, a violation of the fundamental tenet that all human beings "were equal in the eyes of God." This conviction, however, was both widely shared and insufficient to lead to structural change.[29]

What made the difference? Appiah sees a convergence between the ways in which the identity of an increasingly powerful working class was tied to the abhorrence of the dehumanization of slavery and the value of labor, and the ways in which the honor of that working class, its political strength and influence, was itself expressed in challenging slavery.

Appiah recounts the ways in which the very identity of the English working class was tied to two ideals—a conviction that to be human means that one must be deeply affronted by and moved to action by the suffering of slavery and, what is equally significant, a recognition of the honor and value of labor. What it meant to be a person of honor was to work with others to take concrete steps to end this institutional assault on humanity. Furthermore, by valuing labor per se, the equation that those who were enslaved were less than honorable because they were workers was broken. To work can be noble, and should not be seen as the mark of those who are inferior. A key dimension of the struggle for abolition was that those whites who allied with Africans in the challenges to the institution of slavery saw their concrete means of protest as themselves an expression of honor—competing in the production of petitions demanding the end of an immoral and unjust system, participating in boycotts of sugar and cotton produced by slavery.

> What really worked, in the end, however, was the national campaign of petitions to Parliament.... The [Anti-Slavery] Society organized petition-signing meetings all across the country, and they became competitive events. In the newly prosperous industrializing towns . . . the campaign allowed new magnates, like Josiah Wedgwood, to express pride in their freshly acquired civic standing.[30]

The numbers of people who joined in these campaigns to affirm the equal humanity of Africans, and to call for the end of the system that violated that humanity at its core, were substantial:

[T]he movement [to abolish slavery] had huge numbers of followers among the "middling classes." (Late in 1787, in the first mass anti-slavery petition, the city of Manchester—with a population of just 50,000, counting children—produced almost 11,000 signatures.) One measure of the movement's success was the fact that, in the early 1790s, between 300,000 and 400,000 people joined boycotts of slave-grown sugar.[31]

Once framed as an expression of honor, the campaign to end slavery gained traction: "The movement for the abolition of the slave trade began in the decade of the 1780s and took hold in the 1790s, the two decades in which the centuries-old English slave trade reached its height."[32] Despite its power, it took more than 50 years, until 1838, for Britain to end its involvement in slavery:

> The Parliament of the United Kingdom abolished the slave trade in the British Empire in 1807; enacted the end of colonial slavery in 1833; and abandoned the Negro Apprenticeship that succeeded slavery in the West Indies in 1838, thus liberating, in the end, more than three quarters of a million slaves.[33]

While Appiah recounts this change as a revolution that "came with astonishing speed," I would argue that the speed was not fast enough, and that one of the imperatives that we have now as agents of social change is to learn from these movements how to both act in ways that are decisive in ending forms of injustice and to learn, by deliberately repeating these lessons of what has worked in the past, to act more quickly to end structural forms of injustice that deny the humanity of millions of people in the present.

Here then, is our task: to discern the multiple dimensions of successful social movements in the past, and, knowing those, determine how we can apply them to our ongoing challenges of economic, racial, and environmental justice. Appiah is describing the same phenomenon highlighted by William Schulz, briefly in his General Assembly address, and in more detail in his book *In Our Own Best Interests*.[34] When social movements are successful, groups with a measure of political and economic power do more than respond out of fear or acquiescence to a superior power. The rising industrial class in England worked to end slavery out of an affirmation of what they too held most dear—the equality of all human beings, and the need to concretely affirm and respect the dignity of labor. When successful, significant numbers of people in power see the legitimacy of the protestors' critique, the desirability of the prophetic vision, and the feasibility and necessity of beginning the implementation of that vision in daily institutional practices and in foundational institutional policies.

Steven Pinker, *The Better Angels of Our Nature*

There have been moments in history in which people have reshaped institutions to embody justice and human rights and to reduce physical violence. The social psychologist Steven Pinker described just this process in *The Better Angels of Our Nature: Why Violence Has Declined.* In his massive study of the decline of various forms of violence, published in 2011, Pinker examined the history of the decline of slavery, capital punishment, and torture as accepted and routine forms of political and economic life. He also examined what he called the ongoing "rights revolution": "civil rights, women's rights, children's rights, gay rights and animal rights."[35] In each case he found a complex interaction of five historical forces: an expansion of the circle of sympathy, an escalator of reason, a system of commerce governed by laws and respect, increasing empowerment of and respect for women, and the Leviathan and Justicia—a state and judiciary that are regarded as fundamentally fair to all members of society, restrained in the use of force, and evenhanded in the enforcement of laws. In each movement, large numbers of people came to value the lives of people formerly exploited and marginalized, and embodied those values in new laws, institutional policies, and cultural norms.[36]

It is very different to read Steven Pinker today than it was in 2011 when *The Better Angels of Our Nature* was first published. In 2011, Steven Pinker claimed that "the decline of violence may be the most significant and least appreciated development in the history of our species. Its implications touch the core of our beliefs and values—for what could be more fundamental than an understanding of whether the human condition, over the course of its history, has gotten steadily better, steadily worse, or not changed?"[37]

Pinker provided solid statistical evidence that physical violence had declined, and he examined the cultural and social forces that led to that decline. His response, however, was not optimism, but one of ongoing vigilance: "*Declines of violence are a product of social, cultural, and material conditions. If the conditions persist, violence will remain low or decline further; if they don't, it won't.*"[38]

It is also very different to read Pinker's 2018 book, *Enlightenment Now*, than it is to read his previous book. In this volume, the judicious caution of the former work has been replaced with resolute optimism. Pinker argues that while there may be short-term setbacks in rights and respect for immigrants, women, and racial minorities, the fundamental gains of the "rights revolution" cannot be eroded.[39] Furthermore, Pinker does not address a significant development in our cultural and political life, the erosion of reason, respect, and compassion through uses of social media that reinforce polarization and occlude the operation of reason.[40]

In contrast to his more recent claims, what Pinker described in 2011 as the possibility of dangerous rises in violence may well now be an actuality. In examining the significance of Pinker's work, there are two major issues for us to consider. Is physical violence now on the rise? Are the social, cultural, and material conditions that have led to declines in violence in the past being eroded in the present? As Pinker stated in 2011, declines of violence are neither inevitable nor immutable. Are we seeing, in the United States, for example, a rise in racialized police violence and in racist terror?

In the case of police violence against African Americans in the United States, it may not be the case that violence is getting worse, but that there is an expansion of the circle of sympathy in which many white Americans are finally seeing what African Americans, Native Americans, and people who are Latinx have long known to be true—that there is a disproportionate amount of police violence against those communities, and that such violence is both endemic and long-standing. Pinker did acknowledge the severity of police violence against African Americans in 2011, stating that this was a major factor in ongoing crime and instability. He also argued that mass incarceration was a fundamental failure of one of the core elements of a peaceful society, the reliable implementation of the Leviathan and Justicia.[41]

Whether or not the amount of violence against African Americans and other people of color is increasing, there is growing consensus that the amount of violence that exists is fundamentally unjust and a violation of our basic values, a moral and political outrage that must be stopped. We live in a time in which the activists in #BlackLivesMatter are leading in both an expansion of the circle of sympathy and the escalator of reason. Activists throughout the United States are drawing attention to both the fact of violence and to the concrete measures of accountability and prevention that must be put in place to stop such violence. We find the expansion of the circle of sympathy in efforts to raise awareness of the human costs of this violence and in demands that it stop, and we find the escalator of reason in sustained attention to concrete steps that can both hold those who commit such violence legally responsible and prevent such violence in the future.[42] It is here that we have the convergence of activist pressure from the outside and professionals acting in deep solidarity to continue work that has already begun for structural change. In fact, efforts for structural change in police-community relations have been in place for decades and are now being given increased attention although there is also ongoing resistance to such profound social change.

Criminal Justice Reform

We live in a time in which many people are applying the lessons of the history of racism to our current struggles for a socially just criminal justice system. Let us look more deeply at the political opportunity and ethical challenges posed by the recent convergence of those from the left, center, and right of the U.S. political spectrum on the pressing issue of criminal justice reform, and the possibly stronger attempt to reaffirm punitive and racially discriminatory forms of policing and criminal justice by many conservative politicians and policy makers.

Since its publication in 2010, *The New Jim Crow: Mass Incarceration in an Age of Colorblindness* by the civil rights attorney and professor Michelle Alexander has raised critical awareness of the ways in which the criminal justice system in the United States disproportionately penalizes and discriminates against African Americans. It was no surprise, therefore, to read in a February 2015 article in the *New York Times* that a coalition had been formed "to reduce [the] prison population, overhaul sentencing, and reduce recidivism." What *was* surprising, however, was the composition of the Coalition for Public Safety. Liberal groups that one would expect to work for criminal justice reform—the American Civil Liberties Union and the Center for American Progress—were joined by staunchly conservative groups—Koch Industries and FreedomWorks, a group affiliated with the Tea Party. At that time, representatives from the left and the right acknowledged the political power, and risks, of such a coalition. The power—there is a genuine commitment from all parties to enact reforms that will substantially reduce the number of people in prison. The risk—while the overall goals and even specific policies are the same, the primary motivation for the work varies. Those on the right decried the financial cost of "the 2.2 million-person prison population" and those on the left denounced its intrinsic racism and human costs.[43] At this juncture in history, both efforts are under assault by those who remain committed to providing military equipment to the police, who want to step back from federal oversight of policing, and who favor a continuation of the policies that have led to mass incarceration.

There is not yet an inkling of a similar convergence on a closely related issue, police violence against people of color, but there is movement in that direction on the part of those who are leftist and progressive. The work of the Black Lives Matter campaign has brought essential attention to glaring acts of police violence in which innocent people have been killed, and people are calling for responses that are equally energized and sustained.

On August 9, 2014, an unarmed 18-year-old black man, Michael Brown, was shot by a police officer, Darren Wilson, while walking down the street in the middle of the day. His body was left on the street for four hours. In the protests and investigations that followed, the guilt of Wilson was revealed, as was the systemic racism of the Ferguson, Missouri police department.[44] Although Wilson was not indicted for murder by a grand jury in St. Louis, the U.S. Department of Justice continued its investigation and found patterns of systemic discrimination. African Americans made up 66% of the Ferguson population, yet were the victims of 88% of the times when force was used by police officers and were subject to 93% of all arrests. In an interview with *Democracy Now*, Michelle Alexander stated that the events in Ferguson, Missouri, show "why the criminal justice system of racial control should be undone." She spoke of the report by the Justice Department that uncovered patterns of racial discrimination in Ferguson: "The report does not give me hope. What gives me hope is that people across America are finally waking up. . . . There is a system of racial and social control in communities of color across America. . . . What we see now is that we do have the power to make things change. The question is are we going to transition from protest politics to long-term, strategic movement building?"[45] A year after the killing of Michael Brown, the Reverend Tommie Pierson, a minister and a Missouri state representative, expressed a similar concern: "Protesting is good, but it only brings attention to the problems. Solving the problem requires doing other things." Rev. Pierson spoke of the importance of voting, of running for office, "of changing the system to work for us."[46]

As we take up the calls of Michelle Alexander and Reverend Pierson for long-term strategic change, we do not have to begin de novo. There are people who have worked for decades on the systemic roots of such racist violence, and who see this moment as an opportunity to enact much-needed change in the recruitment, training, and oversight of police officers. Take, for example, the work of Vern Redekop, Shirley Paré, and Aaron Thompson. Vern Neufeld Redekop is an associate professor of conflict studies at Saint Paul University in Canada. He is the former president of the Canadian Institute for Conflict Resolution. Shirley Paré is a senior trainer at the Canadian Institute for Conflict Resolution and a retired officer of the Canadian Armed Forces. Aaron Thompson is a sociologist who has worked on equitable and racially just police community relations for over two decades. Thompson is the executive vice president and chief academic officer for the Kentucky Council on Postsecondary Education and has worked with police departments in cities such as Richmond, Kentucky; Rockford, Illinois; and Columbia, Missouri.

In 2010, Vern Redekop and Shirley Paré published *Beyond Control: A Mutual Respect Approach to Protest-Crowd Relations*. The urgency that led Paré and Redekop to write the book has only intensified. They pointed out the danger of increasingly militarized police forces and the necessity of sustaining overall positive community relationships with the police in which there is genuine respect by the police for the communities they serve. The paradigm of community policing has been in place since the 1980s, but it can easily be eroded and requires systematic efforts to maintain.[47]

> In the 1980s there was a movement among police to change the paradigm of policing from a strict law enforcement approach to "community policing" in which police were to identify with the community as a part of the community. [This approach] later morphed into problem-solving policing in which police were to look at difficult situations as problems to be solved rather than simply bad people breaking some laws. . . . One Canadian police inspector who took a national lead in community policing used to reward his officers monthly on the basis of who had worked with community members to find a creative long-term solution to an intractable problem. This policy is in stark contrast to police being rewarded for arrests made or cases closed.[48]

At the core of a mutual respect paradigm of policing is a commitment to not just the right of protest but also to the *necessity* of protest as an essential ingredient in a healthy society. Rather than a crowd-control or crowd-management form of policing, there can be relationships in which police and protestors work together to ensure that grievances are expressed and public safety maintained. Redekop and Paré give examples of such paradigms in action, and the complexity of the ongoing training and community police relationships that are required to keep them alive.

On January 7, 2015 Aaron Thompson gave an address, "Is Justified Always Justice: The Role Leaders Play in Building Community," at the Unitarian Universalist theological school in Chicago, Meadville Lombard. Thompson made four main points about the nature of the crisis facing us, and the opportunities it provides for systemic reform. Each point was surprising to his progressive audience of ministerial students and the ministers who are serving as their internship supervisors, all of whom are already committed to racial justice and fundamental criminal justice reform.

First, Thompson said that it is a mistake to cast this as a liberal versus conservative issue. He himself is a liberal, and is committed to reform for liberal reasons. He brings to this work his experience as an African American male who knows firsthand the threats of racist police violence, whether caused by explicit or implicit bias. Yet he has found over the years that many conservatives also support the training and oversight of police departments in ways that monitor and limit the use of force in the service of public safety and order. Second, the unjust use of force can only be limited through ongoing training and systemic attention to creating a culture of respect for a racially diverse population. It is important to systematically check the verbal disrespect on the part of police officers that mars police-community relations. It is crucial to provide ongoing training in identifying the implicit bias that leads police officers to misidentify the threats posed by African Americans. These basic tasks are essential in preventing escalation into the unjust use of deadly force.

Here there is much to learn from the work of the psychologist Curtis Hardin and the social ethicist Mahzarin Banaji on implicit bias. In an essay published in 2011, they reported on a significant study of implicit bias. In a series of studies undertaken between 2002 and 2007, subjects were asked if a person was holding a tool or a gun. The majority of people were more likely to mistakenly identify a white person as holding a tool when they actually held a gun, and a majority mistakenly identified a black person as holding a gun when they held a tool. A finding that surprised these authors, writing in 2011—that "these results applied even to police officers"—has been made undeniably clear in the disclosures of police violence in the past few years.[49] Thompson made it clear that in the case of police officers implicit bias has long been deadly and that containing implicit bias requires far more than changes in individual conscious attitudes. Just as accuracy in shooting requires ongoing target practice, acuity and wisdom in when not to use deadly force requires both rigorous oversight and ongoing training.

Third, Thompson explored a paradoxical challenge for concerned citizens and community leaders. The protests following the 2014 killings of innocent black men by police—the shooting of Michael Brown in Ferguson, Missouri, and the strangling of Eric Garner in Staten Island, New York, and in each case the failure of grand juries to indict the officers responsible for those deaths—were essential in raising awareness of the need for fundamental change, and may provide the momentum for a municipality to take up the ongoing work of rigorous civilian review boards and fundamental policy change. Thompson gave, however, a pointed warning to his audience of current and prospective ministers. In his experience, ministers get in the way of reform when the protests become more about their being seen and making a statement, rather than providing the staying power for the long work of lifting up the history of police-community relations and then working with conservatives and liberals for fundamental reforms.

Since Thompson spoke in January 2015, we have seen such efforts emerge at both the national and local arenas. On the local level, many municipalities are including the use of body cameras by police officers. In a May 10, 2015 article in the *San Francisco Chronicle*, Kevin Fagan reported on significant changes in the reduction of violence: "Since deploying wearable cameras in 2010, use-of-force incidents in the 400,000-population city of Oakland have plunged 72 percent, according to department records. With 700 body cameras, Oakland has the biggest inventory in the nation." This is a case in which there is genuine accord between police officers and the citizenry they serve. As the police chief of Oakland, Sean Whent, explained: "It's not just that the cops are behaving better when they know the camera is on, but people interacting with us know we're filming, so they behave better too. I think it has a civilizing effect on both sides of the camera."[50] Yet, as the advocates of body cameras note, as important as they are, they are not the only policy changes required to limit excessive violence and restore public trust. To that end, the Obama administration had enacted specific policies (i.e., reexamining and reducing the provision of military equipment to police departments) and was engaged in a systemic review of the recruitment, training, and oversight of police officers nationwide.[51]

Fourth, Thompson pointed to another surprising area of shared concern. Just as concern with the control of deadly force by police officers is shared by liberals and conservatives, Thompson reminded us that most police officers want to have positive relationships with the communities in which they serve and want to work with the community to protect people against crime and to maintain the just order that is essential for a democratic society.

There are key roles that religious leaders can play. Remember the core finding of Chenoweth and Stephan regarding the role of violence in movements for social change. While the evidence is not clear on whether or not a radical, violent fringe helps or harms movements for social change, it is clear that the violence must remain peripheral rather than dominant. In the work of Vern Redekop and Shirley Paré we can see what leads to violence in protests, both by the police and by protestors, and what can be done to contain it. They argue that it is first important to understand the scapegoating dynamic, and for protestors and police alike to become aware of their own proclivities to violence and to be proactive in checking them. It is naïve to think that there will ever be a protest without the possibility of violence by protestors, or ever an exercise of maintaining security by the police without the tendency for them to also become violent.

To read Redekop and Paré now is challenging and disconcerting. When the book was written in 2010, they operated from the assumption of a social given—one recognized by police, by protestors, and by the larger public—that protest is a legitimate part of society. They also began with the assumption that the role of the police in the protection of civil order includes the protection of the right of people to protest. That fundamental conviction—peaceful protest is a right in a democracy—came under attack early in the Donald Trump administration.

Even when the police and protestors agree on the right to free speech and protest there are dynamics that may lead to the escalation of violence. There is a need for both sides to be aware of these dynamics and the ways in which they can check them when, and rarely not if, they arise.

Why is this important? Redekop and Paré argue that when there is violence the focus of media attention is the clash with the police, rather than the issues being raised, the systems of injustice that are the focus of the demonstration.[52] For example, in protests in June 2010 in Toronto at the Group of Twenty (G20) summit, a meeting of finance ministers from the 20 major economies, the focus became the violent clashes with the police when what people were demonstrating against was a system of economic injustice that also exploits the police.

Here we have a two-edged sword—the necessity and power of the media to convey to a larger audience the message of protests, and yet the tendency of the media to focus on violence and spectacle, giving far more attention to a few violent incidents than to the larger numbers of peaceful activists. The trick—how do we get attention to what we want to focus on?

Redekop and Paré claim that protestors and police are each necessary for a well-functioning society and for the effective and safe operation of protests. Yet, drawing on the work of the philosopher René Girard, they also address what leads both to slide into violence and scapegoating. For the police, there is, first, an experience of danger and fear; second, a strong group identity as the keeper of order; third, a single violator of that order is made a scapegoat for the entire threat; fourth, there is disproportionate violence against that threat. Redekop and Paré state that police can be trained to know that this is likely to happen, and can have officers ready to contain the violence of other police.[53]

The dynamics for protestors are the same. The only differential is that the strong group identity is that of the bearer of justice, rather than the keeper of order.[54] Religious leaders can play a key role in preventing the explosion of violence on both sides and upholding a paradigm of mutual respect. Here we can learn from the insights of professor of religion and theological studies Theophus Smith and his analysis of the concept of "conjure," "that which heals can also harm."[55] We can both honor the power and energy of protest and know how to act when it becomes violent. We can call both police and protestors away from two dangerous paradigms, crowd control and crowd management, and back to a catalytic paradigm of mutual respect. With crowd control, the public gets the message that violence is on the increase and the protestors are dangerous. With crowd management, the police are seen as helpful in containing troublesome outsiders. With mutual respect, the public gets a vision of new possibilities, a vision grounded in both what is unjust and what is just and the number of people committed to this greater specific vision of an expansive common good.[56]

Containing Physical and Structural Violence and Expanding Support for Human Rights

Can the paradigm of "mutual respect" be applied to other dimensions of our common life, economic, cultural, and political? Here again the work of Pinker is significant, and here it is limited and appropriately open to more questions for those who are activists and leaders of institutions. Pinker explicitly and deliberately stops with an analysis of what has worked in the past to decrease physical violence and increase respect for human rights. He states that he will not "offer advice to politicians, police chiefs, or peacemakers, which given my qualifications would be a form of malpractice."[57] Pinker's malpractice, however, is our professional responsibility. How do we nurture, sustain, and expand the social, cultural, and material conditions that have led to the decline of physical violence?

Might we be able to once again activate forces that have led to declines of violence and increased respect for human rights in the past? Furthermore, might the dynamics that led to the decline in physical violence and the respect for the human rights of growing segments of the population be applied to structural violence, to the ongoing costs of poverty, of institutionalized racism, of environmental degradation?

None of these questions can, of course, be answered in advance of the doing, outside of the hard work of applying these same factors to seemingly intractable political and economic problems. Pinker was clear that this ongoing work was outside of the scope of his professional expertise.

But what might professionals learn from Pinker as we work to contain the spread of violence and enhance the reach of justice in the institutions we manage, govern, and shape? Here we take up a fundamental task of social ethics, grounding our political work in the best science of our time. Pinker's analysis of what has led to either declines or increases in violence is grounded in a theory of mind based on cognitive science, affective and cognitive neuroscience, and social and evolutionary psychology. Based on those sciences, his view of human nature is neither tragic nor utopian. Humans are capable of compassion, but "compassion is not a reflex that is triggered automatically by the presence of another living thing." In fact, just the opposite is the case. People tend to react with compassion to tribe and kin, but hold in suspicion those seen as other.[58]

Furthermore, while violence can decline, it can also increase. Here we have not a change in human nature, but changes in how we work with the complexities of that nature, its capacity for generosity and domination, for fear and compassion. Remember, Pinker claims that violence has declined and can decline, but such decline is neither inevitable nor assured. There is nothing in human nature that guarantees that progress in the past will be maintained in the future. If we want to stanch the horrific increase in racist violence and possible increases in other forms of violence, it is important that we understand what has led to declines in the past, and explore whether or not those same conditions may be similarly effective in the present.

Let us look, then, in more detail at five historical forces identified by Pinker. The first is the expansion of the circle of sympathy.

> The science of empathy has shown that sympathy can promote genuine altruism, and that it can be extended to new classes of people when a beholder takes the perspective of a member of that class, even a fictitious one. The research gives teeth to the speculation that humanitarian reforms are driven in part by an enhanced sensitivity to the experiences of living things and a genuine desire to relieve their suffering. And as such, the cognitive process of perspective-taking and the emotion of sympathy must figure in the explanation for many historical reductions in violence. They include institutionalized violence such as cruel punishments, slavery, and frivolous executions; the everyday abuse of vulnerable populations such as women, children, homosexuals, racial minorities, and animals; and the waging of wars, conquests, and ethnic cleansings with a callousness to their human costs.[59]

A key factor in the expansion of sympathy in the past has been the spread of literacy, and more specifically the rise of a particular kind of fiction and autobiography that humanized the lives of others seen as nonhuman or threatening. From the "powerful autobiographies of slaves to the female protagonists in 19th century fiction," literature enabled people to see and then honor the humanity of others.[60]

Pinker is clear, however, about both the power and limits of empathy. Empathy, even when expanded, is not enough to reduce violence. Emotional openness to the dignity and struggles of others is not enough for fundamental social change. Because of this, Pinker argues for the importance of a second historical force, the "escalator of reason":

> But the limited reach of empathy, with its affinity for people like us and people close to us, suggests that empathy needs the universalizing boost of reason to bring about changes in policies and norms that actually reduce violence in the world. . . . These changes include not just legal

prohibitions against acts of violence but institutions that are engineered to reduce the temptations of violence. Among these wonkish contraptions are democratic government, the Kantian safeguards against war, reconciliation movements in the developing world, nonviolent resistance movements, international peacekeeping operations, the crime prevention reforms and civilizing offensives of the 1990s, and tactics of containment, sanctions, and wary engagement designed to give national leaders more options than just the game of chicken that led to the First World War or the appeasement that led to the Second.[61]

Three other historical forces are of equal importance in the reduction of physical violence. Pinker talks about the ways in which relatively just economic relations within and between nations can lessen the chance of internal violence and war: "Commerce is a positive-sum game in which everybody can win; as technological progress allows the exchange of goods and ideas over longer distances and among larger groups of trading partners, other people become more valuable alive than dead, and they are less likely to become targets of demonization and dehumanization."[62] Pinker points to a key aspect of such exchange, and why he qualifies it as "gentle." Commerce can be beneficial even *if* built on an infrastructure that contains exploitation:

> Beginning in the late Middle Ages, expanding kingdoms not only penalized plunder and nationalized justice, but supported an infrastructure of exchange, including money and the enforcement of contracts. This infrastructure, together with technological advances such as in roads and clocks, and the removal of taboos on interest, innovation, and competition, made commerce more attractive, and as a result merchants, craftsmen, and bureaucrats displaced knightly warriors.[63]

As we have seen in our examination of the move toward a socially just green economy, this attempt to create a form of economic relations that honors the gifts of interdependence is unfinished, yet ongoing.

It is a fourth factor, however, that may well be in the process of being undermined today in the United States—"the Leviathan and Justicia"—a citizen's confidence that the use of force by police departments and the application of justice throughout society are fair, unbiased, and in the interest of the greater good. As Pinker noted even in 2011, "The . . . United States imprisons far more people than it should, with disproportionate harm falling on African American communities." He also argued that higher crime rates in many African American communities were due to a well-warranted lack of respect and trust in police departments by the communities that they should be designed to serve.[64]

A fifth and final factor that is as essential and remains contested in much of the world is what Pinker calls the feminization process: "direct political empowerment [of women], the deflation of manly honor, the promotion of marriage on women's terms, the right of girls to be born, and women's control over their own reproduction."[65]

In 2011, Pinker's work was challenging on three counts. While some questioned the claims of actual declines in physical violence, the more significant political challenges to the book then and now are not the accuracy of Pinker's historical analysis, but the implications of his work for ongoing political challenges. First, Pinker's analysis is primarily based on Western cultures. What processes are at work in other cultures? Are they the same or different? Second, Pinker's focus is on physical violence—might the same processes work to mitigate structural violence (i.e., poverty and the five forms of injustice described by Iris Marion Young)?

"Never forget. Never again." What would it mean if we applied these convictions, so rightly held in regard to the Holocaust, to other times of systemic violence? "Never forget. Always again." What would it mean if we applied these convictions to times when social movements have been successful, when human lives have been honored, when the ecosystem has been respected? In our current era, where is the expansion of sympathy needed? Is literature still a valued medium for that expansion? Are there other forms of human creative expression that are serving the same function for our era as autobiographies and epistolary novels did in the 19th century? In our current era, what new forms can the escalator of reason take in our institutional lives? Where else are we seeing the escalator of reason at work?

This leads to a third question for us to consider. We are seeing in our time the rise of explicit hatred, bigotry, and physical violence. Given this upsurge, might a renewed application of the five historical forces that have led to declines of violence in the past once again make a significant difference? Here the challenge is clear; the outcome uncertain. In each of these cases, we may have the opposite of what occurred in the 19th and 20th centuries. Pinker argues that the rise of epistolary literature led to respect for the humanity and fundamental rights of people formerly ignored, oppressed, and marginalized. Now, however, the current tenor of movies and television shows in the United States that revel in physical violence and psychological cruelty significantly diminish our capacities for empathy. The focus on sensationalism in both the news and the popular media is even leading to a disregard for the truth. Writing in the *New York Times* on September 4, 2017, the journalist Charles M. Blow put Donald Trump's "incessant lying" into a larger political context. It was not merely a lack of character in one person, but a basic affront to the core of democracy, to what Pinker would call the "escalator of reason" as a key factor in reducing violence and institutionalizing the protection of human rights. To quote Blow:

> Trump's incessant lying is obscene. It is a collapse in morality; it is an ethical assault. . . . It seems odd that we have to defend the merits of truth, and yet we do. We must. This is not simply about a flawed man, this is about the function of our democracy and American positioning in the world. How is one supposed to debate policy with someone who almost never tells the truth? How can a liar negotiate treaties or navigate international disputes? . . . we must develop a societal strategy for protecting the truth in a post-truth world, and the first step is that we must never stop saying: Donald Trump is a liar.[66]

We do find, thankfully, counters to the contraction of the circle of sympathy in other forms of social media. The release of videos taken by citizens of police violence provides evidence to a larger world of rampant verbal disrespect and physical violence of too many police officers against African Americans. How can we use social media to increase compassion and respect, keeping alive our sensitivity to the physical and psychological suffering of others? How do we share stories of where people are doing the rewarding and challenging work of living in racially and culturally diverse workplaces and communities? How do we maintain both gratitude *and* vigilance? As Pinker states so clearly:

> The shift is not toward complacency; we enjoy the peace we find today because people in past generations were appalled by the violence in their time

and worked to reduce it, and so we should work to reduce the violence that remains in our time. Indeed, it is a recognition of the decline of violence that best affirms that such efforts are worthwhile. Man's inhumanity to man has long been a subject for moralization. With the knowledge that something has driven it down, we can also treat it as a matter of cause and effect. Instead of asking, "Why is there war" we might ask, "Why is there peace?" We can obsess not just over what we have been doing wrong but also over what we have been doing right. Because we *have* been doing something right, and it would be good to know what, exactly, it is.[67]

In a speech at the Association of Theological Schools in spring 2015, Willie Jenkins, associate professor of theology and Black Church studies, described the work for racial justice in theological education as our efforts to honor and celebrate the blessing of diversity. I expect that we will see more of the expansion of the circle of sympathy in regard to gun violence, Islamophobia, and xenophobic and racist immigration policies. Our challenge will be to accompany that increase in sympathy with the escalator of reason, with the creation of concrete policies and practices that contain violence and uphold the gift, the blessing, of racial, cultural, gender, and religious difference.

Applied Behavioral Science

It is in this move from prophetic critique to catalytic engagement that we have much to learn from other theorists about what enables policy changes to be implemented, assessed, and revised. Here the escalator of reason is applied in examining what enables people and institutions to routinely and systematically act in ways that are socially just and environmentally sustainable. In this work we have much to learn from the insights of the psychologist Daniel Kahneman and the behavioral science of social change.

As we have seen in Appiah's work, extensive and lasting social change occurs when people embrace a new vision of what is honorable and, as we have seen in Pinker's writing, when it embodies that vision in concrete social practices. The move, however, from honorable goals to equitable practices is neither linear nor assured. Experimentation, risk-taking, and mistakes are an inevitable part of the process. Here again we encounter a fundamental challenge—the simple insight that it is far easier to rectify mistakes when you know that you are likely to make them. And, a corollary insight, it is far easier to see the mistakes of others than to acknowledge, and reckon with, our own. Kahneman describes his work as an attempt to address both concerns. While we can rarely check ourselves, we can create an institutional culture in which we check each other. As he states, "it is much easier to identify a minefield when you observe others wandering into it than when you are about to do so."[68]

According to Kahneman, this cultural change requires two interrelated developments, "a richer language" for identifying errors of judgment and a culture that values "the skill of constructive criticism." In such a culture, Kahneman claims that "[decision makers] will make better choices when they trust their critics to be sophisticated and fair."[69] Also, in such a culture, there is a recognition that we cannot escape the vulnerabilities and limitations of human insight and reasoning, but we can learn to see the "distinctive patterns in the errors people make. Systematic errors are known as biases, and they recur predictably in particular circumstances. When the handsome and confident speaker bounds onto the stage, for example, you can anticipate that the audience will judge his comments more favorably than he deserves. The availability of a diagnostic label for this bias—the halo effect—makes it easier to anticipate, recognize, and understand."[70]

In his groundbreaking book *Thinking, Fast and Slow*, Kahneman primarily explores the biases that affect our ability to make rational economic decisions under conditions of uncertainty. He and his colleague Amos Tversky identified 20 biases that they see as intrinsic to "the machinery of cognition" and not simply errors caused by emotions overriding reason. They also found that these biases could not be overcome by individual willpower. They are only checked through the critical insights of others: "Although humans are not irrational, they often need help to make more accurate judgments and better decisions, and in some cases policies and institutions can provide that help." Kahneman is clear—these policies are not simple or easy, but it is possible to create organizations that acknowledge our vulnerability and intrinsic limitations: "[O]rganizations can also encourage a culture in which people watch out for one another as they approach minefields. . . . Constant quality control is an alternative to the wholesale reviews of processes that organizations commonly undertake in the wake of disasters."[71]

In *Thinking, Fast and Slow*, Kahneman did not explicitly address the ways in which cognitive errors lead to the replication of structures that are systemically exploitive, discriminatory, and oppressive. It is just that task, however, that is central to the work of applied behavioral science. In his introduction to *The Behavioral Foundations of Public Policy*, Kahneman describes this move to look at the ways in which intrinsic human errors in judgment "extended beyond purely economic circumstances, to issues ranging from voting and negotiations, to health behavior, labor relations, education, and the law."[72] Kahneman describes the importance of policy makers moving beyond the assumptions of the "rational agent model" of human decision making, and exploring instead the range of forces that actually shape our decisions. These forces include intrinsic cognitive limitations, implicit biases, and exposure to negative racial and gender stereotypes. This study of how our decisions are shaped is the work of the burgeoning field of applied behavioral science. Its implications for those committed to the move from prophetic critique to prophetic engagement are vast. With these tools, we can see why good intentions often fail, and we can create institutional practices that activate our expansive best rather than our defensive and insular worst. As Kahneman states, this work is essential in the following areas: "When it comes to the memories of eyewitnesses, or to employers' ability to avoid discrimination, or to the budgeting challenges of the poor, behavior research presents the serious possibility that we may want to rethink some fundamental concepts and question the basic assumption of current policies."[73]

Guy Adams and Danny Balfour are professors of public affairs and nonprofit administration who have taken this principle of inoculation even further. They argue that the practice of professional ethics, with its attention to efficiency, effectiveness, accountability, and productivity, must be amplified by a rigorous awareness of, and safeguards against, administrative evil, the process by which actions that cause grave harm to other people, and to the environment, are masked by the daily practices of "ordinary people acting appropriately in their organizational role."[74] Balfour and Adams advocate for a new form of professional ethics infused with historical consciousness and claim that we "can recognize the masks of administrative evil and refuse to act as its accomplice."[75] They examine in detail the role that administrative evil played in the implementation of the Nazi Holocaust, the *Challenger* shuttle disaster, and the internment of Japanese Americans during World War II. They argue that our task as professionals is twofold—learning how to recognize administrative evil as it occurs within our organizations, and establishing ongoing safeguards against it.[76]

While well received within the discipline, the work laid out by Adams and Balfour has just begun.[77] When individuals encounter administrative evil, they may protest or resign. But what else might they do? What are more powerful ways of bringing such awareness to the normal practices of attention, vigilance, and oversight within corporate and governmental responsibility? A first step is a resolute and vigilant awareness not just of the mistakes of others but also of the likelihood that we ourselves will fail, will fall short, and will need to revise even formerly successful strategies to better meet the needs of new situations.

Such awareness is not readily embodied, even by those who are well aware of its importance. In their account of the many ways in which a new generation of philanthropists are using their business skills to create social well-being and environmental justice, Matthew Bishop and Michael Green point out that "taking risks is the essence of philanthrocapitalism."[78]

Despite their forthright acknowledgement of the necessity of critique, Bishop and Green interpret essential criticism as devastating indictment, rather than embracing it as an essential ingredient in effective social change. In their account of Laurie Garret's pertinent and serious examination of the approach of the Gates Foundation to global health, published in *Foreign Affairs* in 2007, they describe the critique as an assault. They characterize Garret's critique as "the brickbats came out again" rather than as just the kind of critical examination essential to determine which approaches to global health are most effective in which situations: "her theme was that focusing on particular diseases—so-called stovepiping—was less effective than a broader approach based on building up the overall health care system of poor countries."[79]

This aversion to critique is also seen in their odd account of the attempts by the Gates Foundation to actively solicit critical feedback: "[Gates] has promised to be open about the foundation's failures, of which he expects plenty—given that taking risks is one of the philanthropist's comparative advantages. . . . in 2007 he gave $105 million to the University of Washington to research the performance of global health work, including that of his foundation. It remains to be seen how willing the university will be to tell a major funding source that he is doing something badly (perish the thought)."[80] What is behind this aversion to potentially transformative and even actively solicited critique? Bishop and Green are aware of a core element of this problem—the stories we tell ourselves. They quote the analysts Lael Brainard and Derek Chollett, who raise a central question: "Can a campaign achieve success where there is no Hollywood storyline—no heroes and villains and conclusive triumphs, only the slow struggle of well-meaning people to overcome the vagaries of nature and set the stage for future generations to lead modestly better lives?"[81]

At this point, a further shift in honor codes is necessary. The shift—the measure of our success is not the perfection of our efforts but our honesty, humility, accountability, resilience, and audacity in the face of unintended consequences and ongoing challenges.

One type of prophetic engagement that took this approach is exemplified in the weeklong trainings of the Equity Institute in Oakland, California. Equity brought together activists for LGBTQIA rights, women's rights, economic justice, and equality for all racial, ethnic, and religious groups and for people with disabilities. They taught different strategies to increase popular awareness of multiple forms of oppression, and explored various means of empowerment and resistance. Inevitably, during each week, an exercise designed to address a single issue, such as gender, replicated, in so doing, another pattern of oppression and injustice—class bias, racism, or homophobia. Rather than seeing these failures among even seasoned activists as an aberration to be denounced, the Equity trainers saw them as the norm—dynamics to be recognized, acknowledged, and worked with in honesty and humility as the source of deeper learning and more supple forms of social justice.

Key Insights for Progressive Practice

How do we embrace what is honorable and embody it in concrete social practices? First, it is important that we name and avoid the Windigo of paralyzing infighting over strategies and tactics and the Windigo of falling prey to either the complacency of reform or the delusions of revolutionary victory. Ongoing critique is valuable when it is used as the catalyst for further experimentation. Ongoing critique is debilitating and destructive when we stop with the denunciation of others.

Second, as we move from critique to building just institutions, there are key practices to follow. We can use the social science available to us to understand what leads to the expansion and embodiment of sympathy and respect for other human beings. We can also choose methods of denunciation, of prophetic rage, that are consonant with the goals of inclusion and building just institutions. As we rightly denounce structures of injustice, we can call even oppressors to accountability and solidarity. As those who have been and are oppressed take up the mantle of power, they can remain aware of their own capacity for partiality, error, and even ego-driven domination.

Third, there are areas where creative social engagement is desperately needed at this juncture in history. The work of fundamental criminal justice reform, of genuinely embodying Justicia and Leviathan at all levels of our political life, is a massive task, yet there are people throughout the United States taking it up with honesty and discipline. The civil rights attorney Alphonse Gerhardstein has created a toolkit that describes the multiple steps that can be taken to curtail police violence and racist policing. And, with his son Adam, he leads workshops on criminal justice reform.[82]

There is another related issue, challenging the overall militarization of police forces, and re-creating a "mutual respect paradigm of policing" in which protests are seen as a core ingredient of successful democracies and the role of police is to protect the right of peaceful protest and to contain violence by protestors, counterprotestors, and other police officers.

A final challenge is finding ways to use new media to increase sympathy and deepen critical thought. Just as literature in the past led to the expansion of the circle of sympathy, how can we shape our new forms of communication to counter, rather than reinforce, polarization and sensational, simplistic thinking?

The history and theory of social change are evolving, as are our current forms of living justly. In the next chapters, we take up further challenges of constructive and catalytic civic engagement, turning to concrete examples of people who are living out the mandate of social justice and environmental sustainability in the businesses they create and the institutions they manage and lead.

3

"Go Social, Go Green"

Environmentally Sound and Socially Just Economic Development

It is startling for many activists to see a commitment to the social good being expressed by the owners and managers of businesses directly through their professional lives. Progressives have long, and rightly, criticized businesses for putting short-term profit over justice for workers and due attention to environmental sustainability. What we see today in the world of social enterprise and B corporations, however, are people in the business world who fully share that critique and are committed to creating a different way of producing goods and services.[1] They are living out, willingly and creatively, the imperative voiced by the secretary-general of the Organization of Economic Co-operation and Development, Angel Gurría, "Go Social, Go Green." This commitment reflects a change in honor codes, the basic values that shape collective life, as compelling as those recounted by Kwame Anthony Appiah in *The Honor Code*.

In their book *The Solution Revolution*, William Eggers, global director at the professional services network Deloitte Research, and Paul Macmillan, global industry leader at Deloitte, describe a major shift in how society is solving core social problems. They describe a "solution economy" in which "new innovators are closing the widening gap between what governments provide and what citizens need. This approach promises better results, lower costs, and the best hope we have for public innovation in an era of fiscal constraints and unmet needs." Eggers and Macmillan state that this move to businesses voluntarily working to meet the needs of citizens is a fundamental shift from a prior honor code in which "thinking beyond the bottom line was viewed as unfocused or, even worse, a disservice to shareholders."[2]

In contrast to a narrow focus on short-term gains for the few, there is now a growing and genuine commitment to long-term social justice for the many. "We can make market forces work better for the poor," explains the businessman and philanthropist Bill Gates, "if we can develop a more creative capitalism—if we can stretch the reach of market forces so that more people can make a profit, or at least make a living, serving people who are suffering from the worst inequities."[3]

Progressives are accustomed to seeing work for social justice and environmental sustainability being expressed in political advocacy and in direct service to victims of injustice. We often are not aware of the ways in which we are not alone in our work for justice, but have allies in the business community. This chapter explores this burgeoning world of social entrepreneurship, its drivers, its impact, and its practical and ethical challenges.

This commitment to social impact is long-standing and is taking on even greater urgency in the face of rising authoritarianism, hatred, and fear. The words of the founders of the B Lab, an organization that supports and certifies businesses that are committed to an interdependent economy, are unabashed in their call to business leaders to expand their work for social justice. Andrew Kassoy, Bart Houlahan, and Jay Coen Gilbert, the founders of B Lab, posted "An Open Letter to Business Leaders" on February 6, 2017. They began by reiterating the B Corps values:

> That we must be the change that we seek in the world,
> That all business ought to be conducted as if people and place mattered,
> That, through their products, practices, and profits, businesses should
> aspire to do no harm and benefit all.
> To do so requires that we act with the understanding that we are each
> dependent upon another and thus responsible for each other and future
> generations.[4]

While these values are of long-standing, Kassoy, Houlahan, and Gilbert were unabashed in their warning of the direct assault on them in this time of rising authoritarianism, and equally forthright in their challenge to business leaders:

> At this moment, we call on all business leaders to do two things. First, in this chaotic moment, to stand up and to speak out, together and unequivocally, when we see injustice, hate, and the violence they produce.

Second, to take concrete action in our businesses to create an inclusive economy that is equitable and creates opportunity for all for the long term.[5]

The numbers of business leaders who share these goals are significant, their impact is real, and they are a significant source of support for generative interdependence. To understand this movement more deeply, let's begin with the basics.

First, what is social entrepreneurship? In their account of the growing power of social entrepreneurship, Roger Martin, institute director of the Martin Prosperity Institute, and Sally Osberg, president and CEO of the Skoll Foundation, describe the ways in which social entrepreneurship relates to, yet differs from, both direct service and political advocacy.[6] As we know, social advocacy is focused on directly challenging the structural causes of poverty, marginalization, and environmental degradation by pushing for changes in state and national laws, and by pushing for international accords, that would make such practices illegal. Social advocacy is also focused on implementing laws and regulations that will enhance the greater common good.

> In contrast to social service providers, social advocates work *indirectly*, advocating for legislative changes that can *transform the environment in question*. . . . Only with new legislation in place would such fundamental and permanent beneficial change take hold. . . . Social advocates work with all levels of government to create lasting, significant change in a variety of domains, from marriage rights to clean water to local development issues.[7]

In the work of social service providers, we find people and organizations committed to working directly to ameliorate the immediate and dire effects of oppression and injustice, providing food for those in need, a place to sleep for those who are homeless, a place of refuge and support for those who are the victims of domestic and sexual violence.

> *Social service providers* have a long and noble history of working to make communities and the world more equal, safer, healthier and, well, better. . . . Social service providers take *direct action* in a given situation. But

they *leave the existing system in place* while seeking to reduce its negative effects. For example, a food bank works directly to ameliorate the
effects of poverty. . . . This food relieves the family's hunger that day, but it
doesn't fundamentally change the dynamic that leaves the family so poor
that it needs to use the food bank the next week, and the next, etc.[8]

Martin and Osberg have described existing ways of seeking to live
justly that are in the process of expansion and transformation. There
are some social service providers that also seek to address the causes
of the suffering that they redress on a daily basis. There is a growing
commitment by people and institutions throughout the world to work
directly to meet basic needs and to change the structures of injustice that
have created those needs in the first place. Social entrepreneurs share the
goals of social service providers and social advocates, seeking to both
rectify the immediate costs of economic and environmental injustice
and to fundamentally reshape the economic structure that has led to
social injustice and environmental damage.

> *Social entrepreneurs* . . . both take direct action *and* seek to transform the
> existing system. They seek to go beyond better, to bring about a trans-
> formed, stable new system that is fundamentally different than the world
> that preceded it. . . . social entrepreneurs explicitly aim to permanently
> and systematically transform a miserable or unfair societal condition.[9]

Let's dig deeper. What does it take to "systematically transform an
unfair societal condition" in the daily practices of our economic lives,
not just in one business, but in all businesses, not just in small businesses, but in corporations? If a company decides, like Bill Gates, "to
serve people who are suffering from the worst inequities," two institutional shifts are necessary. First, there is an external shift. The business
must be incorporated in a way that allows focus on a larger social good
and not on short-term profit. Second, there is an internal shift. There
must be ongoing self-critique and self-evaluation to ensure that social
goals are genuinely being met.

We can see what it takes to institutionalize this concern with a larger
social good in many sectors of the economy. Let us begin with a small
business.[10]

The Oneota Community Co-Op

Beth Rotto waits for me in the Oneota Community Co-op's small dining area overlooking the quaint main street of Decorah, Iowa. The space is sunny and welcoming, with complementary water and Internet. Around us, people are eating, reading, working at laptops, visiting. Delicious smells waft out from the small deli, which serves mostly organic food.

Beth is in charge of the cheese department. She selects, stocks, and displays a variety of cheeses. Like all the store buyers, she orders organic, sustainably raised, and local products whenever she can. She is also sensitive to humane treatment of the animals whose milk is used for the cheese.

Beth was attending the local college when she first learned about the Co-op. "We were very idealistic," she told me, "and the Co-op let us live some of those values." Like many young people in the 1970s, "we wanted good food, we wanted to work cooperatively. We were concerned about world hunger, and many of us were vegetarian, believing there would be enough food for everyone if we would stop eating meat. We didn't want our money going to big corporations; we wanted our money to be spent for things we believed in."

Figure 3.1 Beth Rotto, Oneota Community Co-op. Photo by author.

The Co-op began in 1973 as a "Food Buying Club," with about 30 families rotating the labor of taking orders, making a six-hour round-trip to Minneapolis to pick up supplies, repackaging, and distributing the food. Within a year, they decided to make less frequent trips by stocking some inventory. Their first "store" was a small shed with an old woodstove for heat that "was scary to light," Beth remembers. "We called around to find someone to meet the truck when it delivered an order. We mostly carried dry goods, which we kept in metal garbage cans to keep out rodents. There was a code to let members know in which bin the key to the cash box was hidden, so they could pay for what they took."

From the beginning, Co-op members wanted to know where their food was coming from: "We would tour wholesale facilities. Many of them had childcare on-site for their workers, and even provided meals for them. There was a lot of excitement about the world we were building."

Yet they quickly learned that their new way of doing business had drawbacks as well as benefits. As membership grew, so did the time needed for filling orders. Decision making became cumbersome. "Our goal was consensus," Beth recalls, "so it only took one person to put a serious kink in the works. We spent a lot of time in meetings."

Over the next 10 years, members wrestled with the problems of growth. Volunteers became overworked, especially a core few. They began to pay a manager, or, at times, several co-managers. They outgrew their shed and moved twice (into the upstairs of the old Armory, then into a storefront on Water Street, several blocks from the current location). Their rent went up each year while sales barely kept pace.

"We constantly had to decide whether to keep solvent or to make decisions based on principles," Beth said. "For example, in 1983 the board decided to discontinue buying from two suppliers, both all-woman collectives, feeling it was a discriminatory hiring policy." In 1984, the Co-op established a base pay for employees, sick leave and snow day policies, and began to offer an extra bonus for members working on their day off to meet deliveries.

In 2007 they expanded again into the present store building, which had been a grocery store. "The first day this location opened, it felt like the happiest day of my life," Beth says. "There was a solid line of people moving up and down the aisles just in jaw-dropping amazement! It was much more accessible, and set up like a real store!"

"It has changed, there have been some trade-offs, but it still reflects my values," Beth says. She points to the Co-op Mission Statement, posted on the wall: 'The mission of the Oneota Community Food Co-op is to build vibrant communities and ecosystems by providing organic, locally produced and bulk foods, as well as other products and services that are sustainable for those who consume and produce them."

"It's a good place to work," she says, looking around her with a smile. "And I do love cheese!"

Steve McCargar, who has been with the Co-op since 1982, met with me for coffee, and explained some of the difficult trade-offs. Steve has been deeply involved with the governance of the Co-op as it has evolved over the years, and has been consistently committed to keeping the social responsibility core of the Co-op from being overtaken by profit-making concerns.

"One of the losses we have sustained along the way is that we had to change from having several co-managers to having only one manager," Steve explained. "When we applied for admittance to the National Cooperative Association, they denied us membership because of co-management. This movement is all about alternative management. There should be room in a collective movement for collective management."

When it comes to paying employees, the Co-op has made a lot of progress. The first managers were paid a dollar an hour and a discount on food. "Managing the Co-op became very much a matriarchal thing," Steve noted with a twinkle in his eye. "Not many men were willing to work for a dollar an hour!" Today, employees are paid above minimum wage, with paid vacation, sick pay, and health insurance for all employees who work over 35 hours. Those who work at least 20 hours a week are given prorated benefits.

"In the 42 years since the Oneota Community Co-op was first formed, we have gone from being an outlier, a bunch of hippies invested in a back-to-the-land alternative culture, to being today a core asset to the community," he says. "We have really stepped up to community connection and engagement, and have been through a real operational maturation process."

He notes several places of tension in the process of growth, when decisions were made that kept the Co-op both solvent and ethical. The need to stay financially afloat while serving the common good has driven

Figure 3.2. David Lester, Oneota Community Co-op.
Photo from David Lester.

many of these changes: decisions to carry inventory, to pay managers
and later employees, and especially the decision to retain the Co-op's
identity as a niche market for those who wanted their food to be grown
in healthy, sustainable ways.

Steve gives an example: "Years ago, I worked on toxic plastic research. I suggested to the Co-op that we begin wrapping cheese etc. in
non-PVC wrap. The only thing we could find was a small company that
was making a small, noncling, expensive wrap. We made the decision to
invest in the protection of customers. For 25 years, we used this wrap.
When it was clear that the place was going under, we bought a stockpile!
Recently, we ran out, and our current manager, David Lester, contacted a
business called Natural Value to produce it. They will now begin manufacturing it in commercial sizes for use in co-ops."

"This is part of the potential of what a mission-driven business can
do," Steve said. "Profit-driven business practice externalizes costs when-

ever possible, often on the backs of the environment and people. We are going to figure out a way to do what we do in a regenerative, socially responsible way. We are holding our management accountable for keeping true to the mission."

I caught up with David Lester in the Co-op Kitchen Classroom, located in a recently acquired space next door to the Co-op store. "This space has been a big boost to our ability to live into our mission," he says with obvious pleasure. "Oneota Community Co-op is a consumer cooperative. It has created a 'solution economy,' steadily working at stretching our reach to benefit small farmers, organic farmers, sustainable agriculture, college students, and people on food stamps."

I asked him to explain a bit about the consumer cooperative business model. "A cooperative is community focused, not investor focused," he explains. "Our investors are all member-owners, and each investor owns an equal share, with one vote, no matter the amount of the investment. Each year, any profits are first invested in the health of the business and furthering our mission, and the excess is shared equally among our member-owners in the form of dividends."

David outlined the six guiding principles that inform the day-to-day decisions he makes as manager, as well as the policy decisions of the board of directors:

(1) Organic, locally sourced, sustainably produced, affordable food and other products.
(2) A community that is educated about food and other products that are healthy for people and the environment.
(3) A business that promotes the development of cooperation and cooperative enterprise.
(4) A business that promotes environmental and financial sustainability.
(5) Employment in a workplace that provides the personal satisfaction of collaborative work directed toward common goals and provides extraordinary customer service.
(6) A diverse, local community whose fabric is strengthened through caring, and sharing gifts of time, energy, and resources.

Explaining some of the ways that the Oneota Community Co-op is fulfilling its mission in each of these areas, David's enthusiasm came through loud and clear. Out of the Co-op's $1.2 million in sales in 2016, David explained that 23 percent of it was grown or packaged, or both, within 100 miles of Decorah:

> We now have 72 local producers, many of whom sell at the Farmer's Market we host in our parking lot two days a week, April through October. We offer the option for those vendors to sell their unsold wares to us for fair wholesale market value, so they don't have to deal with storage or waste.

> For several years we have offered the use of our cooler space free for CSA [Community Supported Agriculture] boxes, where farmers sell a share of their harvest each week to consumers for a set price. We began a partnership with the Iowa State University Extension Office to begin a Food Hub in the Co-op basement, serving as a warehouse for organic, sustainably produced food for small producers. We now have two refrigerated trucks per week hauling these products to Hy-Vee [a large grocery chain], which expands the market for local farmers by a lot!

> We do a lot of education. We put a lot of time and effort into training our employees on the benefits of whole food, why fair trade is important, why we are against GMOs, about gluten-free products and other health concerns; almost everyone can answer the questions people may ask. We have a quarterly newspaper that addresses these and other topics. We bought this space to make a classroom kitchen, where we hold classes on cooking and nutrition, health, organic beauty products, etc. We also do classes at the college, area employers, etc. We did a training at the nursing home on how to use herbs and spices to make food taste good without lots of salt, as many seniors are on salt-restricted diets.

> We try to live our values in every aspect of our business activities. We accept food stamps, and we try hard to keep our basic food items affordable through bulk sales, having co-op deals each month where we have very little markup, and passing along savings from suppliers. Members can earn extra discounts by putting in volunteer hours. We also keep overhead costs down by using our own excess or damaged produce in our café menu. Solar panels and our day-to-day practices reduce our energy costs.

We consider our employees to be our most valuable assets. Employees really feel like they have a voice in their employment; they feel like they can be safe bringing their ideas for improvement. We teach all our employees to read a profit and loss sheet, how to understand their department's growth goals, so that when tough decisions need to be made, people understand why, and how to help turn things around. Our ratio between highest and lowest paid employees—including me—is four times. We want to keep employees as long as possible; it is expensive and time-consuming to hire and train new workers.

We have our challenges. The competition in the natural grocery industry has become fierce. Several co-ops across the country closed their doors after decades of serving their communities. Online sales of organic groceries and "food boxes" have eroded sales at stores like ours, and there are no signs of this competition letting up; but we are focused more than ever on doing what we have always done best: serving our community and our members.

This is what keeps me going. It is my job to do good in the world! It's a job that I go home from every day feeling I have done good work, I have done something important.

* * *

We can see in the work of co-ops inspiring goals and significant challenges. Some are unique to cooperatives, others are common to the basic enterprise of food service. As for the former, it is important to balance inclusion in decision making with policies and procedures that enable decisions to be made in a timely basis. This requires the participants to confront the Windigo of confusing differences over strategy and tactics with commitments to basic principles. Groups must learn how to critically evaluate different ways of living out values, and be willing to experiment with different ways of meetings those goals. Also, while there is a clear move away from the Windigo danger of exploitative capitalism, it takes ongoing efforts to both pay employees well and maintain a fair manager/owner pay ratio, in this case as low as 4:1. Furthermore, it is difficult for cooperatives to receive funding and to scale up and provide jobs for more than a small number of people.

Let us now turn to what it takes to institutionalize this concern with a larger social good in investment strategies and in the mission and organizational structure of large and small businesses.

Social Enterprise Alliance

Marc Lane is a business and tax attorney who is a director of the Social Enterprise Alliance (SEA) and a cofounder of its Chicago chapter. Lane is one of the leading authorities in the United States on the legal and financial ramifications of creating social enterprises and benefit corporations.[11]

Marc Lane

Marc Lane has a favorite quote: "How wonderful would it be if the growth of scientific and technological innovation would come along with more equality and social inclusion." These words from Pope Francis encapsulate the vision Lane has been working toward for most of his life.

Lane is finding innovative ways to help people harness the power of the marketplace to drive positive social change. One of the ways this can happen, he says, is to help investors channel their money toward businesses that are socially responsible. Lane is the pioneer behind the Advocacy Investing approach to socially responsible and mission-related investing.

Many small investors, Lane says, especially millennials, are unwilling to put their money to work for companies that are not socially responsible. The inheritors of large wealth often feel the same way. Yet, traditionally, socially responsible investing has often been linked to lower returns. When companies and even whole industries were screened out because of particular business practices and corporate values, investors were often left with a very narrow slice of possible investment opportunities. This lack of diversification made for a less than healthy portfolio.

Lane's investment approach flips this dynamic. Rather than screen out companies whose values an investor doesn't agree with, Advocacy Investing screens for positive company behaviors in the areas of social justice (which includes human rights, employment practices, and diversity) and respect for the environment. It adds social/environmental

Figure 3.3. Marc Lane, Law Offices of Marc Lane, and founder of the Chicago chapter of the Social Enterprise Alliance. Photo from 2013 SBND Appreciation Awards Expo

factors into other investment criteria. Lane's approach makes sure each investment meets financial and industry criteria as well as passing social and environmental muster. It allows socially conscious investors with modest investable assets an opportunity to give voice to their values, while still realizing a healthy return on their investments.

It is a very practical approach, and it is based on 10 years of research in the field of responsible investment. "It turns passive assets into active assets, and unlocks a huge amount of capital to drive positive social and environmental change," Lane explains. And it's easy: "Decide which issues are most important to you, and align [your] investment portfolio with that mission. Over time, you actually tend to get larger returns because those companies avoid fines, class-action suits, etc."

Encouraging investment in existing socially responsible companies is not the only way that Lane is changing the face of business. He has come up with a novel new business structure, called the Low-profit Limited Liability Company, which helps start-up companies attract investment funds while focusing on social and environmental values.

"Every business structure is transactional," Lane says. "A business needs money to operate, and must provide something people need or want. Why not transact that business in ways that can be transformational?"

Lane is the force behind Illinois's Low-profit Limited Liability Company (L3C) law, and has been instrumental in promoting L3C legislation nationwide. Currently, L3Cs are authorized in eight states.[12] Of the different business legal structures that address social concerns, the L3C is the only one that permanently places social good above all others. It legally mandates a social or educational purpose for the company, meaning that profits for investors, while important, cannot supersede the stated mission of the business.

Lane, a lifelong advocate for social justice efforts, noticed that beginning in 2009, in the wake of the 2008 recession, social ventures became increasingly constrained by lack of capital. There was increasingly feverish competition for grants fueled by the recession. The L3C, by writing one or more significant charitable or educational purposes into the legal organization of the company, opens the door to an investment source not available to other forms of business: money from philanthropic foundations.

Foundations get tax breaks for investments related to their mission, which is traditionally disbursed as grants. Once a grant is paid out, the money is gone. However, making a program-related investment with a purpose related to the foundation's programs will also qualify for the same tax breaks—with a couple of added benefits. When the money is invested rather than given as a grant, it returns to the foundation as earnings on the investment and both the principal and earnings can then be reinvested, creating a multiplier effect, while still carrying the investment on the books as an asset.

"It's a win/win situation that opens floodgates of capital for social purpose businesses," Lane explains. "Low-profit Limited Liability Company (L3C) legislation can leverage foundations' program-related investments to access trillions of dollars of market-driven capital for ventures with modest financial prospects. It is one way to harness the power of the marketplace to drive positive social change, and has the possibility of major social impact. Today there are about 1,500 L3Cs across the country."

About half of L3Cs are owned by 501(c)(3) organizations. When a nonprofit corporation decides it needs to diversify its source of revenue beyond grants and philanthropy, it can now do so through a business that provides liability protection. This creates a subsidiary or strategic alliance partner; it can own a business that is guaranteed to further the mission of the 501(c)(3). The L3C can tap into markets untouched by the nonprofit corporation. The two entities can move money back and forth easily, increasing the flexibility and effectiveness of both.

In addition to harnessing and leveraging capital and business activities to serve the social good, Lane works to bring together and magnify people power. He founded the Chicago chapter of the Social Enterprise Alliance in 2009; it convenes thought leaders and practitioners of social entrepreneurship to share ideas, lessons learned, and networks in order to increase their impact.

Lane is a great believer in complex systems. "There are a lot of ways to tackle problems that can be mutually reinforcing," he says. "Together, we can unleash the country's enormous social and financial capital for the common good. There is strength in numbers. When you help any aspect of the social ills cities face, public health, crime, the many faces of poverty, every little thing you do in one area helps all the others. When you bring the players together, they share their experience, brainstorm, and find ways to cooperate and leverage what they are doing. It raises awareness and also morale." Lane suggested that SEA implement a chapter strategy, which helped them to organize and spread their influence. While Chicago's chapter was the first, today there are 16 SEA chapters in operation across the country.

Lane didn't stop there. He became chairman of the Illinois Task Force on Social Innovation, Entrepreneurship, and Enterprise. The Task Force was created to bring together people around a common cause, addressing the social ills that cities face: public health, crime, hunger, inner city blight—the many faces of poverty. They especially looked at innovative solutions to change the lives of the most vulnerable, those living on the outskirts of hope, such as children in the foster care and criminal justice systems.

The Task Force worked so well that, in 2016, County Commissioner Jesus "Chuy" Garcia created the Cook County Commission on Social Innovation, for job creation, workforce development, entrepreneurship, community revitalization, and industrial development, naming Marc Lane as vice-chairman. Together, they have assembled a cohort for the Commission made up of thought leaders in the nonprofit sector, Cook County government heads of departments, economic development experts, and community builders.

Since its creation, the Commission has been generating headlines such as "Jesus 'Chuy' Garcia: We Want Socially Responsible Businesses. Here's How to Grow Them" (*Crain's Chicago Business*) and "Chicago's Commission on Social Innovation: Enlisting Impact Entrepreneurs to Boost the Economy" (*Forbes*). Lane explains:

> The Commission is not only an incubator, but serves as a think tank to weigh in on how to maximize positive social impact and minimize negative impact. We have broad and deep community and business representation, people with experience, leaders in their field, and those living and working in the trenches. It is all hands on deck. We have open meetings, and often over 100 people will attend. We educate about social problems, and bring in information and knowledge about what is working elsewhere. We are talking about the many faces of poverty, and how if you nibble away at one of them, you help the other aspects as well.

> This is the only government unit to help vet legislation and see how to help the county board make the most of their policy-making power. It puts into place a preference for procurement of social enterprises, for co-ops and crowdfunding, for local stores. For instance, we have a Good Food Initiative to put nutritious, local, sustainable foods in schools, jails, and hospitals. We are finding ways to encourage urban agriculture. All of this adds jobs and tax revenue while decreasing crime, homelessness, hunger, and a host of related ills.

> We're marrying the social mission of a government program with the market-driven approach of business. It's all about engaging businesses to pursue market-driven strategies that have a financial and social return. When you hold out a helping hand, you help yourself, your tax base, your economy. You create safer neighborhoods. Everyone's lives get better when we do the right thing. The reality is, we're all "us." Poverty and ill health hurts us all down the road. Make your ripple effect a positive one.

On a personal level, Lane feels that there is nothing he could do with his life that would bring him more satisfaction than what he is doing: "There is so much joy when what you do actually works! If I can contribute to others' lives and derive satisfaction, completion, purpose—that's transformative. I believe that together, we can unleash the country's enormous social and financial capital for the common good. What could be better than that?"

In his book *The Mission-Driven Venture*, Lane addresses the complex task of doing good through using sound business principles. Lane finds in the California Benefit Corporation law a helpful list of the type of public benefits that may be at the core of a company's mission and daily operations:

1. Providing low-income or underserved individuals or communities with beneficial products or services;
2. Promoting economic opportunity for individuals or communities beyond the creation of jobs in the ordinary course of business;
3. Preserving the environment;
4. Improving human health;
5. Promoting the arts, sciences, or advancement of knowledge;
6. Increasing the flow of capital to entities with a public benefit purpose; or
7. The accomplishment of any other particular benefit for society or the environment.[13]

In addition to having such laudatory goals, benefit corporations must demonstrate that the goals are being met. Again, Lane's words are instructive:

[I]t's critical—and required by law—that the company's social and environmental performance be periodically measured against a third-party standard and reported to shareholders, usually on an annual benefit report posted on the company's website and thus also made available to all the company's stake-holders, including the public at large.[14]

To be certified as a B Corp, firms must score 80 out of 200 points on a rigorous certification test. Among other measures, the test looks for a core commitment to a social purpose, whether in type of goods and services provided, or in groups that are employed, or both. B Corps must demonstrate equitable compensation of employees, and are noted for paying from more than 100% to 230% of the minimum wage to the lowest paid employees, having compensation ratios between lowest and highest paid employees that are equitable and far less that the average ratio in U.S. companies. Here we have a key shift in honor codes, a recognition that the existing pay ratio is ethically bankrupt. According to Lane, "CEOs and their friends in American executive suites continue to pocket increasingly larger shares of company gains: in 2011, U.S. CEOs earned 209.4 times more than American workers, compared to 21.5 times more in 1978."[15]

Lane makes a compelling case that such ratios can be dramatically decreased, and gives as an example Mondragon's co-operative network. Mondragon, located in the town of Mondragon in the Basque region of Spain, was founded in 1956 as a cooperative that produced paraffin heaters. Now Spain's seventh largest industrial group, it is composed of over 100 small, medium-sized, and larger co-ops. Mondragon employs 84,000 people in enterprises that include banking, insurance, telecommunications, manufacturing, construction, retail, horticulture, education, and technological innovation. At the core of the Mondragon enterprise is a commitment to social equity: "top-paid workers earn only 6.5 times the lowest-paid workers' pay."[16] Lest we think this is only possible for a small business, Lane reminds us of the efficiency and scale of Mondragon: "the Mondragon network, now operating seventy-seven businesses outside of Spain, effectively competes on equal footing with companies all over the world."[17]

In August 2015 the Securities and Exchange Commission enacted a rule that companies would have to disclose the ratio of their chief executive officer versus median workers' pay. While there is resistance to the rule, there is also voluntary compliance with it by some corporations, and a determination to move to a more equitable pay ratio. In an article in the *New York Times*, Rachel Abrams reported on companies that have been making such reports already (Whole Foods, the North-Western Corporation, and Noble Energy). The companies that have voluntarily reported their ratios are far different from most. According to the Economic Policy Institute, in 2013 chief executives were paid nearly 300 times their employees, while the ratio 50 years ago was roughly 20 times. Whole Foods has moved back to that standard of 50 years ago, with a cap of 19 times pay for their chief executive as compared to the average worker.[18]

Within the world of benefit corporations we see a shifting honor code that values both pay equity and environmental sustainability. As Lane states, we have, in the more than 1,000 certified B Corps, the emergence of a "triple-bottom-line," a genuine valuation of people, planet, and profit.[19]

To understand the nature and scope of this movement in the United States, let's return to the analyses of Gregory Dees, one of the founding scholars of social entrepreneurship. As Dees noted, here we find two things—*a focus on creating new institutions, rather than trying to force old institutions to change, and a focus on acting ourselves to find more effective ways of living justly.*

Dees provides a clear definition of what unites social innovators and entrepreneurs:

> Social entrepreneurs play the role of change agents in the social sector by:
> Adopting a mission to create and sustain social value (not just private value),
> Recognizing and relentlessly pursuing new opportunities to serve that mission,
> Engaging in a process of continuous innovation, adaptation, and learning,
> Acting boldly without being limited by resources currently in hand, and
> Exhibiting heightened accountability to the constituencies served and for the outcomes created.[20]

In 1998 the first social enterprise conference was held in Colorado Springs. The field has been rapidly growing since then and the mission is clear:

> Three characteristics distinguish a social enterprise from other types of businesses, nonprofits and government agencies:
> It directly addresses an intractable social need and serves the common good, either through its products and services or through the number of disadvantaged people it employs.
> Its commercial activity is a strong revenue drive, whether a significant earned income stream within a nonprofit's mixed revenue portfolio, or a for profit enterprise.

The common good is its primary purpose . . . baked into the organization's DNA, and trumping all others.[21]

Note the key factor here for these efforts of the owning class and professional managerial class to live justly, "heightened accountability to the
constituencies served and outcomes created." These concerns of social
equity and environmental sustainability are not limited to small enterprises. There are now 1,156 corporations in 37 countries that are committed to "using the power of business to solve social and environmental
problems." Nineteen states allow benefit corporations, and the number
is growing.[22]

An economy of interdependence is being created not only in small
businesses, but in corporations throughout the world. Here we have
another shift in honor codes, business leaders voluntarily committing
themselves and their companies to a higher and more rigorous definition of excellence, and a radically different view of success. People who
have chosen to create B corporations see themselves as a "growing community" that is an "increasingly powerful [agent] of change": "We are
passing laws. We are driving capital."[23]

In August 2013, owners and managers of B corporations wrote a letter
to fellow business leaders on the occasion of Delaware enacting benefit corporation legislation. They saw the value of Delaware's move as
twofold—enhancing the social good and making sufficient profits. They
forthrightly acknowledged the failure of old business models: "Until recently, corporate law has not recognized the legitimacy of any corporate
purpose other than maximizing profits. That old conception of the role
of business in society is at best limiting, and at worst destructive."[24]

Now, they saw new opportunities, "a new freedom to build businesses
with a higher purpose than simply maximizing profit. We are part of
a growing movement of business leaders that see this as a big market
opportunity, because a large and increasing number of people want to
support a better way to do business—better for our workers, better for
our communities, better for our environment."[25]

To take this goal seriously requires a deeper understanding of social
change. Here we see what happens when protests are effective. Once
business leaders recognize the imperative of justice for workers and
environmental responsibility, what next? In order to be certified as a

B corporation, the actions that are taken in corporate governance, in environmental impact, in worker compensation, and inclusion must be more than symbolic. The challenge of these business leaders to others is clear:

> Put your higher purpose into practice, and compare and improve your social and environmental performance by using a free educational tool like the B Impact Assessment.
>
> Bake your purpose into the legal DNA of your business and help ensure it remains central as you scale, bring in outside capital, plan succession, or even sell, by registering as a benefit corporation.
>
> Be recognized as a leader of this new economy by becoming a Certified B Corporation.[26]

Some companies also focus on providing well-paid and rewarding work to people who have difficulty finding jobs. Part of their mission is to integrate people into the social fabric of their communities. In his exposition of the multiple forms of environmentally sustainable and socially just businesses, Khanjan Mehta, a founder of the field of humanitarian engineering and social entrepreneurship, gives a concrete example of one business that does just that:

> Greyston Bakery sells brownies and cookies just like normal bakeries, but their motto says it all: "We don't hire people to bake brownies, we bake brownies to hire people." Their goal is to hire and empower people who would not otherwise be employable because of previous criminal history or lack of relevant skills. Greyston focuses on giving such individuals a chance at a job and helping them onto the path of self-sufficiency.[27]

In addition to a focus on who is hired, there is deliberate attention to diversity at all levels of these institutions: the board, owners, managers, and staff. Careful attention is given to fair governance, and rigorous assessment of environmental impacts of not only the business itself, but of its suppliers.

This movement, as large as it is, is occurring in the context of other changes in how people throughout the world are "performing economy." J. K. Gibson-Graham describe a "diverse economy," shaped by common questions and aspirations, rather than by common answers. They highlight the common questions, and the ethical goals that are driving a diverse economy that acknowledges, honors, and fosters interdependence.[28]

Community Economies

J. K. Gibson-Graham have led action research projects in the Pioneer Valley of Massachusetts, in the Latrobe Valley in Australia, in the Asian Migrant Centre in Hong Kong, and in four projects in the Philippines (Jagna, Bohol, Linamon, and Mindanao).[29] They describe economies in which subsistence needs are met through alternative market transactions and the ethical or fair trade of products, with producers and consumers agreeing on price levels that sustain the livelihood of the producers. They also highlight the growth of green or socially responsible capitalist firms—businesses concerned with profit, but "also concerned with environmentally responsible production, with increasing workers' ownership of the firm, or distribution of surplus to replenishing and maintaining the social commons."[30]

For many critics of unjust economic structures, it is often difficult to move from critique to constructive work. J. K Gibson-Graham refer to the "familiar mode of being of the anticapitalist subject, with its negative and stymied positioning."[31] Have you witnessed or experienced this stance of cultured despair—being fully aware of the magnitude of the problems that face us, but being equally aware of the lack of commensuration between the depth of the problem and the impact of our efforts for social justice? Such despair sometimes takes the form of even criticizing efforts at social change as foolish, taking a perverse satisfaction in being able to predict one's own defeat. J. K. Gibson-Graham give an example of the claims that they often hear: "the assertions that capitalism really is the major force in contemporary life, that it . . . has no outside and thus any so-called alternatives are actually part of the neoliberal, patriarchal, corporate capitalist global order."[32] J.K. Gibson-Graham then ask a series of probing questions: "What was this all-knowingness about the world? Where did this disparaging sense of certainty come from, the view that anything new would not work?"[33]

Although we often recognize the importance of challenging the necessity and inevitability of unjust social structures, it is difficult for many, activists and leftist intellectuals alike, to forgo the satisfaction of theoretical comprehensiveness and certainty, even when what we are certain about is the impossibility of fundamental social change!

J. K. Gibson-Graham explicitly acknowledge the multiple ways we are invested, literally and metaphorically, in existing economic structures. The inability to imagine an alternative form of markets, of economic relations, is also shared by many workers. They cite the example of the Argentinean workers who participated in the "recreation of Argentinean manufacturing."

> When unemployed workers in Argentina took over abandoned factories after the economic crisis of 2001, the obstacle they encountered was not the state or capital—which were, after all, in disarray—but their own subjectivities. They were workers, not managers or sales reps or entrepreneurs, and as one of them said, "If they had come to us with 50 pesos and told us to show up for work tomorrow, we would have done just that."[34]

J. K. Gibson-Graham state that this "struggle against themselves" is explicitly acknowledged as one of the principal tenets of the workers' collective, the "cultivation of new forms of sociability, visions of happiness, and economic capacities."[35] In order to create community economies, J. K. Gibson-Graham describe a beginning point that is as daunting in practice as it is simple in theory: "start where you are and build on what you have."[36] Why is this simple task so difficult? We often begin from communities marked by deep despair and hopelessness. J. K. Gibson-Graham describe the understandable deep resistance to work for social change among those most marginalized and exploited, a resistance grounded in the trauma of years of rejection, failure, and exclusion. They describe, for example, the endemic hopelessness of laid-off workers and unemployed youth in the Latrobe Valley of Australia. With the loss of an industrial base, a high percentage of the population is unemployed. Many older workers, laid off after years of relatively well-paid employment, feel themselves the victims of an all-powerful system: "Look what *they* have done. What are *they* going to do about it? What's the use? No one is going to be bothered with community enterprises. People will want to be paid."[37]

Among young people who have never been employed and have no prospects of meaningful work, J. K. Gibson-Graham find despair and a sense of worthlessness: "What can I do? I can't do anything. People look at me cause I'm a dole bludger—a bum."[38] They did, however, find sources of hope in another group, single mothers, working together to support their children and each other. For others, caught in the trauma of rejection and failure, the breakthrough to new economic enterprises did not come from either the denunciations of unjust economic structures nor through ringing declarations of the moral imperative of new economic forms. The breakthrough came through different forms of acting together—work projects clearing abandoned lots for a community garden and workshop, and collective trips to a conference on cooperatives and to a community garden in inner city Melbourne.[39]

J. K. Gibson-Graham challenge us to embrace the intrinsic ambiguity of creating new institutions, and name some of the barriers to such an embrace: "Fearing implication with those in power, we become attached to guarding and demonstrating our purity rather than mucking around in everyday politics."[40] They ask us to follow the guidelines of the queer and feminist critical theorist Eve Sedgwick, recasting our tasks as intellectuals:

> What if we believed, as Sedgwick suggests, that the goal of theory were not only to extend and deepen knowledge by confirming what we already know—that the world is full of cruelty, misery and loss, a place of domination and systemic oppression? What if we asked theory to do something else—to help us see openings, to help us to find happiness, to provide a space of freedom and possibility?[41]

As you will have noticed by now, the intent to do good is not enough. Attention must be paid to actual impacts to ensure that our efforts are both financially sustainable and genuinely transformative, meeting the needs of all people, and not just those of the middle and upper class. Here we have another recognition of the fourth Windigo. Our ideals may be pure but our strategies and tactics inept. We can be shortsighted and ineffective in our attempts to meet a larger social good. The words of Marc Lane are stark and essential for us to hear and reckon with. He states that it is always harder to run a mission-driven venture than a short-sighted and exploitative one:

> They [mission-driven ventures] are tough to set up, slow to get going, and expensive to run, especially if their mission includes employing and supporting people facing barriers to employment, the mission most commonly pursued by social entrepreneurs.[42]

Not only are such ventures a challenge to create, but their ongoing operation remains full of risk:

> It never gets easier. Even the most successful mission-driven venture cannot responsibly count on continuing success. As with any business, consumer appetites can change, ties with suppliers can break, key employees can move on, costs can rise, and competition can stiffen. So the need for talented, consistent, and proactive management will never go away.[43]

Take for example a study of a failed social enterprise in the spring 2015 issue of the *Stanford Social Innovation Review*. A core ingredient of proactive management is paying attention to, and learning from, failure. As the editor of the *Review*, Eric Nee, notes, "roughly half of all new businesses are gone after five years."[44] Given that reality, we are well served by taking stock of what factors can be identified as likely to lead to failure. Michael Cobb, Caitlin Rosser, and Andreas Vailakis, master's candidates in social enterprise at the School of International Studies at American University, with the director of the School of International Studies, Robert Tomasko, take up just that task in their analysis of the failure of Cause, a restaurant and bar in Washington, DC, that was created to both attract a clientele committed to social justice and to give all of its profit to nonprofits working for social change. The restaurant closed after 14 months, unable to generate enough revenue to continue operation, much less make specific donations to nonprofits. The goal of the business was clear:

> From the start (and until the very end), Cause stayed remarkably true to the value proposition laid out during that first conversation between [the founders] Vilelle and Ratwani: Cause would make an impact by en-

abling people to give to charity through an everyday activity; at the same time, it would provide much-needed funds to nonprofits. Each quarter, according to the initial plan, Cause would choose four organizations and distribute that quarter's profits to those groups. In addition, Cause would help raise awareness of social purpose organizations and would serve as a community space where people could engage with issues of local and global scope.[45]

The problem, however, was that the envisioned clientele, members of the nonprofit community, did not have the financial means to sustain a full-service restaurant and bar:

> "We came to realize that members of the nonprofit community—the first people to fall in love with Cause—weren't exactly what you'd call big spenders. And who can blame them? Making $35,000 a year and living in D.C. isn't easy," Vilelle noted later. Consequently, the restaurant failed not only to get enough people in the door but also to generate enough revenue once customers arrived.[46]

Others in the restaurant business have also noted that relying on events hosted by nonprofits is also financially insufficient: "customers who attended events hosted by nonprofits often spent very little money and required a lot of time and effort to serve—a situation that proved to be especially frustrating for staff members who depended on tips to generate a decent income."[47]

What are the lessons? Cobb, Rosser, Vailakis, and Tomasko describe other social enterprises that have succeeded and note that a key factor is making sure that fulfilling the social mission is part of daily business, and not only a result of financial success. They describe two organizations that have accomplished what Cause did not, making "the pursuit of a core mission . . . an intrinsic feature of its business."

> Busboys and Poets, a certified B Corporation, is a restaurant chain that has developed a reputation as a center of community activism. As Cause did when it opened, Busboys and Poets attracts people from Washington's activist and non-profit communities, and it offers itself as an event space for members of those communities. Unlike Cause, however, Busboys

and Poets pays its staff members a living wage and provides benefits—
paid time off, health insurance, and matching 401(k) contributions—
that go well beyond what most restaurants offer. It has also developed
an arrangement through which employees who work during community
events get paid a flat rate instead of relying on tips. . . . Today, after less
than a decade in operation, Busboys and Poets has four locations in the
Washington area.[48]

In their analysis of a similarly successful organization, DC Central
Kitchen, a business that provides culinary training to at-risk and formerly homeless adults, Cobb, Rosser, Vailakis, and Tomasko describe
the redefinition of success. They quote the CEO of DC Central Kitchen,
Mike Curtin, "Even if we're just breaking even, we're still winning because we're accomplishing that mission."[49]

How do we know, however, if that mission is being met? How do
we know if we are serving the interests of all? The economists Abhijit
Banerjee and Esther Duflo have taken attention to impact to a new
level of rigor and precision in their study of global initiatives to combat poverty. In 2003 they founded the Poverty Action Lab, and by 2010
researchers with the lab had studied "over 240 experiments in forty
countries around the world."[50]

Like J. K. Gibson-Graham, Banerjee and Duflo's immersion in the
empirical study of communities that are different from their own has led
them to make a shift "away from universal answers." These studies have
led them to a conclusion similar to that held by J. K. Gibson-Graham:
there will be more than one way to create community economies, more
than one way to establish excellent health care, education, and environmental practices. Furthermore, what works in one situation may not
work in another. As Banerjee and Duflo insist, attention to particulari-
ties of motivation, context, and resources are necessary to overcome the
barriers of "ideology, ignorance, and inertia."[51]

In spite of these difficulties, Banerjee and Duflo find that incremental
change is possible and can serve as the foundation for further substantive change, what they call the creation of a "virtuous cycle":

If we resist the kind of lazy, formulaic thinking that reduces every problem to the same set of general principles; if we listen to poor people them-

selves and force ourselves to understand the logic of their choices; if we accept the possibility of error and subject every idea, including the most apparently commonsensical ones, to rigorous empirical testing, then we will be able not only to construct a toolbox of effective policies but also to better understand why the poor live as they do. Armed with this patient understanding, we can identify the poverty traps where they really are and know which tools we need to give the poor to help them get out of those.[52]

At the core of overcoming poverty traps is a basic commitment, simple in theory, complex in practice: recognizing the full humanity, and enabling the equal participation, of the poor in all efforts at economic development. Banerjee and Duflo have addressed this dilemma directly and challenge the way that the poor are characterized in much of social theory and the implications of uninformed views for initiatives to combat poverty.

The poor appear, in social theory as much as in literature, by turns lazy or enterprising, noble or thievish, angry or passive, helpless or self-sufficient. It is not surprising that the policy stances that correspond to these views of the poor also tend to be captured in simple formulas: "Free markets for the poor," "Make human rights substantial," "Deal with conflict first," "Give more money to the poorest," "Foreign aid kills development," and the like. These ideas all have important elements of truth, but they rarely have much space for average poor women or men, with their hopes and doubts, limitations and aspirations, beliefs and confusion. If the poor appear at all, it is usually as the dramatis personae of some uplifting anecdote or tragic episode, to be admired or pitied, but not as a source of knowledge, not as people to be consulted about what they think or want or do.[53]

In contrast to these reductive generalizations, Banerjee and Duflo claim that immersion in the lives of the poor is necessary to craft economic policies that successfully combat poverty. In so doing, they found that "the poor often resist the wonderful plans we think up for them because they do not share our faith that those plans work, or work as well as we claim."[54] They have concluded that there are good reasons for that mistrust: policies based on ideology that ignore the material constraints of people's lives. They give one striking example, a failed attempt to address the absenteeism among health care workers in the Indian Udaipur District by the nongovernmental organization Seva Mandir. They cite the discovery by Neelima Khetan, the head of Seva Mandir:

> She had discovered . . . that what they [the nurses] were expected to do was crazy: Come to work six days a week. Sign in, then take your medicine bag and head out to one of the hamlets to do the rounds. Walk anywhere up to 3 miles to reach the hamlet, even if it's 100 degrees Fahrenheit in the shade. Go from house to house checking on the health status of women of childbearing age and their children. Try to convince a few uninterested women to be sterilized. After five or six hours of doing this, walk back to the center. Sign out. Take a bus to go home, two hours away.[55]

Banerjee and Duflo see in this specific intervention an example of an endemic pattern that leads to the failure of social policies:

> The nurses' workload was based on an *ideology* that wants to see nurses as dedicated social workers, designed in *ignorance* of the conditions on the ground, that lives on, mostly just on paper, because of *inertia*. Altering the rules to make the jobs doable might not be sufficient to get the nurses to come to work regularly, but it has to be a necessary first step.[56]

Their work illustrates another intrinsic barrier to successful social change—expecting people to trust that change is substantive and long-lasting in a period of months, rather than years. Their research reflects the insight of John Paul Lederach, expert in conflict mediation and resolution, about the persistence and time constraints endemic to successful conflict resolution. Taking as an example a local police force that undertakes a system-wide initiative to improve its relationship with the community it serves, Lederach states that

> [the] test of authenticity of this change . . . will not lie at the level of the words spoken by the leaders or written on the side of the patrol cars, the distribution of the brochures announcing the program and the new

guidelines, or the budget that paid for the training, which demonstrates the system's commitment to the change. Ultimately the authenticity litmus test will ride on how people experience the behavior of police officers in real-life situations. The great paradox is this: . . . Authenticity involves a long waiting period until people believe the change is real, but judgment of inauthenticity is continuous and immediate.[57]

Despite these difficulties, and with ongoing attention to them, change is possible. And while not perfect, while not applicable in every situation, even modest changes can serve as the catalyst for ongoing efforts to distribute resources and opportunities with respect and care. Take for example the work of Carrie Dahlquist and Choice Employment Services.[58]

Carrie Dahlquist and Choice Employment Services

Carrie Dahlquist sits across the table from me in the modest office of Choice Employment Services in Decorah, Iowa. "I'm just a mom," she said. "I never went to college. Who would have dreamed that I could start a company, helping others in a real way? Choice has grown from just me at my kitchen table to having this office with 20 employees."

Choice specializes in finding jobs for people who are disadvantaged in the job market by physical or mental disabilities, including mental illness. Like many agencies of its kind, Choice sends job coaches to work with their clients, helping them learn the job and become successful at it. But they have a rather unique approach to providing these services: they offer their clients choices in the type of job they will be doing.

"I really believe everyone has a path, and everything you do in life helps prepare you for that path, that purpose," Carrie says. Her son Taylor suffered a traumatic brain injury when he was three months old. He learns more slowly than most people do, and needs a lot of repetition. He had good support while in school, but once he graduated, he couldn't find work. He finally got a job through State Consumer Choice Options, at Walmart, and he learned his job and no longer needed his job coach.

Carrie was impressed with the difference it made for her son to be working and able to earn money. She saw what could be done for people like Taylor, and she wanted to give back. So she became a job coach for the agency that had helped her son.

Carrie soon found that Taylor's experience was far from the norm. The goal of most agencies that work with the differently abled population is to get them working at any job the placement person thinks they can handle. The person whose life this is affecting has no choice, no say in what kind of job they will be given. And once placed, there is no provision made for learning new skills, taking more responsibility at work, or moving to a better position in the future.

The more Carrie looked into vocational services for the disabled, the more she realized the ways in which our system lets them down, shoves them aside. Not everyone even gets a job; many are placed in shelter-workshops where they live dormitory style and work for $3 a day doing piecework. "Who profits from this work?" Carrie asks. "In many ways, this is modern-day slavery."

By contrast, Choice prides itself on being consumer driven. The goal is individual empowerment. They ask each person, "What's your dream? What do you need in order to get there?" They start with where the person is right now, and help them work toward more and more success. The job counselor helps them look at different angles, different approaches to honestly get closer and closer to doing the type of work they find most fulfilling. "To be successful, people need to be happy," she says.

Choice offers individual job coaching, for as long as the consumer needs it, but the final goal is independence from the job coach. Choice counselors and job coaches must have a passion for people, and be willing to put the consumer's needs first. They have become adept at thinking outside the box. Choice can create opportunities, jobs that meet the client's needs and also the needs of the employer. They will set up trial jobs, which may become an actual job because the employer sees that the person is filling a need—maybe one the employer didn't even know they had.

For example, one person Choice helped had been a healthy young man until he got hurt in a farming accident, which left him blind and in a wheelchair. His life is now taken up with doctor visits, therapies, and being cared for by nurses and aides. But he loves to talk to people. Choice set up a program for him where he would talk to other residents of the nursing home for 15 minutes each. He visits each person at the same time on the same day each week. He started out on a volunteer basis, but the staff began to notice a marked improvement in the mood, vitality, and interest in life of those that this man visits. These residents became much more compliant and were easier for the staff to care for. They recognized the value of these visits, and created a position for him, paying him for the service he provides. For this young man, his life now has a purpose, and he knows he performs a valuable service, doing something he really enjoys doing.

Once an employer has had experience with a Choice-placed worker, they often see the benefit not only to the consumer and to society, but to their business as well. They find that job-supported employees are generally more punctual, more dedicated to doing a really good job, and less apt to call in sick than other employees. They are earning their own money, meaning fewer taxpayer dollars must be spent supporting them. They grow in self-esteem, and become truly valuable members of the workforce.

Choice staff members work with employers individually, finding out their needs. They help employers to recognize the possibilities for their business. They explain that a job coach will stay with the employees for as long as they are needed. They show them a study that found that hiring people with disabilities actually increases quality and productivity store-wide, and decreases staff turnover and absenteeism.

Carrie says, "I'm a mom, and I run this business from a mom's perspective. What would I want for this consumer, if I were their mother? That's how we treat them. We are as interested in their dreams and their success as their own mother would be." She feels that focusing on consumers' strengths, rather than their disabilities, allows for growth and a feeling of competence, which brings out the best in each person.

With this strengths-based orientation, Choice is at the forefront of what Carrie calls "the newest civil rights movement." More and more, people across the country are becoming aware of the need to include those with disabilities in every public venue and to give them the widest range of opportunity possible. Recently, the American Dream Employment Network reached out to Choice to partner with them in their Ticket to Work program. ADEN's purpose is to provide high-quality services to Social Security disability beneficiaries. ADEN recognizes that the people-centered focus of Choice makes a huge difference in the lives of disabled people, is beneficial to the businesses that hire them, and saves taxpayer dollars.

Local employers are beginning to catch the vision of how disabled workers can contribute to their business in a very real way. The head manager at the local Walmart has been so happy with the results that he has spread the word among his business associates. As a result, the Walmart in Prairie duChen, about 40 miles from Decorah, has not only hired Choice job-supported employees, but has "gone above the call of duty," as Carrie put it. They employed someone who had issues that resulted in attendance problems. Rather than letting him go, his supervisor worked with the job coach to develop a protocol to deal with his issues. This consumer just passed his first-year review, and got a raise in pay.

Choice is groundbreaking in another way, as well. They have hired some of their own consumers: 25% of their staff is composed of people who are disabled or are impaired by mental illness. This is far above the goal that the government has set of 3% disabled workers in workplaces nationwide. Carrie believes that goal can be met and even exceeded by attention to making the job fit not only the employers' needs, but the needs and desires of the disabled workers, as well.

"When people are happy in their work, they show up on time, and do an excellent job, consistently. This makes them wonderful employees," Carrie says. She tells of one young woman who really loved to cook, and had a dream of being a chef, but with no experience or training in institutional cooking, she wasn't ready for a restaurant cook job. But she was willing to start out with a job cleaning bathrooms in a restaurant. The owner was impressed by her diligence and thoroughness. So when he needed someone to do some food prep work for a few hours a week, Choice suggested they add an hour to this woman's work schedule, washing and cutting up vegetables. She did so well at this that soon she was doing salad prep; then she was moved up to work at the fryers.

But at this point she had no more room for advancement in this small restaurant. Choice then worked with her case manager at Social Services to find her a job at Strawberry Point, a local nursing home. Now, she is working in dietary and cooking, performing a job with considerable responsibility. She is doing what she loves, and feels needed and appreciated. Strawberry Point has become very supportive of Choice, hiring their people whenever they can, and letting other business owners and managers know about the advantages of employing people through Choice Employment Services.

Carrie's passion for helping each person have the widest possible choice has rubbed off on her family. As the client base grew and more help was needed, Carrie's husband quit his job and came on staff full time. Three of their children have graduated from college and now work at Choice, offering their skills in business and social work to the mix. "It's great to be working together for something we all believe in," Carrie says with a smile.

What can we learn from Carrie's work for social equity? For modest changes to serve as catalysts for ongoing efforts, three factors are required:

1. Immersion in the lives of those who are most exploited and ignored, working together, not working for, sustainable human flourishing.
2. A culture of ongoing evaluation and critique and institutional practices that enact that critique on a routine and ongoing basis.
3. A redefinition of success.

These factors are at work in others who own and manage social enterprises and B corporations, and are a manifestation of the way that the economic and political power of the professional managerial class can be used in the interest of what the theologians Kwok Pui Lan and Joerg Rieger call "deep solidarity."[59]

Before we explore such emerging forms of economic change in more detail, let's step back and think about two factors: the basics of social change and the role of particular classes in engendering that change. With regard to the role of particular classes, this book is largely focused on the role of the professional managerial class, those who have achieved some measure of institutional power and want to marshal it in the service of progressive social change. True to the basic tenets of theologies of liberation, it is crucial that we acknowledge our social location, and the roles that we can play from that location. It is important for us to see the nature of our political, social, and economic power and to learn how to use it for justice.

Beginning in the late 19th century and continuing into the 21st century, the professional managerial class has played a distinct role in capitalist societies. In their 1977 work, "The Professional Managerial Class,"

Barbara and John Ehrenreich provided a classic description of this class and its economic and social power. Members of the professional managerial class are neither the primary owners of the means of production, nor the workers who produce goods directly. Rather, as managers in corporate and civil life, as physicians, nurses, teachers, ministers, architects, engineers, attorneys, and professors, *they are the agents of social order*. This may be a social order based on social control, and hence be accompanied by relationships of either deference or hostility from the working class, or it can be a social order in solidarity with the working class, agents of a social order based on justice, equity, and compassion. They have the relative leisure and social capital to make their voices heard and can lead demonstrations and acts of public witness. More importantly, in their professional lives they are in decision-making positions in which they can respond to demonstrations and acts of public witness. They can shape policy to respond to the dual imperatives of social justice and environmental sustainability.[60]

Key Insights for Progressive Practice

What does it take for consumers, investors, workers, managers, and owners to move away from the Windigo of extractive capitalism and excessive consumerism to the creation of community economies of mutuality and reciprocity? What does it take to make such efforts genuinely liberative? How can we avoid the trap of seeking a larger social good, yet only meeting the needs of our own social class? Here the basic tenets of liberation theology are essential: first, ongoing involvement of those marginalized and excluded groups in the creation of social policies and institutions, and, second, ongoing attention to the impact of our joint efforts on those most marginalized. This requires direct contact, building relationships of accountability and mutual critique.

In the *Oxford Handbook on Professional Economic Ethics*, the economist Ravi Kanbur makes a strong case for sustained immersion in communities served by development professionals. Kanbur is a professor at Cornell University, and served on the senior staff of the World Bank, including as principal adviser to the Bank's chief economist. He has also served as director of the World Bank's World Development Report. He finds that well-designed immersions as short as 2–3 days make an immense difference for development professionals in "keep[ing] them in touch with the lives of the people their work is supposed to help." He goes on to argue that periodic immersions in which development professionals are made aware of "the changing realities of development" are critical for the professional rigor of development work.[61] This same immersion is true for those who own and manage social enterprises and B corporations. In order for our commitment to the common good to remain effective, we must be continuously grounded in learning with and from people whose life experiences are so very different from our own. Without such continuous connection, our work can lose its transformative power, becoming merely charity rather than genuine empowerment.

How do we know if we are living in genuine solidarity? How do we know if our work is mutually empowering? Here again the analyses of Eggers and Macmillan are instructive. In their description of the solution economy we see the fourth Windigo at work, the inability to forthrightly embrace our ongoing capacity for failure. Eggers and Macmillan manifest both an embrace of critique and a fear of rigorous critique. They are clear about why ongoing evaluation and critique are necessary. Without it, corporate efforts may be only "self-serving efforts in corporate PR," and their positive impacts can be vastly overstated.[62] Furthermore, even when intentions are genuine, specific ventures will fail. Given these dual realities, the creation of independent and rigorous means of tracking impact is critical and ongoing.

> Real-time feedback, still relatively rare among solution economy organizations, is nevertheless likely to grow. . . . Consider the GlobalGiving Foundation, which connects individuals to more than one thousand prescreened grassroots charity projects around the world. . . . GlobalGiving solicited feedback from residents in a Kenyan slum. The foundation asked what it was doing right but also where there were delivery gaps or program complaints. However, instead of simply interviewing individuals, GlobalGiving went a step farther and partnered with a UK-based analytics firm, Cognitive Edge. The partner's software helped GlobalGiving turn the raw information of residents into data that could be broken down, analyzed, visualized and, in turn, inform decisions on where funds should be allocated.[63]

These measures, providing mechanisms for listening to, and learning from, intended beneficiaries, is an ongoing imperative.

> RARE, a conservation group that deploys its program fellows to areas with biodiversity deemed at risk, is differentiating itself among environmental funders by measuring not only ecological improvements, but also the economic benefits to local communities. . . . When RARE is seeking to establish a no-take fishing zone to repopulate overfished areas in the Philippines, it also tries to provide alternative income streams for locals, in some cases by providing honeybee boxes.[64]

What is important here is a comprehensive set of metrics, not only "acreage of land preserved" but also economically viable sustainable practices. The challenge is twofold—developing measures that are suited to the opportunities and needs of a particular community, and creating a "common language" so that efforts by social enterprises and nonprofits can meaningfully be compared and evaluated. One group that is working to create such a common language is Impact Reporting and Investment Standards (IRIS). The value of such standards is clear:

> Stakeholders can use IRIS to aggregate sector-wide data and compare it across organizations—the same way the SEC extracts data to analyze public companies. Organizations get an accredited way to assess their social performance and maximize their funds. Investors get transparency.[65]

What is crucial in this shift is getting accurate and timely feedback from beneficiaries, feedback that can allow timely changes in how the work of the organization is done: "The sooner an organization is aware of a mishap, the more quickly it can course-correct and repair relationships with jilted users."[66]

Eggers and Macmillan's language here is revealing—while there is a shift to listening to beneficiaries, the reference to them as "jilted users" reflects a mind-set in which beneficiaries are not yet full participants in the constructive work of nonprofits and social enterprises. It is that effort to move from working for to working with that is the next step in creative capitalism, and it is an effort that is being given thorough attention in the world of engagement scholarship. We will turn to those efforts in a subsequent chapter. For now, we are in the world where some moves are being made and much yet remains to be done. It is crucial to note, however, that there is an emerging honor code that is a shift from old ways of doing business, of "operating in isolation, ignoring entire classes and groups of people, and shrugging off ruinous externalities of the market."[67]

There is a further measure of the impact of social enterprises—not just the impact of the individual mission-driven venture itself, but the larger social change that such ventures spark and support. Here we find a direct confrontation with the seventh Windigo, the complacency of being satisfied with partial changes and mere reform. Marc Lane advocates a commitment to a much larger social good—not just doing well as a single entity, but working with governments to transform the very nature of what types of economic practices are not only laudable and feasible, but are the only ones that are normative and legal.

> Mission-driven ventures won't be judged only by purity of thought, revenue, profit, or even the number of people they serve. It will be their effectiveness as change agents that separates those that earn support and acclaim from those that do not. They will engage and empower commercial businesses to improve their practices; they will lobby governments to change their laws and policies as they help eradicate poverty and unemployment and improve public health and education; and they will leverage their successes, spreading beyond their markets and service areas the solutions they have learned will work.[68]

Those involved in the work of social entrepreneurship share two convictions: fundamental social change is possible, and fundamental social change takes time.

What are the multiple drivers of this form of constructive social engagement? What leads people to take up the demanding, long-term work of institutional change? Here we find an emerging, broad-based sense of what actually constitutes the abundant, flourishing life. Diverse publics may be motivated for closely related reasons: a concern with the integrity of good work (work that is socially equitable and ecological sustainable) and the discovery of a larger good—the joy of being a part of a wider human community. It is here that we turn to the third element of socially responsible economic life, a fundamental redefinition of economic success and of what constitutes the abundant life. People throughout the world are moving away from endless material expansion to genuinely interdependent plenitude. The goal is no longer maximum short-term economic gains but socially just economic and environmental sustainability.[69]

4

"Belonging, Not Belongings"

An Economy of Gratitude and Reciprocity

The redefinition of abundance and success that we see in the world of social entrepreneurship may seem new, but it is not. There are many other cultures that have lived out an economy of gratitude and reciprocity. We can learn from them, from their mistakes, from their successes, and from their honest accounts of what it takes to live with a greater awareness of interdependence.

Paul Hawken claims that one of the core characteristics of impact-driven nonprofits is learning from indigenous people's resistance to globalization. While those lessons are certainly important, what is equally important is to learn from other cultures different ways of shaping our collective lives together. What we find in many indigenous cultures is far more than resistance. We find creative alternatives to our current economic system, alternatives that are grounded in an awareness of deadly mistakes and sustained by ceremonies of gratitude and responsibility.

I first encountered this way of living through teaching and working with Carol Lee Sanchez. In her writing and teaching, Sanchez was clear not to share particular indigenous rituals and stories, but rather invited nonindigenous people to live out of a deep respect for "all our relations" and with keen awareness of what it means to "use technology in a sacred manner," using our many tools in ways that are equitable and ecologically sustainable. At the core of her teaching was the forthright acknowledgment that indigenous peoples are not intrinsically closer to nature, not intrinsically more adept at living with respect for the rhythms and limitations of the natural world. Indigenous populations have sometimes been as destructive as current populations. The difference, as noted earlier, is that they have learned from those mistakes, tell the stories of those excesses, and commit, through ritual and daily practices, not to repeat them. Sanchez claimed that the indigenous respect for nature and ritualized checks on human greed and shortsightedness was grounded in the honest remembrance of when indigenous populations had gone awry, and had made their environs uninhabitable for humans through overfishing, overgrazing, and overcultivation of the land.[1]

Sanchez described an alternative way of living with the world, an attitude of respect and vigilance described as the Beauty Way. She invited those who are nonindigenous to enter the Beauty Way, telling our own stories of mistakes and greed, celebrating as well the joy and wonder of living within limits, and with attention to the overall impact of our decisions on other peoples and on the ecosystem that sustains us all.[2]

Robin Wall Kimmerer also describes the wisdom of living with gratitude and reciprocity, a wisdom embraced by many indigenous peoples and one that others may learn from and embrace.

> Each of us comes from people who were once indigenous. We can reclaim our membership in the cultures of gratitude that formed our old relationships with the living earth. Gratitude is a powerful antidote to Windigo psychosis. A deep awareness of the gifts of the earth and of each other is medicine. The practice of gratitude lets us hear the badgering of marketers as the stomach grumblings of a Windigo. It celebrates cultures of regenerative reciprocity, where wealth is understood to be having enough to share and riches are counted in mutually beneficial relationships. Besides, it makes us happy.[3]

Kimmerer weaves together the knowledge gleaned from her work as a botanist and as a student of indigenous traditions to describe what it means to live out a radically different understanding of abundance and success. As in the work of Sanchez, Kimmerer's understanding of an alternative way of being is grounded in a forthright acknowledgment of the capacity of humans to make dire mistakes, to live in ways that are socially and environmentally destructive. She describes the ways in which these lessons are carried in the Anishinaabe stories of the Windigo: "The Windigo is a human being who has become a cannibal monster. Born of our fears and our failings, Windigo is the name for that within us which cares more for its own survival than for anything else. . . . The old teachings recognized that Windigo nature is in each of us, so the monster was created in stories, that we might learn why we should recoil from the greedy part of ourselves. . . . See the dark, recognize its power, but do not feed it."[4]

Kimmerer sees in the Windigo stories a core insight about survival and what threatens it, an insight common to many indigenous cultures, and an insight that is emerging in our own industrialized culture: "Cautionary Windigo tales arose in a commons-based society where sharing was essential to survival and greed made any individual a danger to the whole."[5] While such awareness is not universal, more and more people throughout the industrialized world are recognizing that what was true of indigenous societies is true of our own. We, too, are in actuality a commons-based society, and it is the utmost folly to deny those connections and fail to check our own greed. Kimmerer's analysis is pointed. While she is critical of overarching systems, she also points to the ways in which we sustain those systems through our daily choices: "We are all complicit. We've allowed the 'market' to define what we value so that the redefined common good seems to depend on profligate lifestyles that enrich the sellers while impoverishing the soul and the earth."[6]

Indigenous cultures checked individual and collective greed because of its destructive effects. Indigenous cultures also checked individual and collective greed because such a way of life is less rewarding and less fulfilling than a culture of gratitude and reciprocity. Taking as a test case the hard work of "restoring the Onondaga watershed to its pre-industrial condition," Kimmerer names the value of this risky, uncertain work:

> Species composition may change, but relationship endures. Here is where our most challenging and most rewarding work lies, in restoring a relationship of respect, responsibly, and reciprocity. And love.[7]

Kimmerer describes the joy of a culture of gratitude and gives a concrete example of such a culture in her account of the giveaway:

> I don't know the origin of the giveaway, but I think we learned it from watching the plants, especially the berries who offer up their gifts all wrapped in red and blue. . . .
> When berries spread out their giveaway blanket, offering their sweetness to birds and bears and boys alike, the transaction does not end there.

The berries trust that we will uphold our end of the bargain and disperse their seeds to new places to grow. . . . They remind us that all flourishing is mutual. . . . Their gifts multiply by our care for them, and dwindle from our neglect. We are bound in a covenant for reciprocity, a pact of mutual responsibility to sustain those who sustain us.[8]

While Kimmerer extols both the beauty and the possibility of living in a covenant of reciprocity, she also is forthright in her acknowledgment that it may be too late for us to correct the damage caused by a culture of individualism and heedless exploitation of the human and natural world.[9]

Kimmerer challenges us, however, to not succumb to the certainly destructive power of despair, but to choose the uncertainty and promise of the "green path":

Our spiritual leaders interpret this prophecy as the choice between the deadly road of materialism that threatens the land and the people, and the soft path of wisdom, respect, and reciprocity that is held in the teachings of the first fire.[10]

Kimmerer offers an evocative vision of what it means to live both with the possibility of irredeemable destruction and the choice of honest recognition and accountability:

The moral covenant of reciprocity calls us to honor our responsibilities for all we have been given, for all that we have taken. . . . Gifts of mind, hands, heart, voice and vision all offered up on behalf of the earth. Whatever our gift, we are called to give it and to dance for the renewal of the world.

In return for the privilege of breath.[11]

While we may choose to accept the covenant of reciprocity, while we may choose to honor our responsibilities, Kimmerer is clear: we may not know how to restore damaged ecosystems.

The land, plants, animals, and their allies among the human people are making small steps, but ultimately it is the earth that will restore the structure and function, the ecosystem services. . . . We're not in control.

What we *are* in control of is our relationship to the earth. Nature herself is a moving target, especially in an era of rapid climate change.[12]

We may not know how to live with the natural world in a way that is equitable and sustainable. Knowing what is good, and wanting to do the good, does not mean that we know how to enact the good. Much of social ethics and community organizing stops with knowledge and motivation. None that I know of addresses organizational and fiscal competence. That is assumed! For those who take up the task of actually implementing desired social change, issues of competence quickly assume paramount importance: managing finances; knowing how to support, motivate, and engage coworkers; knowing how to read ecosystems; weighing possible changes from different interactions; and learning how to assess the impact of those interactions in a timely and accountable fashion, and then making timely and necessary corrections.

It is from the work of implementing policies as a leader within institutions that I have had a major shift in my understanding of an ethic of risk. While an outsider, I saw it as a matter of not knowing the impact of our efforts, yet acting anyway. Now, as a relatively empowered insider, I have learned that we can discover the impact of our decisions and policy changes. It is important, therefore, to pay attention to actual impacts and to make the necessary changes to enhance the unexpected results that are positive and to learn from and rectify the unexpected mistakes that will undoubtedly occur.

Environmental Sustainability

What does it mean for us in industrialized societies to concretely live out an ethos and ethic of gratitude, respect, reciprocity, and responsibility? How do we accept Kimmerer's challenge and confront the possibility of irredeemable destruction and choose honest recognition and accountability?

There are people doing just that work, there are solutions ready to be tried, and more plausible solutions are continuing to be developed. In *Drawdown: The Most Comprehensive Plan Ever Proposed to Reverse Global Warming*, Paul Hawken shares the work of a group of scientists, engineers, builders, businesspeople, and organizers who describe in compelling detail what can be done to live as humans in balance with, rather than exploiting and dominating, the natural world that sustains us.

The significance of this work is immense, and the importance of this shift is described well by Michael Pollan. Pollan recounts how terrified he was by Al Gore's 2006 documentary, *An Inconvenient Truth*. What was most frightening to Pollan was not the amount of human-induced climate disasters, but the paucity and lack of imagination of the solutions that were provided.

> I don't know about you, but for me the most upsetting moment in *An Inconvenient Truth* came long after Al Gore scared the hell out of me, constructing an utterly convincing case that the very survival of life on earth as we know it is threatened by climate change. No, the really dark moment came during the closing credits, when we are asked to . . . change our light bulbs. That's when it got really depressing. The immense disproportion between the magnitude of the problem Gore had described and the puniness of what he was asking us to do about it was enough to sink your heart.[13]

Thankfully, hopefully, we have more to do now—a vast array of changes in individual and collective practices that may be able to bring us back into balance with the natural world. None of these solutions are sufficient in themselves. All of these solutions are necessary. None of them are without significant challenges, whether that of mobilizing collective will or paying attention to possible negative effects. Of the 100 solutions proposed in *Drawdown*, it is profoundly reassuring, rather than discouraging, that scientists and engineers are already aware of the need to pay attention to specific risks, dangers, and trade-offs in 67 of the solutions. For example, Hawken describes both the positive potential of wind energy and the ongoing challenges.

> In the United States, the wind energy potential of just three states— Kansas, North Dakota, and Texas—would be sufficient to meet electricity demand from coast to coast. Wind farms have small footprints, typically using no more than 1 percent of the land they sit on, so grazing, farming, recreation, or conservation can happen simultaneously with power generation.[14]

The challenges, though, of relying on wind energy are significant.

The variable nature of wind means there are times when turbines are not turning. Where the intermittent production of wind (and solar) power can span a broader geography, however, it is easier to overcome fluctuations in supply and demand. Interconnected grids can shuttle power to where it is needed. Critics argue that turbines are noisy, aesthetically unpleasant, and at times deadly to bats and migrating birds.[15]

An energy source that can balance the variability of wind and solar energy is geothermal energy. However, the technical challenges here are also significant.

In the process of pursuing its potential, geothermal's negatives need to be managed. Whether naturally occurring or pumped in, water and steam can be laced with dissolved gases, including carbon dioxide, and toxic substances such as mercury, arsenic, and boric acid. Though its emissions per megawatt hour are just 5 to 10 percent of a coal plant's, geothermal is not without greenhouse impact. In addition, depleting hydrothermal pools can cause soil subsidence, while hydrofracturing can produce microearthquakes. Additional concerns include land-use change that can cause noise pollution, foul smells, and impacts on viewshed.[16]

To both experiment with new ways of using and restoring natural resources and to know how to expect and look for the unexpected is a core ingredient in human responsibility. It is how we both honor the gifts, and acknowledge the limits, of human reason.

The solutions described in *Drawdown* include different ways of paying attention to energy, food, buildings and cities, land use, transport, materials, and the empowerment of women and girls.[17] The solutions are concrete and multifaceted, and build on the insight also expressed by Kimmerer. This is not merely "stopping doing bad things"; these are deliberate attempts at restoration. The grounding for such work is threefold: genuine accountability for damage done; honest realization that we may not know the answers; and, what is of utmost importance, these choices are not based on a sense of sacrifice but on the embrace of genuine abundance, "restoring relationships of respect, responsibility, reciprocity. And love."[18]

Hawken describes the goal of creating and empowering a network of people who share common goals and are ready to explore multiple strategies for healing the damage caused by humans to the natural world and for enacting new forms of relationship with ecosystems that are sustainable and mutually beneficial.

> This is why, in creating *Drawdown* and its associated website, we sought to do more than merely perform exacting research and inform. We wanted to captivate and surprise, to present solutions to global warming in a new way with an eye towards helping draw the threads and webs of humanity into a coherent and more effective network of people that can accelerate progress towards reversing climate change.[19]

Among the 70 scholars from 22 countries who are Drawdown fellows, 40% are women. There is also a "120 person Advisory Board, a prominent and diverse community of geologists, engineers, agronomists, politicians, writers, climatologists, biologists, botanists, economists, financial analysts, architects, and activists."[20] What unites this diverse group is a commitment to model "the economics of regeneration":

> Going forward, the staff, fellows and volunteers at Project Drawdown will be modeling the economics of regeneration—jobs, policy and economic complexity—mapping climate solutions onto specific national economies and calculating how climate change technologies and processes can generate dignified, socially just, family-wage jobs. . . . the profit that can be achieved by instituting regenerative solutions is greater than the monetary gains generated by causing the problem or conducting business-as-usual. For instance, the most profitable and productive method of farming is regenerative agriculture. And, more people in the U.S. as of 2016 are employed by the solar industry than by gas, coal, and oil combined. Restoration creates more jobs than despoliation. We can just as easily have an economy that is based on healing the future rather than on stealing it.[21]

This goal of socially just and environmentally sound economic development is also being explored and implemented in the work of Van

Jones. In *The Green Collar Economy: How One Solution Can Fix Our Two Biggest Problems,* he describes the ways in which environmental responsibility can work in tandem with our efforts to stop racism, repair its effects, and create a racially just economy. Jones criticizes fundamental and dangerous assumptions about economic growth: "Democrats and Republicans together assured the American public that we could grow our economy based on: (1) consumption rather than production, (2) credit rather than thrift, and (3) ecological destruction rather than ecological restoration. The present crisis has exposed all three of these notions as dangerous shams."[22]

What Jones advocates is instead a green economy: "There is a wiser and more civilized alternative. Rather than continuing to base our economy on a finite supply of dead things, we can base it on sources that are practically infinite and eternal: the sun, the moon, and the Earth's inner fire."[23]

Jones also claims that the emerging green economy can also address the structural effects of racism and provide the foundation for a genuinely inclusive economy:

> We want to build a green economy strong enough to lift people out of poverty. . . . We want to ensure that those communities that were locked out of the last century's pollution-based economy will be locked in to the new clean and green economy. We know that we don't have any throwaway species or resources, and we know that we can't have any throwaway children or neighborhoods either. All of creation is precious and sacred. And we are all in this together.
>
> Those words would open the door to a cross-race and cross-class partnership that would change America and the world.
>
> Imagine a Green New Deal—with a pivotal role for green entrepreneurs, a strategic and limited role for government and an honored place for labor and social activists.[24]

What does it mean to live out an economy of regeneration and balance? First, multiple actors and institutions are involved, "developers, cities, nonprofits, corporations, farmers, churches, provinces, schools and universities."[25] And those multiple perspectives are all essential.

Second, these are not merely abstract goals of living in harmony, but there are technical means of growing food, using and storing energy, recycling waste, to explore, evaluate, and try. Third, Hawken and his colleagues make the same significant step that we find in the work of Kimmerer. These attempts to live in harmony are based in learning from the wisdom of the natural world. Just as plants can work together for survival, we can do the same. We see, for example, in the work of the biomimicry pioneer Janine Benyus an account of a significant phenomenon:

> The more stressful the environment, the more likely you are to see plants working together to ensure mutual survival. On Chilean peaks, studies of mounded plants huddling together against harmful ultraviolet rays and cold, drying winds reveal complex interactions of support. A single six-foot-wide yareta, or cushion plant, can be thousands of years old and harbor dozens of different flowering species in its mound.[26]

Benyus writes that "[d]iscoveries about the holistic nature of forests have vast implications for forestry, conservation, and climate change. It's time to bring the same penetrating insight to farmlands. Although 80 percent of all land plants have roots that grow in association with mycorrhizae fungi, it's rare to find common mycorrhizal networks in agricultural fields."[27] We can foster, rather than disrupt, such networks, "[returning] to our role as nurturers, one of the many helpers in this planetary story of collaborative healing."[28]

Hawken and his colleagues provide specific ways of both restoring and healing ecosystems, and of living in a continuously regenerative balance with the natural world. This includes regenerative uses of energy, improved means of energy storage and distribution, and the further development and expansion of wind turbines, solar farms, and cogenerative energy production.[29] With food production, there can be both a dramatic reduction in food waste and new forms of regenerative agriculture.

While the specifics vary, the principles are the same. Each solution is a carefully crafted calibration of how to best integrate people and place, drawing on ancient wisdom as well as on new technology.

For example, Mark Hertsgaard describes the work of Yacouba Sawadogo and his practice of tree intercropping in Burkina Faso:

> Trees can be harvested—their branches pruned and sold—and then they grow back, and their benefits for the soil make it easier for additional trees to grow. "The more trees you have, the more you get," Sawadogo explained. Wood is the main energy source in rural Africa, and as his tree cover expanded, Sawadogo sold wood for cooking, furniture making, and construction. . . . "I think trees are at least a partial answer to climate change, and I've tried to share this information with others," Sawadogo added. "My conviction, based on personal experience, is that trees are like lungs. If we do not protect them, and increase their numbers, it will be the end of the world."[30]

Chris Reij, a Dutch environmental scientist, has studied the technique of "agro-forestry" or "farmer-managed natural regeneration." He states "that in Niger alone farmers had grown 200 million trees and rehabilitated 12.5 million acres of land . . . Many farmers in the Sahel are better off now than they were thirty years ago because of the agro-forestry innovations they have made."[31]

Human intervention can be, and has been, devastatingly destructive. Hawken describes the ways in which human intervention can also be restorative and regenerative:

> The usual assumption about human activity is that it makes nature worse, however well intentioned. But that has not always been the case. The productivity of the tallgrass prairies of the Great Plain region can be attributed to the fire ecology practiced by Native Americans. In Norman Myers's book *The Primary Source*, he describes going into a forty-thousand-year-old "untouched" primary forest in Borneo with an ethnobotanist. Both stayed in one spot for the day while the ethnobotanist identified the towering dipterocarps and other flora for Myers. It turns out the entire forest had been placed and planted by human beings before the last ice age. The Swiss agroecologist Ernst Gotsch works with deforested and desertified lands in Brazil and restores them in a matter of years to lush forest forms bountiful with food. In a video segment in

which he describes his work, Gotschs picks up dark, moist soil and pro-claims, "We are growing water."[32]

Our use of natural resources can be regenerative, as in the emerging practice of creating "living buildings." Buildings can actually contribute to the greater good as they fulfill the following functions:

[L]iving buildings should grow food, produce net-positive waste (a water stream that nourishes living systems or land), create net-positive water, and generate more energy with renewables than they use. They need to incorporate biophilic design, satisfying humankind's innate affinity for natural materials, natural light, views of nature, sounds of water, and more. On the unnatural side of things, living buildings have to avoid all "red-listed" materials, such as PVC and formaldehyde. They are required to cater to the human scale, rather than the car scale, and intentionally educate and inspire others—building as teacher rather than container.[33]

While the technological challenges in building practices are immense, the motivation for doing this work resonates with the wisdom offered by Kimmerer, a deeper form of abundance, an embrace of a form of beauty that is consonant with "belonging, rather than belongings."

Buildings that are LBC [Living Building Challenge] certified are spec-tacular to look at and be in. Architect David Sellers summed it up per-fectly when he said the pathway to sustainability is beauty, because people preserve and care for that which feeds their spirit and heart.[34]

Why, then, do we choose a path of environmental sustainability? In the introduction to *Drawdown*, Hawken provides an unusual perspec-tive. His focus is not protesting the actions of others, but taking up re-sponsibility ourselves. He also offers a paradoxical challenge—this time can be a gift, a chance to make amends and move into right relations with each other and with the natural world to which we belong:

Unquestionably, distress signals are flashing throughout nature and so-ciety, from drought, sea level rise, and unrelenting increases in temperatures to expanded refugee crises, conflict, and dislocation. This is not the whole story. We have endeavored in *Drawdown* to show that many people are staunchly and unwaveringly on the case. Although carbon emissions from fossil fuel combustion and land use have a two-century head start on these solutions, we will take those odds. The buildup of greenhouse gases we experience today occurred in the absence of human understanding: our ancestors were innocent of the damage they were doing. That can tempt us to believe that global warming is something that is happening *to* us—that we are victims of a fate that was determined by actions that precede us. If we change the preposition, and consider that global warming is happening *for* us—an atmospheric transformation that inspires us to change and reimagine everything we make and do—we begin to live in a different world. We take 100 percent responsibility and stop blaming others. We see global warming not as an inevitability but as an invitation to build, innovate, and effect change, a pathway that awakens creativity, compassion, and genius. This is not a liberal agenda, nor is it a conservative one. This is the human agenda.[35]

Craig Sieben, founder and CEO of Sieben Energy Associates, is one who has embraced this "human agenda," the "invitation to build, innovate, and effect change" with "creativity, compassion, and genius."[36]

Sieben Energy Associates

Craig Sieben may not fit the popular image of an environmental activist. You will not see one word on Sieben Energy Associates' webpage about global climate change, the environmental ravages of using fossil fuels, or air and water pollution. Yet for people who lead social enterprises or B corporations, Sieben Energy Associates is the place to go to make the triple bottom line (people, planet, profit) a reality. What you will see is how much money a business or organization stands to save by utilizing energy more efficiently. Craig's company offers to help an organization's bottom line, to improve profitability by lowering energy costs substantially. The core of his work—simple in its wording, profound in its impact: "Take the passion and turn it into a practice."

Since Craig first started his business 28 years ago, doing good for the environment is what his business has been all about. There are many

Figure 4.1. Craig Sieben, Sieben Energy Associates.
Photo from Craig R. Sieben.

ways to tackle the environmental impact of nonrenewable fuels, he says, and saving energy is definitely one of them: "Sieben Energy Associates is mission-driven. The work we do takes a stand for reducing energy use. Seventy-two percent of the CO_2 in Chicago comes from buildings."

Craig Sieben puts his hope in practical solutions to the world's problems, and in the power of ordinary people. He grew up believing in the inherent goodness of all people. "I believe in ideas," he says, "and the opening of minds and hearts, and seeking solutions. My parents and my Unitarian Universalist upbringing taught me to question the structures of society, to ask always, 'Am I harming others?' before I act."

In 1977, a physics major at Hampshire College in Amherst, Massachusetts, Craig participated in a nonviolent, civil disobedience-oriented protest at the Seabrook, New Hampshire site of a planned nuclear power plant, where over 1,400 people were arrested and spent a week in the Nassau, New Hampshire National Guard Amory at an impromptu "teach-in" on energy alternatives to nuclear power. Later, when he returned to school and was passionately explaining why he had joined the protest, his physics professor said to him, "Craig, you've defined what you're against; what are you *for*?" Craig began to research better ways to provide energy and discovered the inefficiency of U.S. energy sources. His physics teacher handed Craig a copy of Amory Lovins's just-published article in the fall 1976 issue of *Foreign Affairs* titled "Soft Energy Paths: The Road Not Taken."

Craig became excited about the concepts of "soft energy"—ramping up passive energy sources (solar, wind) and increasing efficiency. Craig joined the college's Board of Trustee's Buildings and Grounds committee and helped develop a plan to improve energy efficiency at Hampshire College, and energy went from 8% to 3% of the college budget during the next 10 years. He ended up writing his own degree program in community energy policy. He was inspired by the idea that by using energy more efficiently and effectively, we didn't have to build so many fossil-fuel energy plants in the first place. And efficiency just makes sense. "The need for energy efficiency won't end when we are using 100% renewable energy sources," Craig maintains.

When Craig decided to make a business out of his passion, he sought out mentors in his nascent field—who subsequently become decades-long resources. "I'm not an engineer," he says. It was of the utmost importance to him to understand how to run a business that would be viable. He wanted a business that works for everyone: owners, customers, and workers.

Craig sees his workers as his greatest asset and treats them accordingly. "People who work with me really care," Craig says. "These are people with advanced technical degrees in engineering, math, etc. Their skills and training in their areas of expertise are the best. They see every building as a challenge, as an opportunity to improve energy efficiency. They also need to be collaborative by nature, to have emotional intelligence. Each building is unique, each client is unique."

Over the past 29 years, Craig has built Sieben Energy Associates into a recognized leader in achieving energy efficiency in buildings. To quote from their website, "Our consultants and engineers are committed to generating for our clients a strong return on their investment. We help organizations save time and money. We help facility teams implement best practices in energy management. And we help the people who work, live, and play in those buildings have a more comfortable and productive day."

And every bit of the energy saved reduces the strain on resources and cuts down on CO_2 emissions and environmental degradation. That is Craig Sieben's bottom line, the great secret that keeps him going: in the long run, sustainable energy practices are better for business. It is why he believes that a saner energy policy will win out in the end. "Technology is the true driver of change. Bureaucracy is a buffer against government meddling. No business can exist without creating something that people need or value in some way," he says. Craig has some advice for people of any age who would like to make a practical difference in the world:

> Find something you enjoy, that gives you a tremendous amount of joy. Help solve problems, improve life for others, put a smile on their faces. Aim for a bigger impact: learn to lead, to organize people, so you can expand beyond what you can do alone. Develop your entrepreneurial skills, learn effective management, how to make a profit. Do your research, know your area, know where the opportunities are.
>
> Realize that with an average lifespan of 80 years, you have several 25-year careers possible in your life. Become interested and interesting, take care of yourself, learn all you can. Look at the world. Learn where the breakdowns are happening, the trends. Respond and provide value and expertise. In the explosion of information, use discernment and good judgment, separate the noise from what's important. How much stuff do you need? What do you love, what makes you happy? How do you define success? And how do you make a living? You can have a big impact on the world well into your 80s or even 90s.

Sieben addresses the basic challenges named by the economist Juliet Schor in *Plenitude: The New Economics of True Wealth*. While we are relatively skilled at identifying what is wrong with our socially and environmental destructive economic system, we are also limited by an inability to imagine plausible alternatives. As Schor states,

> Climate destabilization, economic meltdown, and the escalation of food and energy prices are warning signs from a highly stressed planet. . . . But

the mainstream conversation has been stalled by fatalism. We're better at identifying what can't be done than what we need to accomplish.[37]

In *Plenitude*, Schor describes an emerging environmentally responsible economic order, one not built on sacrifice and scarcity but grounded in a deep appreciation of what creates genuine and sustainable bounty—the plenitude that is possible as we move from an economy of endless consumption and growth to responsible connections to other people and to the natural world.[38]

Key Insights for Progressive Practice

In his professional life, Sieben lives out practices of plenitude, and enables others to do the same, helping them both use less energy and operate with greater economic efficiency. The challenge of this work is as much technical as it is adaptive. Within some theories of leadership, there is an emphasis on adaptive change, the basic changes in culture and vision that are required to fundamentally reshape an institution.[39] While changes in values are essential, in themselves they are woefully insufficient. It is not enough to want to live in reciprocity with the natural world—we need to know technically how to do so in our energy use and production, in our systems of agriculture, and in how we construct buildings and transportation networks. What we see in the proposals in *Drawdown* and in Sieben's work is a creative way of living out the basics of human and planetary survival. As Schor states, these challenges are technical as well as ethical: "The economy is broken in fundamental ways, as are the local and global ecosystems on which it depends. Quick fixes won't solve its problems. Creating a truly sustainable system will require ecological restoration and technological innovation over a period of many years."[40]

The work of Sieben and the participants in *Drawdown* is what happens after people know what is wrong and choose to live in a new form of abundance. This requires as much technical expertise and experimentation as it does a fundamental ethical choice to move from exploitation to reciprocity.[41] It requires a wholehearted rejection of the Windigo of extractive capitalism and a resolute avoidance of the Windigo of forgetting the partiality of all our knowing, and our ongoing capacity for error. Recall Kimmerer's challenge—we may not know how to restore damaged ecosystems. Recall as well the honesty of the scientists in *Drawdown*, already identifying the trade-offs and risks of 67 of the 100 practices that they endorse.

What does it take to keep generative, self-critical work alive? How do we know that our efforts are valuable for more than ourselves? This requires the embrace of the challenge of ongoing critique and immersion in the paradoxical joys of global connection and cultural humility. We are fortunate that there is yet another social movement that has just this as its aim, the network of public and private universities that make up the Engagement Scholarship Consortium. In the next chapter we will explore the work of universities that have expanded their mission from research and teaching to include engagement with society, "rethinking and reinventing the future of a world at risk."[42]

5

Global Connections and Cultural Humility

The Science and Artistry of Community Engagement

In a March 2014 article in *Crain's Chicago Business* weekly, the advertising executive Andrew Swinad wrote that corporate social responsibility is the millennials' new religion. He cited a 2011 study by ad agency network TBWA/Worldwide and TakePart, the digital division of Participant Media, that found that *"7 in 10 young adults consider themselves social activists*—about double since they were last surveyed, in 2010." They express that activism in where they work and what they buy, wanting to spend their time and resources in ways that are socially just and environmentally sound.[1] Studies of millennials done in 2017 show that this commitment is deep; it is growing, and it is well aware of, and highly critical of, corporate efforts that are mere window dressing or a cover for bad publicity.[2]

What is the source of this commitment to living justly? This deep commitment to corporate social responsibility may well be related to another growing expression of constructive social engagement, the work of the Engagement Scholarship Consortium.

While much attention has been given by journalists, theologians, and social ethicists in the United States to the college students involved in the Occupy movement, little has been given to the large numbers of students involved in the work of engagement scholarship. In 1999, the first conference on engaged scholarship was hosted by Pennsylvania State University. Since 2001, there have been annual conferences that bring together scholars and community practitioners to share what they have learned about how to work together with communities to address pressing issues of social inequality and environmental sustainability. Thirty-eight public and private universities are committed to the co-creation of knowledge that is culturally responsive, scientifically sound, and directed to enhancing the common good.[3]

Valerie Paton, speaking at the 2013 conference of the Engaged Scholarship Consortium, spoke of the commitment of universities "to improve the human condition through our community engagement, addressing the most pressing issues in our world, bringing the assets of communities and universities together."[4] Peter McPherson, American Public and Land Grant University president, states that "[e]ngagement with society is one of the three pillars in the mission of public research universities along with education and research."[5] As Judith Ramaley of Portland University stated in her plenary address at the 2013 Consortium, "Together we can rethink and reinvent the future of a world at risk."[6]

This commitment to meet the needs of a world at risk is expressed in a wide range of constructive endeavors. Many institutions, like Ohio State University, have comprehensive precollegiate and collegiate programs to prepare students from low-income families for college success. Other institutions, like Pennsylvania State University, are involved in multiyear endeavors to "research, design, field test and launch technology based social enterprises." These include "low cost greenhouses and solar food dryers, cellphone applications and informal education systems." These endeavors are grounded in a "fundamental philosophy of Empathy, Equity and Ecosystem to . . . truly collaborate to develop sustainable and scalable solutions. Sustainability in this context refers to the notion that solutions must be technologically appropriate, socially acceptable, environmentally benign, and economically sustainable. Over the past decade our projects, led primarily by undergraduate students, have collectively impacted the lives of a few million people across Kenya, Tanzania, Rwanda, India, U.S., Jamaica, Nicaragua and other countries. . . . [produced] more than 45 peer reviewed articles, . . . and has led to the creation of a rigorous multidisciplinary academic program focused on deploying practical and innovative solutions to compelling global programs."[7]

Other schools, like the College of Natural Resources at the University of Idaho, partner with elementary, middle, and secondary schools to create a comprehensive adventure/learning curriculum that "help[s] future generations of citizens learn to address some of the world's most challenging issues, including climate change and alternative energy."[8]

Similar work is being done at private universities like Southern Methodist University. The mission statement of the Dedman College Center for Academic Community Engagement is instructive, capturing the core ethical and intellectual challenges of socially engaged scholarship. Here there is a recognition "that a central mission of the University is to promote teaching and scholarship in the pursuit of effective social policy; cultivate through the classroom a sense of the 'public good'; provide the community with technical skill; conduct research directed at problems that are important to the community and region."[9] A surprising result of such engagement is the emergence of a growing number of middle- and upper-class students whose lives have been changed, and who are not sure what to do next, how to take the values of cultural humility and connection into their ongoing lives as professionals and citizens.

The fundamental goal of engagement scholarship is straightforward: the creation of mutually beneficial partnerships between universities and local communities to solve pressing social issues. The fulfillment of this goal requires learning two complex sets of skills and knowledges: (1) How to be aware of histories of exploitation and injustice, and the likelihood of repeating those patterns in the present; (2) how to create structures of genuinely working together to solve problems for the long haul—not short-term or ideologically driven, naïve, or inappropriate fixes.

The liberation theologians Joerg Rieger and Kwok Pui Lan call us to a core commitment to deep solidarity in the pursuit of the common good. We find this commitment in the world of engagement scholarship. We also find a deliberate and self-critical embrace of the challenge that theologian Dwight Hopkins raises for white people who are committed to "a better future where all races can enjoy one another as human beings." In the foreword to *Disrupting White Supremacy from Within*, he acknowledges the power of the recognition of some whites that their humanity is inseparable from the affirmation of the full humanity of people of color. As they live out this commitment, he states that as whites they must forgo "historical amnesia" and face forthrightly the depth and ongoing power of white supremacy, and challenge it in their personal, professional, and civic lives: "When pushed against the wall, the United States, like its parent countries in Europe, assumes itself a *white* country. When further crises of identity press harder, a great number of white Americans . . . will even proclaim a white *Christian* nation."[10]

It is vital that we counter this historical amnesia by confronting the history of racism in the past, and understanding how it continues to operate to deny the full humanity of all. Hopkins reminds us of the founding tragedy of the United States:

> The thirteen colonies and, then, the nation, in 1787 were not founded for yellow, red, brown, and black human beings. In this history, the seventeenth century saw enslaved Africans replace European indentured servants. The latter's payoff was to accept rights, entitlements, and opportunities in the divine covenant of antiblack racism.[11]

Hopkins is clear. Whites can confront this history, and can join all people in discovering what "it means to claim our own humanity by acts of love for the humanity of others."[12]

In the growing embrace of engagement scholarship we find students who share this larger sense of self and of purpose and professors who are helping them to express this historically grounded commitment to an expansive common good in their professional and civic lives. This larger sense of self and purpose is fundamentally reshaping many academic fields, and STEM is among the foremost that is being redefined. Peter Butler, professor of biomedical engineering at Penn State, gives a clear definition of STEM: "STEM stands for science, technology, engineering, and mathematics, and its effects encompass every sphere of human existence, from economic competitiveness to national security to standard of living. STEM research and innovation is the engine that drives technological progress and economic prosperity."[13]

In the world of engagement scholarship we find increasing numbers of students and professors who are bringing the critical lens of social justice and environmental sustainability to the work of STEM. B. L. Ramakrishna, professor of humanitarian engineering at Arizona State University, and senior science and technology advisor for the Department of State/U.S. Agency for International Development, describes this core commitment well in his articulation of what is being conveyed to students about the purpose of engineering at even the K–12 levels: "Remind students to keep in mind the ultimate goal of universal accessibility when thinking about solutions. Just as Abraham Lincoln noted that a house divided against itself cannot stand, a world divided by wealth and poverty, health and sickness, and food and hunger cannot long remain a stable place for civilization to thrive."[14]

This work is not done merely to help others; it is not charity. This work is also not done out of a sense of being forced to capitulate to the demands of others for change. Rather, there is a growing awareness that economic structures and technological solutions that primarily benefit the 1% or the .01% are intrinsically unjust and fundamentally unstable. Furthermore, for elites to move out of isolation into deep solidarity is more of a gain than a loss. Such a move enables the deep satisfaction of living in genuine community and honest and accountable interdependence.

Humanitarian Engineering and Social Entrepreneurship

We can see what such work entails in the research, scholarship, and teaching of Khanjan Mehta. Mehta is the vice provost for creative inquiry and director of the Mountaintop Initiative at Lehigh University, and was the founding director of the Humanitarian Engineering and Social Entrepreneurship program and assistant professor of engineering design at Penn State University. Mehta is a pioneer in developing and assessing community and university partnerships that embody the principles of empathy, equity, and ecosystems in developing "transformative and sustainable social innovations." He describes the shift in perspective that occurs as students and professors take up the work of becoming "social innovators and sustainable development professionals." An important objective of Mehta's work is to collectively alter the perception of such efforts from a "save-the world mission with students going to poor countries to save people," to "a rigorous, multidisciplinary, integrative discipline that inspires students and faculty to work shoulder to shoulder with communities to deliver impact."[15]

On Khanjan Mehta's website, he describes himself as "Entrepreneur. Educator. Engineer." Mehta is all three, but he combines the three in ways that are innovative and even revolutionary.[16] For example, the program that he created at Penn State, the Humanitarian Engineering and Social Entrepreneurship program is interdisciplinary, drawing on a wide range of skills and expertise to design solutions for "resource constrained" communities. In this work, community members, students and engineers focus on creating independent systems that are sustainable and adaptable to changing conditions within the community.

Figure 5.1. Khanjan Mehta, Lehigh University. Photo from Penn State University.

Mehta first conceived of the idea of "humanitarian engineering" when he volunteered to advise an engineering student team designing a low-cost windmill for villages in rural western Kenya. He traveled to Kenya in order to orient himself to the conditions where the windmills would be used, and see how things really work on the ground. What he found was that the windmill project was trying to solve a problem of adaptation with a technical solution.

"Windmills have existed in Europe for a very long time, but there were *no* functioning windmills in Kenya. Not one. So that said to me that the problem was not that they had no windmills, but something else," Mehta said. As he spent time with the people in Kenya, he saw such a starkness to their lives; all their energy was taken up getting food on the table day by day. There was no energy left to do anything that might make a big difference in the future. He realized that in order for any solution to have a chance to actually work for them, the Kenyans needed to have a reason, an incentive, to put a new way of doing things into practice.

What Mehta realized is that for people facing compelling problems in "resource constrained" communities, charity is not what they need or want. They want and need opportunities to do something for themselves. They want choices, and the dignity that comes with agency. They need access to capital and technology. They need partners who let them have final say, who respect their intelligence and desire for self-improvement. They need ways to improve their ability to put food on the table and improve their lives. In essence, market-based solutions are more likely to be sustainable in the long run.

Pursuing this approach, Mehta discovered others who were moving in a similar direction, such as the Grameen Bank and its great success with microlending. This and similar grassroots approaches to change were making a huge difference in people's lives. This approach goes beyond mere criticism of things as they are, beyond protesting, marching, and agitating for change. It gets into the nitty-gritty of making things happen, taking deep dives, building trusted relationships, and working together with the community to find solutions that change systems of oppression into systems of opportunity.

Mehta found that volunteers are too limited in their ability to give the time needed to listen to the people who are impacted by poverty and lack of resources. Volunteers are limited by their need to make a living, and also by their discouragement when quick results are not seen. What was lacking was a real incentive for volunteers to engage deeply and to sustain that engagement over enough time to effect change. Mehta provided just these real incentives to his students.

He realized that students were a huge pool of volunteers who were passionate about wanting to change the world. Their incentive and even some of the funding comes from studying in a university program that concentrates on grassroots change making. Mehta has developed the Humanitarian Engineering and Social Entrepreneurship program into an integrated interdisciplinary academic program where learning, research, and entrepreneurial engagement happen concurrently. The fact that the students are doing this for credit encourages knowledge, grappling with the differences in culture and life experiences, accountability for outcomes, and responsibility to stick with a project through its completion.

One of the biggest challenges that students face is trying to understand how things work in low-resource settings. Knowing the facts about an area, such as demographics, incomes, and resources, is important but it does not capture how things work in that culture, and it is not sufficient to design solutions that will work in the long term. Students (and their mentors) need to delve into a culture, its philosophy, how new concepts are introduced, how people think, what problems they face, what their choices are, how they make decisions: the fundamental ways things work in the culture. Students need to be familiar with these things before they go "on-site" in the community they will be working with.

Mehta found quickly that stories were a very practical and efficient way to really capture how things work within a culture. He found that the way people think, make decisions, adopt new systems, accept or reject new ideas can best be captured in stories. He does not consider himself a storyteller, but he came up with a series of narratives, *The Kochia Chronicles,* that highlight these vital but hard-to-describe social structures that are so important to the success or failure of a project.[17]

In his introductory class, students read two stories a week for the first six weeks and then spend a portion of the class discussing the lessons learned. Grounded in this deep contextual understanding and with additional research in the relevant subject areas, students advance their projects forward. When they finally travel to the community for the on-site phase of the project, the understandings gained from engaging with the stories are used to inform their work with the local population. All the projects are multisemester endeavors with one team passing the baton on to the next team in the next semester until the project reaches independent self-sustaining operations (or there is a "spectacular" failure). Every semester students advance ventures forward while disseminating lessons learned in refereed journals and conference proceedings.

Mehta stressed that the work must be one of co-creating working solutions that the local community has ownership of:

We don't go into a community and say, we're going to build you a greenhouse and teach you how to use it. We go into the community and understand its challenges, and we learn that a lot of people can benefit from a greenhouse if, instead of buying them for $3,000, they could buy one for $600. So we designed low-cost greenhouses, and then we identified and worked with local partners to build companies that make and sell these affordable greenhouses to farmers. We helped them connect with agricultural extension services, and we helped them get low-interest loans, and we helped them do a whole lot of other things that supported their burgeoning enterprises. The farmers' return on investment was typically 6–9 months. [We expanded] choice for farmers (as well as people who are interested in farming) and [gave] them another approach if they would like to try something new. All along, we focused not on building greenhouses, but on building companies and systems where people can buy greenhouses and get the support to make sure those greenhouses are successful. Our ultimate metric of success is not the number of greenhouses sold but the number of working greenhouses where the farmers have recovered their capital investment and now have substantially improved livelihoods.

Mehta explains that the social entrepreneurship part is just as important as the humanitarian engineering part. This is a market-based approach. Solutions work best when those who are to implement them have a chance to improve their livelihood. This is the only way to make those solutions economically sustainable. "We need all kinds of organizations," he says, "government, nonprofits, large corporations, start-up ecosystems, UN agencies. Making money is not bad. We need to start making a commitment to equity, paying a living wage, and building and nurturing an inclusive and resilient society. Customers increasingly want to patronize businesses that support and strengthen civil society."

Mehta points out that we can all become more responsible for the impacts we have on the environment and on people who are most vulnerable to exploitation or the effects of poverty. But clear analysis and understanding is important. "Should we boycott Walmart because it sells items made in sweatshops? That might change those sweatshop employee's lives for the worse. There are young women whose only choice is working in a sweatshop . . . or working the streets."

Instead, Mehta urges us to educate ourselves on the real dynamics of survival. "If we want to help homeless people or people living in poverty, step into their shoes; ask them what they need. Trust them to know what works for them. Let go of the need to come up with the "perfect" solution; be willing to experiment; pay attention to the impact on people; be willing to change tactics or even abandon a plan that is not working. Try a new way of doing things. Offer resources, partner with them in their efforts to solve the very real problems of surviving and thriving."

Mehta has seen what can happen when people are offered the chance to partner in the development of solutions that work for them. The idea of humanitarian engineering and social entrepreneurship is working in a lot of different places and in a wide variety of forms. Mehta hopes that more and more people will discover the satisfaction of "doing good while doing well." He is certainly doing his part to make this happen.

Just as technical expertise is not enough for mutually beneficial community partnerships, good intentions and solid ethical commitments are also insufficient. In the world of humanitarian social engineering we find a complex recognition of the interdependence of value problems and technical fixes. Those in the humanities often focus on what we call "wicked problems"—large-scale environmental and economic problems that cannot be solved by a single technological innovation or policy change. In our focus on the values at stake in genuinely taking up the imperative of environmentally sustainable and socially just forms of business and economic development, we forget that these challenges are also truly technical. What are the best ways for a particular locale to generate and expand the use of renewable energy? How are the variations in the supply of wind and solar energy compensated for? What are feasible ways of cleaning up the vast stores of plastics that mar our environment? How do we create and scale up efficient worker-owned cooperatives?

Phil Weilerstein is the executive director of a network that invests in social innovation. He describes the evolving motivations of students and professionals in the fields of science and engineering. He reminds us of the positive "social impacts" of scientific innovation in the past ("chlorination of drinking water, oral rehydration therapy, solar energy") and highlights how these aspirations are being deepened by a sense of community with those who are underserved and exploited, with those whose insights, energy, and expertise is largely unrecognized and untapped.

Students want to be taught how to develop products that will empower people to lift themselves out of poverty. Scientists and engineers have always been motivated by the idea that their inventions would be useful to society; what has changed are their propensity and opportunity to participate actively and directly in that process. We are seeing young college innovators develop new approaches to preserving vaccines; expanding access to light, power, and clean water; and developing more sustainable and better forms of building materials.[18]

This emerging culture is the manifestation of an honor code that goes against the use of science and engineering for short-term gains for the few at the expense of the many. It is collaborative, creative, and unafraid of taking risks and learning from mistakes:

> The combination of a scientific approach, a problem-solving mindset born from creativity and design, and the rigor and embrace of entrepreneurial risk is creating remarkable outcomes. This new culture is collaborative, celebrating successes and respecting failures as opportunities to learn and change.[19]

At the core of STEM at its best is a recognition that technology has been used for good and for ill. Peter Butler, professor of biomedical engineering, is clear: "Together with scientists, engineers, and mathematicians, the STEM community informs, designs, and uses products that (for better or worse) irrevocably impact the world and our lives."[20] What we see in the field of humanitarian social engineering is a self-critical and deliberate attempt to make sure that technology is being developed in a way that serves a larger social good.

Weilerstein's words are, again, instructive. Ethical and technical instruction are equally essential. He encourages students who are committed to innovative social impact to follow an increasingly common educational path:

> [G]et a T-shaped education. That is: become a technical expert in your field; go deep. And then develop your competencies in leadership, entrepreneurship, global awareness and engagement, ethical decision making— the horizontal of the "T." Do not just learn about entrepreneurship—do it! Universities are leading the way in not just educating future change agents, but directly helping them create, develop, and build ventures. This kind of experiential education cultivates empathy, innovation, and entrepreneurship, a mindset and skill set that travels with you everywhere you go.[21]

Uniting Across Our Differences

Let us explore the challenge of developing empathy and uniting across our differences in more detail. One of the first challenges in this task is simply that of seeing differences. We can then learn how to engage those differences with respect and openness to learning more about the world, and learning to see both the strengths, and the limitations, of our prior worldviews and knowledge systems.

Stephanie Brown and Virginia Cope, professors at Ohio State University, have addressed directly the challenge of enabling students to see and learn from difference. They conduct service learning trips in Berlin and New Orleans, and found that even students from currently or formerly marginalized groups found it difficult to fully engage with different communities. Their article in the September 2013 issue of the *Journal of Community Engagement and Scholarship*, "Global Citizenship for the Non-traditional Student," described their initial failures to prepare students for deep engagement, and the pedagogical strategies that enabled students to see difference, respect it, and be changed by it.

Brown and Cope thought they had designed their service learning trips well, and were surprised by the difficulties of respectful and transformative engagement.

> Once in an unfamiliar culture—whether foreign or domestic—a significant number of students failed to embrace the very opportunity that they had paid dearly, and worked hard, to achieve. It became apparent that many students come to international education and even domestic travel with expectations that generally do not line up with the reality of the experience, and frequently they lack the resources to usefully process the difference. Accordingly, some students retreat emotionally or physically, or behave in ways that can only be described as rude—they laugh or made inappropriate comments; they refuse to speak or make eye contact with individuals or take refuge in an electronic device.[22]

Brown and Cope emphasize that this failure was not due to character flaws on the part of the students, but was due to their failure as professors to give the students the competencies required for deep cross-cultural learning. While at first surprised by this reaction, Brown and

Cope delved into the research on transformative learning and found that such reactions are only not unusual but are, rather, to be expected. They turned to the work of Jack Mezirow for a description of deep learning. Deep learning is not merely the acquisition of new information. It is also a challenge to old information, old patterns, assumptions, and convictions about the world. For that reason, when real, it is profoundly unsettling.

Brown and Cope are forthright about their mistake as educators:

> We initially developed our programs in the hope that students, when confronted by unfamiliar experiences that threatened them with disorienting dilemmas, would spontaneously undergo Mezirow's transformative learning experience—that having confronted their own limits, they would expand their frame of reference, change their expectations of themselves or others, and with some guidance from us, engage in "critical self-reflection, which results in the reformulation of a meaning perspective to allow a more inclusive, discriminating and integrative understanding of [their] experience" (Mezirow 1990, xvi).[23]

They learned that nothing could be further from the truth! They designed, therefore, classroom experiences to teach students how to learn from unsettling differences. The exercises were simple—helping students identify behaviors that showed hospitality and learning from others, and then practicing those behaviors in learning from the ways in which they themselves had a degree of difference.

> After introducing the idea of cosmopolitan courtesy into the classroom, we ask students to suggest ways in which one indicates a willingness to show "hospitality" to another. . . . They may suggest that the best way to show interest in another person's words is to ask a minimum of one question about whatever is said, even if the answer to the question seems obvious, since the purpose of the question in this context is as much to indicate attentiveness as to gather information. They may also, if they are preparing to go to a country in which English is not the native language, suggest learning . . . a minimum of three basic phrases useful in social situations, such as "please," "thank you" and "you're welcome."[24]

These steps seem obvious to most instructors, and, indeed, once articulated, they often seem self-evident to students. Yet practicing the markers of cosmopolitan courtesy takes effort, as they discover when they begin to put their suggestions into action in the classroom in the pursuit of what may be designated, using sociologist Elijah Anderson's term, "cosmopolitan canopies" or safe "pluralistic spaces where people engage one another in a spirit of civility, or even comity and goodwill."[25]

They applied these techniques in hospitality and openness in learning from the differences they had with each other.

> We asked them to reflect upon their own peculiar cultures—whether by
> neighborhood, family, class, gender, or ethnicity—and share with a small
> group any unique traditions that would not be understood by those out-
> side the culture. We also then asked them to "consider an example of
> deep culture that has been a topic of debate between groups with differing
> ideologies—in the news or in your experience," providing an example of
> a couple's conflicting holiday traditions. . . . Finally, after these reflection
> sessions, we asked the class, in groups of three, to take turns explaining
> a tradition or perception from their own experience that others in the
> group might be unfamiliar with; listening and responding to that expla-
> nation; or observing that interaction and reflecting on the rewards and
> challenges of the discussion.[26]

The results of these seemingly simple exercises in what the authors call cosmopolitan courtesy were profound. With this preparation, students did engage respectfully with others. They did learn in times of discomfort and challenge, and did see "that they are inextricably part of a global community, representatives of one or more 'others' among many."[27]

There is another dimension to our inability to see and creatively engage difference—the social and political effects of implicit bias. In his introduction to *Behavioral Public Policy*, the editor, Eldar Shafir, states that "persistent biases in social perception" are unrecognized, unchecked, and therefore "often end up playing a big role in exacerbating long-standing political and social tensions."[28] Helping people to create organizational structures and policies that identify and check such implicit biases or prejudices is essential in our work of creating a society and economic system that truly embodies our values of justice, equity, and compassion. He cites the work of Curtis Hardin, professor of psychology, and Mahzarin Banaji, professor of social ethics, who explore the decades-long research that demonstrates the extent to which prejudice and discrimination are reinforced by the operation of implicit bias among those who are explicitly committed to racial and gender equality:

> Curtis Hardin and Mahzarin Banaji argue that our views of prejudice and discrimination are based on outdated notions, with important policy implications. Rather than arising from ignorance and hatred, which would be best addressed by changing the hearts and minds of individuals, prejudice and stereotyping, according to these authors, emerge from cognitively salient structures in our social milieu and do not necessarily involve personal animus, hostility, or even awareness. Rather, prejudice is often "implicit"—that is, unwitting, unintentional, and uncontrollable—even among the most well intentioned. At the same time, these authors suggest, research shows that implicit prejudice can be reduced through sensible changes in the social environment.[29]

It is very different to read *Behavioral Public Policy* now than in 2013 when it was first published. We are living in a time of a deeply disturbing resurgence of explicit prejudice that does "involve personal animus and hostility." As citizens, educators, and leaders committed to social justice, our work has, therefore, a dual focus—challenging explicit bias and hatred through structures of legal accountability and systemic preventive enculturation—as well as systemically and sustainably checking implicit bias that also leads to deleterious, and even deadly, consequences in the lives of millions of people. While research is ongoing on how to contain explicit bias, it is vital that we confront the extent of implicit bias and the reality of its deleterious effects.

Hardin and Banaji's work was profound in its depiction of the ongoing dangers of implicit bias and structural racism, yet they, like so many of us, missed the likelihood of the resurgence of violent and virulent racism by white Americans against all people of color. They argued that there was a need for "a reconceptualization of prejudice—less as a property of malicious individuals and more as a property of

the architecture of cognition and known mechanisms of social learning and social relations."[30]

Hardin and Banaji's work has much to teach us about implicit bias.
Hardin and Banaji find that implicit prejudice is disturbingly widespread: "over 80% of American whites and Asians show antiblack bias
and over 90% of Americans show anti-elder bias."[31] They begin their
examination of the nature of implicit prejudice, and its implications for
personal and public policy, with a reminder of the ongoing presence of
racial discrimination in the United States:

> Some fifty years ago in Arkansas, nine black students initiated a social
> experiment with help from family, friends, and armed National Guards.
> Their successful attempts to desegregate Little Rock's Central High School
> following the decision in *Brown v. Board of Education* is among the most
> momentous events in America's history, leaving no doubt about its his-
> toric importance and the significance of its impact on public policy. Nev-
> ertheless . . . even at the beginning of the twenty-first century, a blatant
> de facto segregation in living and learning persist and in some circum-
> stances has intensified (e.g., Orfield, 2001).[32]

They also highlight the work of the sociologist Robert Putnam that
shows that increases in diversity actually increase social distrust:

> As the ethnic diversity by zip code increases, so does mistrust of one's
> neighbors, even same ethnicity neighbors (Putnam 2007). The naïve op-
> timism that diversity will succeed in the absence of a clear understanding
> of the dynamics of social dominance and intergroup relations is chal-
> lenged by these and other similar revelations.[33]

And, such bias is connected to active discrimination in public life.
According to Hardin and Banaji, Patricia Devine's 1998 research on the
behavioral effects of implicit prejudice marked a "paradigm shift in the
social-psychological understanding of stereotyping and prejudice."

> In the critical experiment, participants evaluated a hypothetical person
> named "Donald" as more hostile if they had been subliminally exposed to

a large versus small proportion of words related to common U.S. stereotypes of African Americans. . . . it was disturbing because it showed that implicit stereotyping occurred to an equal degree whether participants explicitly endorsed racist attitudes or not.[34]

Research since 1998 has been consistent in showing a connection between implicit prejudice and "social judgment and behavior." Though their article was written in 2013, the findings of Hardin and Banaji are disturbingly relevant to what was exposed on a large scale in 2016:

> Across some two dozen experiments in which participants are presented with a series of images of social situations and instructed to as quickly and accurately as possible "shoot if the target is armed" and "don't shoot" if the target is unarmed, the finding is consistent: participants faster and more accurately shoot gun-toting black targets than white targets and *faster and more accurately avoid shooting tool-toting white targets than black targets* (e.g., Correll et al., 2002; Correel, Urland, and Ito 2006). The finding is obtained among both white and black participants alike, and *even among professional police officers* (Correll et al., 2007; Plant and Peruche 2005; Plant, Peruche, and Butz 2005).[35]

As was known even in 2013, such findings are tragically not limited to experimental settings, but are an ongoing and deadly dimension of American public life. Hardin and Banaji argue that "such findings have important implications for police officers, given the broader finding that police consistently use greater lethal and nonlethal force against nonwhite suspects than white suspects."[36]

We may now be seeing broad public demands that this pattern, widely known by those affected and demonstrated by research since 1982, be redressed. The means of doing so are many. At the core is legal accountability and prosecutorial integrity to hold officers liable for the use of deadly force. It is also essential that there be rigorous screening to prevent the hiring of police officers who are explicitly racist. For those whose prejudice is implicit, ongoing training to check the deadly effects of such prejudice is possible and necessary. The results of social science research here are clear—implicit bias is readily activated by the presence of stereotypes; implicit bias leads to discriminatory behavior; and implicit bias cannot be checked consciously. Implicit bias is related to discriminatory actions in terms of "political attitudes, voting, academic achievement scores, consumer preferences, social evaluation, hiring decisions, and verbal and nonverbal affiliation."[37] Implicit bias can be checked, however, through consistent and deliberate policy solutions.

Hardin and Banaji make a claim essential for our progressive work as activists, professionals, and social ethicists. They claim that "[t]he American experiment in desegregation is a reminder that public policies, however noble in intent, may not realize their aspirations if they do not include an understanding of human nature and culture" and the "relevant scientific evidence, which reveals the nature of the problem, the likely outcomes, and how social transformation can best be imagined."[38]

The implications of the research on implicit prejudice for those who are able to shape institutional policies and practices are clear. This is a danger that most of us carry; it cannot be checked by individual willpower; it can be checked by institutional policies that nurture our capacities for sympathy and for self-critique.

> The profound implication of the discovery of implicit prejudice is that anybody is capable of prejudice, whether they know it or not, and of stereotyping, whether they want to or not. Therefore, . . . we believe that solutions should focus on identifying the enabling conditions that call out prejudice and stereotyping across individuals rather than focusing on identifying the rotten apples. Once identified, we must focus on the enabling conditions that promote egalitarianism . . . and healthy individuation.[39]

Let us explore the urgent task of redressing the implicit bias that is all too present in much of the world. As we do this, Shafir urges us to take seriously the psychologists Nicole Shelton, Jennifer Richeson, and John Dovidio's examination of acts of discrimination that "are rarely an obvious act of blatant discrimination" but emerge from 'intergroup biases in interracial interactions."[40] In their study of "Biases in Interracial Interactions," Shelton, Richeson, and Dovidio begin with a stark and troubling reality. They noted that in 2013 there was an increase in "explicit endorsement by whites of racial equality," yet the persistence of biases by whites against people of color in "everyday interracial interactions."[41]

Let us turn to the challenge of creating polices that reduce implicit bias in campus housing, health care, and employment. Shelton, Richeson, and Dovidio state that repeated studies have shown that the short-term difficulty of interracial group relations is often followed by long-term positive impact. They highlight the conclusion of a four-year study of the changes in racial attitudes of white, Asian, black, and Latinx students who had been assigned out-group roommates: "Overwhelmingly, the data revealed that being randomly assigned to have out-group roommates caused improvements in racial attitudes for all individuals . . . both Whites and ethnic minorities."[42]

What can speed or ease the transition from short-term costs to long-term benefits? Shelton, Richeson, and Dovidio describe the value of deliberate activities that enhance the ability of people to understand and work with those from other racial and ethnic groups:

> Among these are "friendly intergroup contact," which can be created deliberately or occur more organically. People who have more "out-group friendships" manifest less implicit prejudice, for example, as do white college freshmen randomly assigned to a black roommate, than to a white one (Shook and Fazio 2007; Henry and Hardin 2006). Simple exposure to positive and nonstereotypical images reduces implicit bias, as does ongoing exposure to and work with "admired black exemplars" (e.g., Dasgupta and Greenwald 2001; cf. De Houwer 2001).
>
> Research has shown that reciprocal personal self-disclosure and working together on shared leisure activities is a way to increase friendship and intimacy (Reis and Shaver 1988). Building upon this idea, Aron et al. (1997) developed a "fast friend" paradigm in which pairs of individuals answer a series of questions that become increasingly more personal and also engage in a relationship building task (e.g., playing a game) together.

Researchers have found that such activities lead to "positive interracial interactions, even among 'highly prejudiced Whites.'"[43]

In addition to greater long-term social harmony, such efforts lead to more creative social engagement and better problem solving:

> [D]iverse groups are better at solving complex problems that require divergent thinking (Antonio et al. 2004) and attending to a broader range

of relevant information in the analysis of issues (Sommers 2006). Policies aimed at achieving immediate harmony may thus preclude achieving other, often more desirable, long-term benefits of diversity.[44]

In their study of "Policy Implications of Unexamined Discrimination: Gender Bias in Employment as a Case Study," Susan Fiske, professor of psychology, and Linda Krieger, professor of law, point to another key aspect of checking bias. Although their example is gender, the recommendations apply to ethnic and racial bias as well. The first insight is key: "Specifically, people do not so much fail to control their biases as fail to notice that they have them." It is crucial, therefore, that we put in place practices that enable people to become aware of the biases that they hold unwittingly. One tool that is helpful in this regard is the Harvard Implicit Association Test, which "is widely used to measure a variety of socially or politically sensitive associations."[45]

Once aware of biases, it is easier to check them. Doing so requires as well ongoing institutional reminders of the positive value of diversity. Fiske and Krieger describe this as "harnessing the motive to belong" by being explicit about the core values of the institution: "Make diversity part of the organization's identity and mission, a mixed-gender, multicultural client base requires a mixed-gender multicultural work force."

They also emphasize the importance of "harnessing the motive to understand"; "[e]ducate decision makers that their evaluative judgments may be influenced by subtle forms of bias, no matter how sincere their conscious commitment to fairness, objectivity, and non-discrimination."

Their conclusion is clear: "[S]tereotype activation does not necessarily lead to stereotype expression. . . . [F]or this to occur . . . [p]erceivers must be aware of the possibility that their initial impression might be biased, and they must be motivated to correct for that bias."[46]

With these insights, while it remains important to check explicit discrimination, our social engagement can be as much proactive and preventative. For example, we can follow the recommendation of Fiske and Krieger and create an Equal Employment Opportunity Policy that can "decenter its current reliance on individual, after-the-fact disputes about whether discrimination occurred in any one particular case and rely more heavily on policy approaches that more systematically harness the power of accountability" to prevent such discrimination.[47]

Hardin and Banaji warned us of the pernicious effects of structural injustice and implicit bias in even those genuinely committed to racial equality. They, like many others, did not see, however, the possibility of a retrenchment in fundamental political rights and economic opportunities. For just such a deeper understanding of human nature and culture, and the ongoing threats of explicit racism, we can turn to the research of two scholars on the history of racism in the United States: Carol Anderson's *White Rage: The Unspoken Truth of Our Racial Divide* and Ibram Kendi's *Stamped from the Beginning: The Definitive History of Racist Ideas in America.*

Kendi discovers a dimension of white supremacy that is essential for us to recognize as we work against racism and for racial justice. Hatred and ignorance are real, yet Kendi claims that the driver of such poisons, and such terror, are policies with racially deleterious effects, chosen out of white self-interest, not out of explicitly racist intentions, and only later defended and maintained by racist ideas.

> Hate and ignorance have not driven the history of racist ideas in America. Racist policies have driven the history of racist ideas in America. . . . Time and again, racist ideas have not been cooked up from the boiling pot of ignorance and hate. Time and again, powerful and brilliant men and women have produced racist ideas in order to justify the racist policies of their era, in order to redirect the blame for their era's racial disparities away from those policies and onto Black people. . . .
>
> Racial discrimination—-racist ideas—ignorance/hate: this is the causal relationship driving America's history of race relations.[48]

Kendi's argument is essential to understand as we take up the work of dismantling racist structures. While the effects of many policies have undoubtedly damaged the lives and limited the opportunities of black Americans, Kendi argues that these policies were most often based on self-interest, not on explicit racist intentions:

> Their own racist ideas usually did not dictate the decisions of the most powerful Americans when they instituted, defended, and tolerated discriminatory policies that affected millions of Black lives over the course of American history. Racially discriminatory policies have usually sprung

from economic, political, and cultural self-interests. . . . Politicians seeking higher office have primarily created and defended discriminatory policies out of political self-interest—not racist ideas. Capitalists seeking to increase profit margins have primarily created and defended discriminatory policies out of economic self-interest—not racist ideas.[49]

When it becomes clear that black lives are harmed by policies, the blame is laid to the supposed inferiority of black people, and not to the effects of the policies:

When we look back on our history, we often wonder why so many Americans did not resist slave trading, enslaving, segregating, or now, mass incarcerating. The reason is, again, racist ideas. The principal function of racist ideas in American history has been the suppression of resistance to racial discrimination and its resulting racial disparities. The beneficiaries of slavery, segregation, and mass incarceration have produced racist ideas of Black people being best suited for or deserving of the confines of slavery, segregation, or the jail cell. Consumers of these racist ideas have been led to believe there is something wrong with Black people and not the policies that have enslaved, oppressed, and confined so many Black people.[50]

Carol Anderson sees another driver for the resurgence of racism in the United States: "The trigger for white rage, inevitably, is black advancement. It is not the mere presence of black people that is the problem; rather, it is blackness with ambition, with drive, with purpose, with aspirations, and with demands for full and equal citizenship. It is blackness that refuses to accept subjugation, to give up." Anderson is clear. The election of President Obama was the "ultimate advancement, and thus the ultimate affront." She names the historical and ongoing costs of this rage—costs that we as whites must see, and a rage that we must learn to confront, challenge, and contain.

The truth is, white rage has undermined democracy, warped the Constitution, weakened the nation's ability to compete economically, squandered billions of dollars on baseless incarceration, rendered an entire region sick, poor, and woefully undereducated, and left cities nothing less than decimated. All this havoc has been wreaked simply because African Americans wanted to work, get an education, live in decent communities, raise their families, and vote.[51]

What do we have here? Kendi sees a resurgence of white racism when African Americans are failing; Anderson sees a resurgence when African Americans succeed. My conclusion—they are both right. Each of these drivers is present in the culture of white Americans and must be, and can be, named and constrained.[52]

Such constraint requires, however, that the dynamics first be seen. To these drivers of racist injustice, I would add the perennial threat of an authoritarianism that targets African American and Latinx peoples, and all other groups perceived both as inferior *and* as threatening.

Let us look at these forms of the Windigo from the perspective of the professional managerial class. These are not merely individual attitudes, beliefs, and practices. They also structure our institutional lives. As those who shape and manage institutions, we who are members of the professional managerial class have a key role in creating structures that activate respect and contain structural injustice and implicit bias. Lawrence Kirmayer, professor of social and transcultural psychology, in his response to a lecture by Paul Farmer, the founder of Partners in Health, on structural violence, posed a clear challenge:

> Who are the "architects of structural violence"? We know their rhetoric and rationalizations, but perhaps we need more appreciation of their ways of being-in-the-world and their decision-making processes.[53]

Many of us may be the unwitting and unintentional "architects of structural violence." Our work for social justice will be stronger, more creative, and more resilient if we learn to distinguish these drivers of injustice and oppression. It is vital that we address all of them with equal power and creativity, and that we do not conflate them in any of the following ways.

First, to be genuinely free of authoritarian violence and hatred, to be genuinely appalled by explicit bias, does not mean that we are not the agents of structural violence.

Structural violence is a powerful metaphor that leads us to look for the brutality in taken-for-granted arrangements. The notion that it involves "sinful" social structures assigns blame and urges a moral response, but how are we to characterize this sin (as avarice, self-interest, gluttony, pride, racism, ignorance, aggression?). . . . Everyone who participates in an oppressive social order is complicit in it, but the more privileged we are the more we are loath to acknowledge our complicity.[54]

The kind of moral denunciation that may contain and constrain racist authoritarianism is not what is required to build on good intentions and check deleterious effects.

Structural violence is not, however, primarily about individual choices—it is built into the functioning of impersonal (bureaucratic, technocratic, and automatic) systems and applied to whole classes of people without regard to the characteristics of any individual case; hence the limitations of the moral vocabulary derived from individual agency for analyzing the larger systems of oppression and exclusion. We need to understand how the system builds and rebuilds itself, neutralizing and absorbing opposition and reform.[55]

Similarly, what contains and constrains implicit bias and unwitting participation in, or the creation of, structural injustice does not work in standing up to blatant calls to white dominance and violence against dehumanized and feared others.

Let us return to the goals of engagement scholarship and the sets of skills and knowledge that are required to fulfill those goals. The fundamental goal of engagement scholarship is straightforward: the creation of mutually beneficial partnerships between universities and local communities to solve pressing social issues. As was stated earlier, fulfillment of this goal requires learning two complex sets of skills and knowledge: (1) how to be aware of histories of exploitation and injustice, and the likelihood of repeating those patterns in the present; (2) how to create structures of genuinely working together to solve problems for the long haul—not short-term or ideologically driven, naïve, or inappropriate fixes.

We have addressed becoming aware of histories of exploitation and injustice, and how to see and engage difference constructively and creatively. For those who are oppressors, there is another dimension to this work. We must confront not just the *fact* of oppression, but the *how* of oppression. How was it justified then, how is it justified now? The theologian Marc Ellis reminds us of a core dynamic of cycles of "atrocity, complicity and hypocrisy," the pretense of innocence on the part of the "purveyors of violence."[56] I discovered the power of teaching students about the pretense of innocence and its role in state-sponsored cruelty, coercion, and exploitation quite by accident. In spring 2004, weeks before the disclosure of the horrific torture of hundreds of Iraqi prisoners of war by United States and British forces at the Abu Ghraib prison compound, I was teaching a class on religious perspectives on peace and war at the University of Missouri. This was, in many ways, a stealth class. It was listed only as Contemporary Issues in Religious Studies and attracted a student body looking for a general humanities credit. As a result, the students reflected the general population of Missouri: 80% considered themselves to be conservative, 10% considered themselves to be very conservative, and only 10% thought of themselves as moderate or liberal. Most of the students also had family members who had a long history of military service, including service in the ongoing wars in Afghanistan and Iraq.

When the photographs were released in late April of the outrageous acts of torture and sexual humiliation by U.S. soldiers at Abu Ghraib, these conservative students were appalled and horrified. They immediately and readily saw these actions as violating all codes of military honor and human decency, and shared wholeheartedly the sentiments expressed by British prime minister Tony Blair—"Let me make it quite clear that if these things have actually been done, they are completely and totally unacceptable. We went to Iraq to get rid of that sort of thing, not to do it ourselves!"[57]

Given that these very conservative students saw the injustice for what it was, I was quite shocked to discover that their reaction seemed to be unique among conservatives, and that, far from being appalled, leaders in the Bush administration dismissed such actions as aberrations, and defended the use of torture. What made the difference between the responses of conservative students in Missouri and conservative citizens and governmental leaders throughout the United States?

In the week prior to the revelations of torture at Abu Ghraib, we had read two essays, William Schulz's "Security Is a Human Right, Too," and Albert Bandura's "Moral Disengagement in the Perpetration of Inhumanities." In his essay Schulz, director of Amnesty International, made the claim that it is equally important to condemn human rights violations in the name of preventing terrorism, and to denounce terrorism itself. He stated, "We have chastised one government after another for using terrorism as an excuse to muzzle peaceful dissent. We have criticized the United States for its arbitrary roundup of Arab and Muslim residents, for the incommunicado detention of prisoners at Guantanamo Bay in defiance of the Geneva convention." In addition to these legitimate criticisms of government actions, he also spoke of the ways in which the human rights community can also combat terrorism: "name the suppliers of arms to terrorist groups, suppliers who include established states, and not just 'rogue' ones; mobilize grass-roots opposition to terrorism by addressing root causes like economic deprivation or social discrimination." He ended his essay with a quotation from Stephen Spender, an opponent of the Fascists during the Spanish Civil War: "When I saw photographs of children murdered by the Fascists, I felt furious pity. When the supporters of Franco talked of Red atrocities, I merely felt indignant that people should tell such lies. In the first case I saw corpses, in the second only words. . . . I gradually acquired a certain horror of the way in which my own mind worked. It was clear to me that unless I cared about every murdered child impartially, I did not really care about children being murdered at all."[58]

The power of Spender's poetic self-disclosure was augmented by the careful arguments of the social psychologist Albert Bandura. Bandura described how easy it is for moral clarity and absolutism to lead to cruelty and violence. He delineated seven practices of moral disengagement—ways genuinely decent human beings commit and justify behaviors that they would otherwise recognize as morally abhorrent. The practices are clear, and examples readily came to mind.[59]

The first and fundamental practice is being convinced that one is the bearer of a just cause, "fighting ruthless oppressors, protecting . . . cherished values, preserving world peace, saving humanity from subjugation, or honoring their countries' commitments."[60] The second practice is avoiding the negative consequences of one's behavior through the use of euphemistic language—the term "collateral damage" for the death and injuries caused to civilians, or the term "professional interrogation techniques" for physical and psychological torture.[61] A third practice is advantageous comparison—our violence pales in comparison to theirs.[62] Recall the response of U.S. attorney general Alberto Gonzales when challenged by Senator Lindsay Graham to decisively condemn the use of torture by U.S. personnel: "While we are struggling to find out what happened at Abu Ghraib, they're beheading people like Danny Pearl and Nick Berg. We are nothing like our enemy!"[63]

The fourth and fifth practices are the diffusion and displacement of responsibility—for subordinates, one claims to have been only following orders. For those in charge, orders to commit atrocities are most often implicit, rather than direct, and officials dismiss harmful actions as the actions of a few irresponsible personnel who are either "misguided or overzealous."[64] In the case of Abu Ghraib, the early outrage of Tony Blair was quickly supplanted by a displacement of responsibility on what were seen as a few ill-trained and misguided soldiers, and the policy decisions by government officials that not only allowed but fostered such abuse have even yet to be thoroughly and independently investigated.[65] A sixth practice is the disregard or distortion of consequences. If euphemistic language no longer works, the "evidence of harm can be discredited."[66] And, finally, when the severity of the consequences can no longer be avoided, one dehumanizes or demonizes the victim, or both: they are all terrorists, or they all share an irrational hatred of us.[67]

These processes of moral disengagement are pervasive, and extremely hard to dislodge once in place. It is, however, possible to inoculate people against these practices.[68] As in the case of the conservative students in Missouri, early warning served to heighten moral intelligence. With this preparation, students could easily see the operation of moral justification in the rhetoric of governmental officials, and were singularly unpersuaded by their legitimacy or morality.

Another core task of equitable social innovation is being aware of the causes of likely failures, and of being fully cognizant of the ways in which good intentions can go horribly awry. Here we see the ways in which the pretense of innocence may keep us from looking for negative effects. A necessary complement to the process of moral disengagement is avoiding all of its evasions, and seeing what is going wrong, and taking direct responsibility for it. It is much easier to do this in the present if we are first aware of how it has been done by people like us. This means that educators must be aware of the ways in which the attempt of educational and religious institutions to share the fruits of their knowledge has led to horrific and ongoing damage.

To that end, my colleagues Nicole Kirk and Mark Hicks and I led a five-hour workshop at the October 2014 Engagement Scholarship Consortium. The name of the workshop was "'Building the World We Dream About': The Pedagogical Challenges of Constructive Social Engagement." This was a preconference exploration of the relationship between the work of engaged scholarship and our ongoing, evolving, and deepening commitments to social justice and environmental sustainability. Since we were meeting in Canada, we took as our case study work that was being undertaken then. We asked the group to explore in depth the following question:

> How do we learn from the work of the Canadian Truth and Reconciliation Commission about examples in the past in which movements intended for social good caused instead great harm? How do we know that we are not replicating the mission schools in the United States and Canada that caused such great harm to First Nations peoples? What concrete measures do we have in place to make sure that our efforts reflect genuinely mutually beneficial community partnerships, and not the imposition of one construct of the social good on less powerful groups?[69]

We designed and led this workshop with Professor Amber Dion, master's in social work instructor and Kahkiyaw Knowing-Doing Project coordinator at the University of Calgary, Faculty of Social Work. Professor Dion is a member of the Cree nation, and involved in ongoing work addressing the ongoing negative effects of residential schools in Canada. From our work together, it was clear that the work of engagement scholarship is most productive when grounded in deep community, in bold visions for the future, and in honest explorations of painful histories of cultural domination and destruction.

There is a striking opportunity, and a surprising challenge, for educators who are committed to fostering social justice and creative and self-critical forms of civic engagement. Unlike other times in history, we live at a moment when large numbers of students come to us with a commitment to equity, to fundamental fairness between all races and social groups. For these students, our challenge is not that of convincing them that people of color, women, people with disabilities, or people who are LGBTQIA should be treated fairly and welcomed as leaders, as partners. Our challenge is learning how to treat each other with fairness and respect, how to embody that commitment to justice in daily practices and institutional policies.

We have, however, another challenge, equally deep, and possibly growing larger. How do we reach white students, often male, who feel isolated and fearful, and turn to violence as a means of expressing strength and gaining social recognition? How do we challenge and interrupt patterns of racial hate, xenophobia, and religious intolerance? How do we prevent the explosion of explicit bias, ill will, and fear? To take up this task is one that is as new to me as it is to many educators, and research that may help is ongoing. At this point we will explore one more example of working with implicit bias and structural injustice.

I have worked with those who have taken up the question posed by Khanjan Mehta and other practitioners of university-community engagement, realizing that social justice and environmental sustainability programs often fail not because of ill will or malice. Many fail because of an inability to see and work with difference. In the educational model at the Unitarian Universalist school of theology, Meadville Lombard, for example, our students come to us with a commitment to justice, equity, and compassion, and a strong belief in the importance of nurturing and supporting the inherent worth and dignity of all human beings. We teach students that living out these commitments requires learning how to exercise the artistry of multiracial and cross-cultural partnerships and leadership.

Like other forms of engagement scholarship and contextual education, our educational model is grounded in service, and grounded in insights from engaged Buddhism, Native American traditions, and feminist theory: we do not think ourselves into new ways of acting, but act ourselves into new ways of thinking and being. To that end, our students begin their preparation for ministry by serving eight hours a week for a full academic year in a nonprofit site that is committed to social justice. Michael Hogue describes the range of sites in which our students serve:

These have included everything from local hospice programs to animal shelters, from AIDS counseling centers to after school programs, from centers for victims of torture and refugees to homeless shelters, from food kitchens and addiction rehabilitation centers to immigrant farmer networks and job training facilities.[70]

In choosing a site, students are asked to look for two things—find a site that is valued by the community for the depth of its partnerships, and choose a site that stretches their boundaries of cultural awareness. In this year of community service, students are embedded in the experience of cultural groups that are both part of their home community and relatively unknown to them. For students who themselves belong to historically or currently marginalized groups, this is a chance to work with people from other groups and learn from their histories of struggle and of thriving, seeing both commonalities and differences in what it means to create communities of self-determination and equity in the face of long-lasting and deeply rooted structural injustice. For students from primarily privileged backgrounds, this is the opportunity to fully see the effects of structural injustice and learn how it is perpetuated, all the while being of direct service in healing the wounds caused by such injustice.

As students work in their sites, we explore multiple forms of injustice and manifold strategies for social change. Students learn from their mistakes, and from those of the sites where they work. Students grow into a larger sense of what it means to belong, with open hearts and minds, to a world in which far too many lives are marred by ongoing forms of exploitation, marginalization, powerlessness, and violence. Students learn the joy of being in deep community with those who choose to live justly, to express our gratitude for the abundance of life by expanding its bounty to all members of the interdependent web of existence. In their second and third years, students are immersed in a 20 hour per week congregational internship in which they design and create a focused initiative, an experience that allows a congregation to grow in its ability to cross borders of race, class, and culture, and create structures of greater justice and flourishing. The goal is to find a place where a congregation is ready to grow, ready to be more just internally, or ready to be a force for justice in the larger community. The ideal—finding an initiative that is so grounded in the capacities of the congregation and the needs of the community that it thrives, long after the intern leaves.

One recent Meadvile Lombard Theological School graduate, James Galasinski, describes the power of such an experience.

> As you may remember my focused initiative was about establishing a chapter of Family Promise (www.familypromiseozaukee.org).
> The chair of my intern committee just emailed me and told me that just now, 3+ years later, they are officially up and running.
> I did not know anything about organizing until I got to Meadville. You taught me to look at the big picture, to look years down the road, and to put my own agenda on the back burner. Instead of taking on a huge topic like Homelessness, you taught me to take a small quantifiable bite out of it. You taught me to cross the aisle and frame the issue to include conservatives and other voices. I trusted the rest of the faculty's wisdom as well. I made relationships with people at the internship site and with other churches in the area. I sent out surveys, held meetings in the community, and worked with the social justice committee to get ideas and buy in. I looked for people to be leaders after I left. My work was mostly behind the scenes. But if there wasn't a focused initiative as part of the curriculum, I would have never pushed the way I did. When I ended that internship, I thought that project was going to do die. It is very humbling and gratifying to know that I help[ed] start something. Though I was learning, this was not mere academic exercise, I was actually engaging in ministry and initiating change.

It is humbling, and heartening, to work with students who are learning how best to express the artistry of cross-cultural and multiracial partnership and leadership, and are sharing that artistry with others. Learning how to see, how to feel, how to think in ways that are deeply transformative is an ongoing task for us all.

Key Insights for Progressive Practice

Let's unpack the multiple dimensions of integrating local knowledge, perspectives, and frameworks. Projects that succeed are contextually appropriate, paying attention to the cultural nuances of embodying basic ethical norms of empathy, equity, and ecosystems:

(a) ensuring that the project is understood and owned by a group, and is not merely the imposition of the ideas of an individual;
(b) finding ways of engaging all stakeholders, with special attention to marginalized groups, in the analysis of the situation and the design of the solutions;
(c) paying attention to and checking particular dynamics of power and privilege.[71]

Such attention must be constant and expressed in four ways—in preparation for engagement, in the design of specific projects, in the implementation of social innovation, and in the ongoing evaluation of the impact of such ventures. Much of this work is now being done in preparation, design, and implementation. At the Engagement Scholarship Consortium conference, Mehta proposed adding another layer to the work of evaluation. Rather than evaluation being something undertaken at the end of the project, he argues that evaluation must be an ongoing, iterative process that addresses the following questions: "What kinds of things go wrong in community-engaged projects? What competencies do students and faculty need to develop? How do we avoid such situations? How do we go about building such a culture of concern? How do we get buy-in?"[72]

Mehta describes this as a process of developing both global citizenship and cultural humility. Given the complexity of genuinely beneficial partnerships, Mehta proposes that we consider the formation of "Engagement Review Boards" that would bring together expertise on how to create partnerships, work with mistakes, and evaluate the impact of social innovation. The work of an Engagement Review Board would be threefold: examining the education process and development of competencies prior to work with a community; examining the application of these competencies in the design, implementation, and review of a specific proposal for social innovation. So far, the structure of an Engagement Review Board is similar to institutional review boards that are in place for research on human subjects. This board would have, however, another task—in fact the largest part of the work would be what Mehta calls the provision of "Snafu Support"—providing hotlines, websites that enable people to learn from mistakes and unintended consequences and opportunities.[73]

Our ability to check unintended consequences in the present depends upon our ability to acknowledge and learn from the intertwined histories of racist domination and extractive capitalism. To counter the ongoing temptations of the Windigo of excessive consumerism and extractive capitalism, we must see its costs and the ways it has been consistently related to the fifth Windigo, multiple forms of racial domination, implicit bias, structural racism, and white violence against people who are African American, Native American, and Latinx.

Far too few white people in the United States know the violent history of "Redemption," what southerners called the violent suppression of basic human, political, and economic rights for African Americans following Reconstruction. Even fewer are aware of the racist pogroms of whites against prosperous African American communities from Tulsa to Chicago to Wilmington, North Carolina between 1898 and 1923. In his recent book, *We Were Eight Years in Power*, Ta-Nehisi Coates also draws parallels between the eight years of modest racial justice during the Reconstruction period and the white violence that ensued to restore white domination of economic and political life. He states that during "the Red Summer of 1919 [there were] a succession of racist pogroms against dozens of cities ranging from Longview, Texas, to Chicago to Washington, DC. Organized white violence against blacks continued into the 1920s—in 1921 a white mob leveled Tulsa's 'Black Wall Street,' and in 1923 another one razed the black town of Rosewood, Florida— and virtually no one was punished." And, while some may be aware of the terror of lynching, few know how lynching was embraced as a form of community celebration, with special trains even bringing whole families to witness these acts of sadistic terror.[74]

In order to check outbreaks of sadistic violence and the ongoing impact of structural violence, it is crucial that we unmask the processes of moral disengagement that enabled people who saw themselves as upstanding citizens to enact extreme violence. It is vital that we find ways of holding people who commit such violence accountable. We must thoroughly acknowledge the depth of racist violence, mourn and rage against its historical and ongoing costs. We cannot move forward to create a truly just democracy unless white citizens join African American, Latinx, Native American, and Asian American citizens in forthrightly confronting this tragic history and ongoing threat. It is only then that we will be able to more fully live out the mandate of social justice and generative interdependence in multiple dimensions of our collective lives.

6

Just Living

Practices of Catalytic Social Engagement

What enables people to take up open-ended, self-critical work for social justice? The logic of working with partial resources for an unfolding series of social goods does not have to be invented. Although we use different terminology, we can draw on the work of the sociologist Patricia Hill Collins to understand this foundational dimension of constructive political engagement.

In 1998, Collins sounded a clarion call for the revitalization of visionary pragmatism, a tradition deeply rooted in the African American tradition, but largely absent in many urban African American communities and sorely needed in progressive politics and in our common life. Collins advocates moving from the reactive stance of critique to the creative task of shaping policies and practices. She claims that "visionary pragmatism" cannot be reduced to a "predetermined destination," but signifies participation in a larger, ongoing collective struggle: "Black women's visionary pragmatism points to a vision, it doesn't prescribe a fixed end point of a universal truth. One never arrives but one constantly strives." Collins extols a pragmatism grounded in "deep love, intense connectedness and a recognition that those in the future will face struggles and challenges that we can neither imagine nor forestall."[1]

Collins argues that it is possible to find an alternative to utopian thinking or cynicism and despair. She analyzes her own childhood experiences, and interprets them as the expression of "visionary pragmatism."

As a child growing up in an African-American, working-class Philadelphia neighborhood, I wondered how my mother and all of the other women on our block kept going. Early each workday, they rode long distances on public transportation to jobs that left them unfulfilled, overworked, and underpaid. Periodically they complained, but more often they counseled practicality and persistence, stressing the importance of a good education as the route to a better life. . . . Their solution: we, their daughters, were to become self-reliant and independent. . . . Despite their practicality, these same Black women also held out hope that things would be better for us. . . . They always encouraged us to dream.[2]

Collins stated that "visionary pragmatism" cannot be reduced to a "predetermined destination," but signifies participation in a larger, ongoing collective struggle.

Thus, although Black women's visionary pragmatism points to a vision, it doesn't prescribe a fixed end point of a universal truth. One never arrives but constantly strives. At the same time, by stressing the pragmatic, it reveals how current actions are part of some larger, more meaningful struggle. Domination succeeds by cutting people off from one another. Actions bring people in touch with the humanity of other struggles by demonstrating that truthful and ethical visions for community cannot be separated from pragmatic struggles on their behalf.[3]

Although she extols the power of this vision, Collins argued that it no longer shapes black civil society.

Sadly, both my childhood neighborhood and the version of visionary pragmatism expressed by its African-American female residents no longer exist. . . . Since 1970, the quality of life in Black working-class communities like the one I grew up in has changed dramatically in the United States. . . . Who could have anticipated how deeply the combination of racial desegregation and drugs, violence, and hopelessness in poor African-American neighborhoods would tear the very fabric of Black civil society? . . . Now that Black women's community work seems increasingly ineffective, what will replace it?[4]

Despite these political changes, her goal is to live and work out of this vision: "[T]he fundamental question raised by the Black women on my block remains: how can scholars and/or activists construct critical social theories that prepare future generations for lives that we ourselves have not lived?"[5]

How can our critical social theories inform creative political action? Collins argues that "remain[ing] in a stance of critique leaves one perpetually responding to the terms of someone else's agenda. . . . The next step lies in moving beyond critique and crafting something new." If we live out of this ethos of visionary pragmatism, Collins claims that our theories do not function as "a dogma or a closed system, but as a story or narrative."[6] Collins adds here a telling element of these narratives:

> Certainly their [the black women on her block] visionary pragmatism was shaped by a commitment to truth, a belief in freedom, a concern for justice, and other ethical ideals. They clearly had an arsenal of pragmatic skills that helped them deal with difficult situations. However, I think that their ability to persist was rooted in a deep love for us. . . . I talk of the power of intense connectedness and of the way that caring deeply for someone can foster a revolutionary politics.[7]

Collins is not alone in her commitment to transformative social theories grounded in deep connections. Since she wrote in 1998, other African American scholars have taken up the task of developing visionary pragmatism. In the work of the theologians and ethicists Monica A. Coleman, Barbara Holmes, and Victor Anderson, we have a ringing affirmation of the creative possibilities for human and nonhuman flourishing that grace our lives. And yet, Coleman, Holmes, and Anderson also point to the ambiguities and complexities of this gift. Holmes claims that "freedom takes on a different guise in each generation" and acknowledges that "I'm not certain that I know much more than my family members did about building a peaceful, interconnected society." She maintains, however, a resolute and joyous commitment to the journey of "liberation for all."[8] Coleman reminds us that there are multiple bests in any given situation.[9] Victor Anderson invites us to remain open to "a world that shows itself as processive, open and relational." He celebrates the power and promise of "creative exchange," those moments "when the self and community transcend isolated self-interests and seek human fulfillment and flourishing in relation to larger wholes." Anderson also explicitly calls us to face the reality of ambiguity even within the process of "creative exchange," what he calls the "grotesque."[10]

The problem is that when moving from critique to the creation of policies and institutions, even when we share the same goals, and even when we hear the same cries of suffering, the particular responses to that suffering, the specific strategies for making health care accessible, education transformative, and economic systems equitable are often radically, and incommensurately, different. Furthermore, we cannot know in advance which policies, which institutional frameworks, will fulfill our goals. It is this intrinsic uncertainty that leads to a predictable pattern in political life, one described centuries ago by the political philosopher Niccolò Machiavelli in *The Prince*:

> And it ought to be remembered that there is nothing more difficult to take in hand, more perilous to conduct, or more uncertain in its success, than to take the lead in the introduction of a new order of things. Because the innovator has for enemies all those who have done well under the old conditions, and lukewarm defenders in those who may do well under the new. This coolness arises partly from fear of the opponents, who have the laws on their side, and partly from the incredulity of men, who do not readily believe in new things until they have had a long experience of them. Thus it happens that whenever those who are hostile have the opportunity to attack they do it like partisans, whilst the others defend lukewarmly.[11]

It could be that the relative lack of passionate support for change is grounded as much in reason as in incredulity. In addition to known limits, any course of action may have devastating unintended consequences. It is in light of this reality that the ecologist and ethicist Anna Peterson and Wes Jackson, agronomist and cofounder of the Land Institute, call us to a fallibility-based worldview: an acknowledgment that all that we know—whether through the resources of reason, imagination, intuition, or compassion—is partial, always vastly exceeded by that which we do not know. For example, we can only ever have partial knowledge of the long-term impact of our agricultural and industrial practices, the ripple effects of changes in social and economic policies, and the unpredictable consequences of our attempts to nurture and sustain the generations that depend upon us.[12]

As we acknowledge the complexity of institutional change, we encounter a paradox, a fundamental lack of parity between the moral certainty of our denunciation of existing forms of injustice and our ethically reasonable uncertainty about justice and the feasibility of our cherished alternatives.

In short, these are the challenges of leadership, for which we need resilience and practical curiosity:

- While we can reasonably expect significant challenges to any innovation, we can neither predict the reasons for the resistance, nor the identity of the bearers of resistance.
- We cannot know in advance which visions will spark the imaginations of others, nor which plans will prove to be plausible and energizing.
- We can neither predict nor control the actual impact of our efforts.

Here, then, is our challenge as activists: it is easy to mobilize political will against a common enemy and for certain goals. As Nelson Mandela stated: "It is a relatively simple proposition to keep a movement together when you are fighting against a common enemy. But creating a policy when that enemy is across the negotiating table is another matter altogether."[13] We have yet to learn how to mobilize political energy when we acknowledge that even we, the "righteous vanguard," are flawed, and while our goals of common flourishing are unambiguously clear, the means of attaining those same goals are intrinsically ambiguous and fluid.

Our role is not only to support policies that we cherish, but also to find ways to bring others along. As we do this work, conflict and resistance may be experienced not as obstacles to be bemoaned, but as realities to be accepted, even played as the ingredients of greater creativity.[14] To seek the fitting response, not the definitive response, places us in the good company of those who, to use the words of the novelist Patrick Chamoiseau, "know through which vices to rifle in order to stumble upon virtue."[15] In our work as leaders, stumble we will, yet create we may, evoking the beauty and justice to be found in a group, a situation, a moment in time. This is our great challenge, our rich legacy, and our sustaining and empowering hope.

President Obama excelled at this work, and this may well be one of the ongoing legacies of the Obama presidency—a catalytic form of civic engagement—not utopian but committed to the creation of microtopias that bear the seeds of ongoing critique and engagement. It may also be that the virulent racist attacks on President Obama and the ongoing attempts to dismantle his legacy may also be the catalyst for a deeper institutionalization of inclusive democracy and more resilient attempts to see, preempt, and contain authoritarian bigotry and violence.

There are two equally significant political challenges that we face as we attempt to reinforce and regain the progressive achievements of the Obama presidency. First, how can we learn from our failures to stand up to racist obstruction and the ongoing attempts to dismantle efforts to achieve and maintain social inclusion, criminal justice reform, and environmental responsibility? It is essential that we recognize that significant social change will often (always?) be met by virulent and contagious resistance. In order to combat such resistance with greater effectiveness, we need to explore how best to apply to the realm of politics what educators have found to be essential in identifying and containing bullying. Within the past three decades, there have been extensive efforts throughout the world to prevent bullying in schools from kindergarten through high school. One of the most prominent methods was created by the Norwegian educator Dan Olweus, and there are meta-analyses of what forms of intervention are most successful.[16]

These meta-analyses demonstrate the power of models that are like that of Olweus in key ways. These are the factors that are essential. First, there is a recognition that there will always be bullying. Bullying among students occurs regularly and is to be expected. Second, given the fact that there are always bullies, processes to identify and contain bullying, and to heal its damages, must be ongoing and proactive. These are a regular part of educational life, not episodic or reactive. Third, these efforts are comprehensive, involving teachers, staff, administrators, parents, and students. Fourth, all students are consistently rewarded for positive behaviors, and fifth, there are consistent negative consequences for bullying. Sixth, there are three groups of students with specific needs. There must be support and healing for those who have been bullied as well as support and education for those who are bystanders. These students can learn the skills of how to intervene to stop bullying in ways that are creative and effective. In all this research, the meta-analyses of what is required for students who are bullies are the most surprising, and the most evocative. Work with peers actually leads to increases in bullying. Given the power differential between those who bully and those who are victimized, researchers have found that attempts to get bullies and their victims to directly work together in conflict resolution and peer mediation leads to more victimization, not less. Bullies can only be called out, their behavior denounced, and social rewards withdrawn.[17] The challenges for political life are clear—how do we heal those who are victimized, empower bystanders to move to effective action, and remove the social, economic, and political rewards of bullying?

The second challenge is, what can we learn from the legacy of the Obama presidency on how to gain power and then use it for justice? The Monday after the November 2016 presidential election, I joined President Obama and 16,000 other supporters in a conference call organized by the Democratic National Committee. Obama's message was simple, its implications profound: "We have better ideas, but they have to be heard."

What are these better ideas? The ideas are not new. They are rooted in the best of who we are as a people, and who we have been as a country. The ideas are an ongoing commitment to the very soul of democracy—to justice, freedom, and genuine opportunities for all people for meaningful work, economic security, inspiring education, and excellent and affordable health care.

We cannot gain power, and we cannot maintain power, if these ideas are not heard. Why were the ideas of hope and change that resonated so powerfully in 2008 and 2012 not heard in 2016? In the call on that Monday night, President Obama described one reason, and in a November interview for the *New Yorker*, he laid out another.[18] The first is simple. He stated that those in the Democratic Party did not try hard enough to reach all Americans through the conventional means of communication that have worked in the past. In the interview in the *New Yorker* he reiterated the importance of on the ground, person to person communications to fellow citizens in all areas of the country, spending time in areas where one is not likely to win, and not just in swing states and districts. He described how he learned the value of this approach in his early campaigns in Illinois for the Senate—traveling to meet people in areas where it was thought he was not likely to garner support, but making the effort nonetheless.

In that same interview President Obama described a new challenge for communicating a progressive vision of American greatness—the limiting power of new media. Now, in a way not true in 2008, it is increasingly easy to stay confined in self-reinforcing bubbles in which the only messages that are heard reflect preconceived ideas, and it is increasingly difficult to challenge both distortions and outright lies.[19]

As we take up this dual challenge, it is important to remember that it has always been difficult to bring a vision of an inclusive, expansive democracy to life. Sometimes the challenge lies in communicating the vision; at others it lies in extending it to all people, and not just to a privileged few. The legal scholar Patricia Williams describes this challenge well in her book *The Alchemy of Race and Rights*:

> To say that blacks never fully believed in rights is true. Yet it is also true that blacks believed in them so much and so hard that we gave them life where there was none before. . . . This was the resurrection of life from ashes four hundred years old. The making of something out of nothing took immense alchemical fire—the fusion of a whole nation and the kindling of several generations. . . . But if it took this long to breathe life into a form whose shape had already been forged by society, and which is therefore idealistically if not ideologically accessible, imagine how long the struggle would be without even that senses of definition, without the power of that familiar vision.[20]

Williams fully acknowledges how hard it has been to extend rights to all human beings, and urges us to embrace more fully the power of that commitment to the rights of "privacy, integrity and self-assertion," extending those rights, renewing them, and resolutely defending them with all of our imagination, intellect, and will.

> In discarding rights altogether, one discards a symbol too deeply enmeshed in the psyche of the oppressed to lose without trauma and much resistance. Instead, society must give them away. Unlock them from reification by giving them to slaves. Give them to trees. Give them to cows. Give them to history. Give them to rivers and rocks. Give to all of society's objects and untouchables the rights of privacy, integrity and self-assertion; give them distance and respect. Flood them with the

animating spirit that rights mythology fires in this country's most oppressed psyches, and wash away the shrouds of inanimate-object status,
so that we may say not that we own gold but that a luminous golden
spirit owns us.[21]

As we take up the ongoing challenge of living out our democratic
ideals, it is crucial that we understand more clearly what it is that stands
in the way of living those out with power and resilience. There are two
key factors to address: first, a failure to be thorough and persistent in
conventional means of communication, and second, the need to find
how to challenge the way new media reinforces lies, division, hatred,
and simplistic solutions, and develop approaches to use new media in
radically different ways—using it to enable critical thinking and empa-
thetic connections.

These factors are crucial, and there are two other challenges as well.
The third challenge is recognizing the appeal of an alternative view
of American greatness, an alternative view of national identity that is
spreading in democracies throughout the world. It was ironic to see the
extent to which news commentators would criticize candidate, and then
elected official, Trump for what was precisely his appeal, the expression
of a form of leadership that was, to quote Amanda Taub, "simple, powerful and punitive."

Now, here is a fourth challenge. Once there is a more progressive administration back in power, how can we work to both foster and then,
importantly, maintain catalytic social engagement? Take for example the
analysis of the economist and journalist Paul Krugman, one of the most
persistent critics of the Obama presidency. In an October 2014 issue of
Rolling Stone, however, Krugman made a startling claim:

> When it comes to Barack Obama, I've always been out of sync. Back in
> 2008, when many liberals were wildly enthusiastic about his candidacy
> and his press was strongly favorable, I was skeptical. . . . But now the
> shoe is on the other foot: Obama faces trash talk left, right and center—
> literally—and doesn't deserve it. Despite bitter opposition, despite hav-
> ing come close to self-inflicted disaster, Obama has emerged as one of
> the most consequential and yes, successful presidents in American his-
> tory. His health reform is imperfect but still a huge step forward—and it's

working better than anyone could have expected. Financial reform fell short of what should have happened, but it's much more effective than you'd think. Economic management has been half-crippled by Republican obstruction, but has nonetheless been much better than in other advanced countries. And environmental policy is starting to look like it could be a major legacy.[22]

What happened in the Obama presidency is what has long been true of political change, at least in the West, yet obscured if we limit our vision to only part of the political process, the essential work of prophetic critique and vision. After the protests are heard, the equally complex task of catalytic civic engagement begins—creating structures that can embody that critique and vision, and knowing that these efforts will only succeed in part. Therefore, we need to create mechanisms for ongoing critique and revision. What is true of social enterprise is also true of constructive civic engagement. We need a more nuanced vocabulary of failure: sometimes a failure is a defeat, sometimes it is a clarification, a grounding in what is going on and what is actually possible.

Let me give you an example. Francis Perkins was the secretary of labor under President Franklin Delano Roosevelt, and was the one who actually envisioned and implemented many of the measures that have defined his presidency—Social Security, unemployment insurance, support for labor unions, the minimum wage, and the Works Progress Administration. Early in her career, Perkins learned how to take partial failure and use it as a lever for further success. When she was a social worker in New York, she was involved in passing legislation that would limit the work week for women to 54 hours. The bill passed the state senate, but was opposed in the state assembly. The measure that finally passed had an amendment that excluded women in the canning industry from the legislation.

Some activists thought the pitch should be all or nothing. Perkins disagreed. She accepted the partial success—400,000 women who worked in manufacturing were covered, and the 50,000 in the canning industry were excluded. She was proven right. Only one year later the same provisions were extended to all women workers.[23]

How do we tell honest stories of alchemical fire, of the many times in which people have persevered and learned from partial success and even catalytic failures? We are in the midst of a major paradigm shift. People all over the word are spending more energy on creating solutions themselves than on demanding that others change. They are responding to the truth and power of protests by living out the simple guidance of J. K. Gibson-Graham: "start where you are, and begin with what you have."

Recall Paul Hawken. He analyzed only impact-driven nonprofits and claimed that we are in the middle of the largest social movement in history. When we add to the examples of creative social and civic engagement the self-critical practices of social enterprise, B corporations, impact investing, and engagement scholarship, we have a movement that is even larger and more comprehensive. Recall again Paul Hawken's pertinent question: If this movement is so large, why can't it be seen? His answer was simple. This movement for social change does not fit our standard Western narratives of social change. This is not good versus evil, pure revolutionaries versus corrupt capitalists, not us against them on the road to certain victory.

This movement is made up of flawed human beings coming together to address major social and environmental problems with all that we know and with the best of who we are, and in this process expecting that others will know more than we do, expecting that we have as much to learn from people on the ground as from experts, expecting that there will be both mistakes and surprising successes, and that we have as much to learn from our failures as from our achievements.

Solutions Journalism

When he published *Blessed Unrest* in 2007, Hawken rightly pointed out that these kinds of stories were not being widely told. This is not what we hear on nightly news, it isn't what we read in mainstream newspapers or find in social media. All of this, however, has begun to change since 2013 when David Bornstein, Courtney Martin, and Tina Rosenberg founded the Solutions Journalism Network. These three award-winning journalists are themselves committed to both covering and enhancing the process of social change. They are learning how to do that themselves, and are sharing what they have learned with others. The mission of the Network is clear: "The Solutions Journalism Network works to legitimize and spread the practice of solutions journalism: rigorous and compelling reporting about responses to social problems." By the end of 2017 3,000 journalists had participated in live trainings, and another 5,500 had taken their online curriculum.[24]

The basic shift in solutions journalism accords with what we see in all of these movements for social change, a focus on experimentation and risk-taking, a commitment to working with people directly affected by policies and learning as much from them as from experts in the field, and a recognition that all results are partial, and that what works in one situation may not work in another. We can, however, be inspired by partial efforts for social change to continue their momentum, to continue this critical work ourselves of being fully alive, fully awake, and fully accountable.

In the *Solutions Journalism Toolkit*, Bornstein, Martin, and Rosenberg describe the basic contours of this way of understanding responses to social problems. Here we have a shift from "whodunit" to "howdunit," a shift from what do experts think to what also do people directly affected think, and a shift from did this initiative succeed or fail to in what ways did it succeed, in what ways did it fail, and what are the lessons to be drawn from both failures and successes.

> In solutions journalism, what matters most is not the quirks and qualities of the main character, but the transferable wisdom found in his or her actions. How did a small organization revolutionize the way a city recycles? What are the slow, systematic steps they took? What are the teachable lessons?[25]

Bornstein, Rosenberg, and Martin are well aware that this way of analyzing political engagement goes against dualistic and simplistic Western models of social change. They describe seven "solutions journalism imposters." To read these descriptions as a social ethicist is to encounter popular reflections of deep-seated cultural illusions about the nature of the conflict between good and evil.

Here are seven types of solutions journalism imposters we've all seen in the media before:

Hero Worship: These are stories that celebrate or glorify an individual, often at the expense of explaining the idea the individual exemplifies. . . .

Silver Bullet: These stories are often seen in the tech and innovation sections. They describe new gadgets in glowing terms, often referring to them as "lifesavers." . . .

Favor for a Friend: . . . Like the silver bullet story, it doesn't have much in the way of a "to be sure" paragraph—i.e. the caveats to success—and appears as thinly veiled PR. . . .

Think Tank: Opinion journalism can explore solutions if it contains real reporting about existing responses to problems (and the results). But "think tank journalism" refers to journalism that proposes things that don't yet exist. . . .

The Afterthought: This is a paragraph or soundbite at the end of a problem story that gives lip service to efforts at solving it. The solutions aren't considered with real seriousness, but rather thrown in as an afterthought. . . .

Instant Activist: A lot of people think, when seeing the phrase "solutions journalism," that we're promoting pieces that ask the reader to click a button at the end and give $5 to a cause. . . .

Chris P. Bacon: This kind of journalism is heartwarming, quirky, and one-off. It often appears at the end of the evening news or on Thanksgiving, in the form of a kid with a lemonade stand. It tells the viewer that the world has good people doing cute things, but doesn't really get to the structural issues that we want solutions journalism to address.[26]

As we reflect on our ongoing work to resolve structural issues, we know that multiple actors have to be involved, and multiple strategies employed. As a case in point, we cannot enact substantive criminal justice reform through one action, but through the ongoing coordination of efforts to heal the damage that has been done and put in place new forms of community policing and judicial responses that are racially just. When we internalize the awareness that change is complex and takes time, we can avoid the kind of misleading critique that dismisses certain efforts as partial, rather than exploring what other kinds of changes need to take place for them to be effective. Take, for example, short-sighted criticisms of increasing the use of body cameras by police. Sim Gill, the district attorney of Salt Lake Country, Utah, was quoted in the *New York Times* as stating that "[b]ody cameras are helpful, but they are not the magic elixir."[27] Why would we think that anything is a magic elixir? Once we give up the false hope of magical solutions by heroic actors, we can realistically engage in the multifaceted and time-intensive task of creating new networks of social perception, responsibility, and accountability.

"An Ecology of Opportunity" (Theaster Gates): Altermodernity and Relational Aesthetics

There is in the world of art a deep resonance with these commitments to social equity, environmental responsibility, and practical curiosity. We are in a political and artistic moment best characterized not as postmodern but by what the French art critic and curator Nicolas Bourriaud calls altermodernity. Rather than either the modern imposition of a Western view of human excellence and linear progress, or the multiple fragmentations of postmodern identities and narratives, the altermodern is an emerging global formation, a shift in politics, aesthetics, and culture shaped equally by Latin America, Asia, Africa, and the West. At the core of the altermodern is a nomadic, dynamic, constructive living out of multiple identities. Many of the ideals of modernity are reclaimed, but are now implemented in light of postcolonial critiques and in light of the failures of the modernist project.[28] Bourriaud names our culture as one shaped by "new intercultural connections" and draws on the botanical analogy of the radicant to describe the dynamism of this global culture. The radicant is "an organism that grows its roots and adds new ones as it advances. To be radicant means setting one's roots in motion, staging them in heterogeneous contexts and formats, denying them the power to completely define one's identity, translating ideas, transcoding images, transplanting behaviors, exchanging rather than imposing."[29] Art, and politics, in this altermodern moment can be seen as a form of relational aesthetics, an exploration of multiple forms of sociality, of playing with the identities that have shaped us and others. When Bourriaud introduced the notion of the altermodern and relational aesthetics in 2002, many academics in the United States thought that its claims for political relevance were overstated. In a nuanced and insightful essay, Claire Bishop, for example, described Bourriaud's position thoroughly, yet advocated the greater political relevance of antagonistic aesthetics.[30] I contend that it is the move from "antagonism" to dynamic, self-critical creativity that is precisely that which is most relevant for constructive ethics and political engagement.

Let me give you an example of political activism as an exercise in roots in motion. In six towns in Kansas, energy use in 2010 declined by 5%, a seemingly slight figure, yet the usual reduction of only 1.5% is considered a success. This reduction was achieved without challenging the widespread and deeply held conviction in much of Kansas that global warming is a hoax. Nancy Jackson of the Climate and Energy Project decided that the focus did not have to be humanly induced climate change: "If the goal was to persuade people to reduce their use of fossil fuels, why not identify issues that motivated them?" A simple tactical shift, choosing to emphasize "thrift, patriotism, spiritual conviction and economic prosperity," led to a significant embrace of both conservation and renewable fuels.[31]

What an altermodern relational aesthetic and politics calls for is the inhabiting a "space of negotiation" where normative ideals and critiques can not only be discovered, but can be embodied in institutional practices of all sorts—private and public, economic and political, educational and cultural. Relational aesthetics and politics bring us into the realm of microtopias, the creation of policies, social arrangements, institutions that "play the world, that reprogram [already existing] social forms."[32] Drawing on Gilles Deleuze and Felix Guattari, Bourriaud claims that these microtopias, far from being universal, "serve as the breeding ground for experiments in justice in all its forms."[33]

Our political, ethical, and aesthetic task is that of "producing the conditions" where we not only see exploitation and suffering, but where we create alternative, concrete forms of daily practices that embody our ideals of freedom, equality, and flourishing. These experiments in justice do not emerge de novo but are grounded in deep, creative immersions in where we are from and who we are.

As we participate, as radicants, in what Guattari calls the "creative uncertainty and outrageous invention" of experiments in justice, we face a stark reality: a shift as big as the switch from an ethic of control to an ethic of risk.[34] The core of our ethical choices is not doing the unambiguously right thing, or valorizing the prophet as one who points out ethical ambiguities in any course of action. Altermodern ethics and relational aesthetics alike call us to a forthright reckoning with the undeniable reality of lesser evils in service of a possible greater good.

The dynamism of relational aesthetics, in art as in politics, lies in "learning to inhabit the world in a better way. . . . The role of artworks is no longer to form imaginary and utopian realities, but to actually be ways of living and models of action within the existing real."[35] Others use the term "social practice" to refer to the work of Theaster Gates, whom we met earlier, and other artists using art to transform communities in the interest of justice.[36] Let us explore further this example of relational aesthetics that is taking place in Chicago. Theaster Gates is an artist, activist, and administrator involved in just such a multifaceted, catalytic process, what he calls the creation of an "ecology of opportunity." Gates is internationally known as a practitioner of relational aesthetics, with projects in Chicago, St. Louis, and Omaha. His home base is the 6900 block of South Dorchester Avenue. In an article for the *New York Times Magazine*, Ben Austen describes the scope of Gates's work.

> Gates was trained as a potter and as an urban planner. In South Dorchester, he now owns 12 properties as part of the Dorchester Projects. His goal is a bold one—"converting a block of decaying two flats into a new creative cottage industry." According to Gates, this is not gentrification but the creation of a community of artists and long-term residents of the area. Gates lives in the project and created Rebuild Foundation, which has led to the building of community art space, an arts incubator in Washington Park, a Black Cinema House with space for film, poetry and story-telling community events, a restored bank will be the home of the library of John H. Johnson, the founder of *Ebony* and *Jet* magazines. A new project that has just begun is one of turning a closed public housing project into a 32 unit mixed income complex for low income families and emerging artists.[37]

Gates's work involves the community in the creation of art as well as providing employment in the renovation of buildings for ex-convicts, teenagers, and artists. There are 20 full-time employees and many more part-time.[38] Gates's work is audacious and comprehensive: "Gates was trained as a potter, but his artistic practice includes . . . sculpture, musical performance, installation and . . . large-scale urban intervention."[39] As noted earlier, Gates describes all dimensions of this project as a work of art—"identifying talented people in the community, [working with them], empowering them, figuring out how they can help to maintain and enlarge a community of innovation, enterprise and security." As he states, these multiple efforts are all necessary for the creation of an "ecology of opportunity."

In all of this work, that of Theaster Gates, of engaged scholarship, of social enterprises, of B corporations, of accountable nonprofits, we see a commitment to create a social order based, not on control, but on an "ecology of opportunity"—relationships of connection, accountability, reciprocity, and empowerment. Gates's work shows the potentially creative power of the professional managerial class. Like many who are in this class, Gates was raised in a working-class family. His father was a roofer who ran a BBQ pit and owned a four-unit rental property.[40] Gates has degrees in urban planning, fine arts, and religious studies, and has worked at the University of Chicago since 2006, now as director of the Arts and Public Life Initiative.[41]

Prior to coming to the University of Chicago, Gates worked at the Chicago Transit Authority as an arts planner. In that position, he not only excelled as a bureaucrat, but saw that skill as a core part of his work as an artist: "Understanding how bureaucratic systems work and even how to invent them and tweak them is a very big part of my practice. I'm not a good perspective drawer, but I can write a really good memo."[42]

Gates describes his work as a melding of multiple elements—"performance and ritual and the spiritual and the metaphysical combined with building and pragmatism and labor."[43]

The impact of Gates's work is still unfolding. In the March 2014 issue of *Chicago* magazine, he was named number 10 of the 100 most influential people in Chicago. This is their description of the importance of Gate's work:

> [T]o those who know him, the South Side-raised Gates is a classic operator who has seized upon the art world's desire to latch onto meaning.
>
> He provides meaning all right: With his sculptures and ceramics selling for upward of $150,000 apiece, Gates has created a circular economy in which urban renewal projects are financed by collectors' checkbooks. So far, he has bought a dozen properties in and around his South Side

neighborhood of Grand Crossing . . . and helped raise $20 million for revitalization projects there. But most impressive is Gates' ability to do what few politicians can: spin the city's most intractable problems into a sales pitch for change—one that captures the imagination of everyone, even his neighbors.[44]

For another example of altermodern catalytic social engagement, or visionary pragmatism, let us examine the work of Toni Preckwinkle. In November 2014, Toni Preckwinkle was elected to a second term as president of the Cook County Board of Commissioners. That reelection was an affirmation of the depth and range of her public service and the quality of her leadership, first as a Fourth Ward alderman since 1991 and then as president of the Cook County Board since 2010. The presidency of the Cook County Board of Commissioners is an immense responsibility. Cook County, which includes Chicago, has a population of over five million, and is the second most populous county in the United States. The 17 commissioners set policy and laws regarding property, public health services, and public safety.[45]

Toni Preckwinkle

Toni Preckwinkle moved to Chicago while she was in high school. Living in a racially mixed neighborhood, Toni saw firsthand the impact of systemic racism on black youth. "I felt, for good reason, that the police could shoot and kill black people with impunity," she told me. "I still feel that way."

Preckwinkle's response to this terrible injustice has been to devote her life to doing everything she can to change it, as well as other injustices to people of color, poor people, working people, and the environment. "Both my family and my Unitarian Universalist church encouraged public service," she explained. Her first foray into politics was as an election canvasser at age 16.

She received a BA and an MA from the University of Chicago, and taught high school history for 10 years, helping her students think critically about the world. She read voraciously on social and economic theory and history. So when she ran for the Chicago City Council for

Figure 6.1. Toni Preckwinkle, president of the Cook
County Board of Commissioners. Photo from
Wikipedia.com.

the third time and was finally elected in 1991 as alderman, she was prepared to educate and persuade constituents and fellow city councilors to
grapple with the structural racism in the Chicago prison system.

One of the initiatives Preckwinkle focused on in her nine years as
Fourth Ward alderman was bail bond reform and reducing the reliance
on pretrial detention. "Contrary to most people's assumptions, the jail is
not primarily a place where we lock up violent criminals. . . . In fact, only
7% of the people in the jail are currently serving a sentence. [And] 70%
of those in the jail awaiting trial [are] accused of a nonviolent charge and
they are detained because they cannot pay their bail. As I've said before
and I will continue to repeat—our jail is the intersection of racism and
poverty: 86% of those in the jail are black and brown."

Preckwinkle's fairness, honesty, grasp of the issues, and no-nonsense
"let's-get-the-job-done" pragmatism have earned her the trust of con-

stituents and peers alike. She was given the Best Alderman Award six times between 1993 and 2008 by the Independent Voters of Illinois–Independent Precinct Organization, a nonpartisan organization dedicated to open and honest governance. And in 2010 she was elected to the Board of Commissioners for Cook County.

Serving on the Cook County Board, Preckwinkle remains committed to justice, equity, and compassion. She has worked tirelessly toward eradicating structural racism and ending institutional practices that limit economic opportunities to the few, rather than expanding them for the many. She has challenged a culture of political corruption and has brought greater funding for education, affordable housing, and public health.

Preckwinkle's work is threefold: (1) bringing to the core of governmental policies attention to the integrity and value of people who are too often ignored, devalued, and discriminated against because of gender, race, and class; (2) implementing governmental policies that create and maintain justice; and (3) reforming the very nature of government to be fair, accountable, financially sound, and politically just.

For those who, like her, might find themselves taking the opportunity to run for public office, Preckwinkle has some advice. It is of the utmost importance, she says, to be scrupulously honest in all that you do. Cut no corners, and pander to no one. Realize that politics is public education at a higher level. Translate the issues into language that the public can understand. Persuade people at every turn that you are doing the right thing, and bring people along. Bring as many as you can into the fold as supporters.

This is exactly what Preckwinkle did when she advocated for a new ordinance addressing the issue of wage theft. Defining exactly why this legislation was necessary, she told the public and the Cook County Board of Commissioners, "Unscrupulous business owners have exploited low-wage workers by refusing to pay overtime, classifying legal employees as independent contractors, paying less than minimum wage, and, in some instances, even refusing to pay wages outright. This is unfair to hard-working employees and their families and it's unfair to competing businesses, which are operating within the confines of the law."

The ordinance was passed into law in February 2015. Now, she says, "companies and individuals found guilty of wage theft will not be allowed to obtain Cook County procurement contracts, business licenses, or property tax incentives for five years."

As Cook County Board president, she has pushed hard for better police accountability. When the U.S. Justice Department published its findings after investigating the pattern of excessive force and misconduct in the Chicago Police Department and others, Preckwinkle expressed hope that the federal courts would insist on exercising oversight and require accountability from police departments. "I don't have any confidence that it can be done without outside oversight," she said.

When I interviewed Preckwinkle in August 2017, I asked her: In this new political climate, where federal oversight looks unlikely, what can be done at the city and county level to address the system that protects police misconduct? Is it possible for communities to do this on their own? "It's a tremendous challenge," she told me. "In Chicago, police misconduct is commonplace and is just not addressed. I feel we will be unable to address the problem with internal processes alone. Our way forward is not clear now. We have to take it on ourselves—which entity could successfully take on such a role? Vigorous third party oversight is needed."

Meanwhile, she says, there are things we can do as private citizens and civic and religious groups that can help keep people informed and aware and put consistent pressure on elected officials. For instance, in Chicago there is a citizen group that stays on top of statistics, which are public record, mining police data for patterns and practices as well as the outcomes of any investigations.

Groups such as the League of Women Voters have done court monitoring. This consists of quietly sitting in on court proceedings. In addition to providing information as to which judges might violate the rights of defendants, the mere presence of a neutral observer encourages better behavior and increases the chance that justice will be done.

"Racism, exploitation of the weak and powerless, these things are not new or unique. The difference is that recently these types of things have had explicit support by national leaders. The message for all of us is, more than ever we need to inform ourselves and speak up. Now is the time we are called upon to stand up for what we believe, to speak truth to power," Preckwinkle says. While we are limited in what we can do at the national level, "there is much we can do at the local and county level," she maintains.

Another important thing that we can all do, she says, is to spread the word to our neighbors and friends. Speak about the importance of civility and involvement in public life. Find out about your local economic development plan, and hold public officials accountable for focusing resources on areas with the highest economic challenges. "The most vibrant economies have the least inequality," Preckwinkle says, "so economic development equals working on justice. It turns out that everybody benefits."

Asked to sum up her philosophy of life, Preckwinkle admits to being an optimist: "I feel it is a privilege to be in a position to do something positive for the world. I am grateful for the chance to help address these challenges." With that, Preckwinkle is off to the next project, changing the world for the better, one day at a time.

In Preckwinkle's achievements as a political leader, we can see clearly the expression of two core Unitarian Universalist principles: "We affirm and promote justice, equity, and compassion in human relations; we affirm and promote the right of conscience and the use of the democratic process." Preckwinkle's ability to live out these principles with such creativity and integrity is likely related to her knowledge as a student and teacher of history. In an interview in the *Chicago Reader*, Preckwinkle named Taylor Branch's three-volume history of the civil rights movement, Michelle Alexander's *The New Jim Crow*, and Doris Kearns Goodwin's book about the Lincoln presidency, *A Team of Rivals*, as being among the works for which she has the most respect. In each of these volumes we find incisive analyses of the depth of injustice and the complex interaction of social movements and institutional political change. In conjunction with philosopher George Santayana's well-known warning, "those who cannot remember the past are condemned to repeat it," in Preckwinkle's leadership we see an alternate trajectory, "those who study the past are able to shape the future."

Key Insights for Progressive Practice

What are the ethical and spiritual challenges of altermodern, catalytic social engagement? Our role is not simply to denounce the real and announce the ideal. Our role is to be catalysts of justice, learning from the courage, the achievements, the limitations, and even the failures of those who have embodied this commitment to equity, flourishing, and plenitude in the past and are living it out now in their work as elected officials, professionals, citizens, and community activists.

In the world of social enterprise and impact-driven nonprofits we see people stepping up to solve problems where government has failed. In the work of Toni Preckwinkle, however, we see what can happen when the goals and methods of visionary pragmatism and catalytic social engagement are lived out in the daily operations of governmental life. We can follow her lead and (1) bring to the core of governmental policies attention to the integrity and value of people who are too often ignored, devalued, and discriminated against because of gender, race, and class; (2) implement governmental policies that create and maintain justice; and (3) reform the very nature of government to be fair, accountable, financially sound, and politically just.

It is this vision of a government of, by, and for all of the people that can shape our political lives and be shared in more creative and sustained ways. It is also true that we do not have to wait for electoral victories to live out an "ecology of opportunity." As we see in the work of Theaster Gates, impact-driven nonprofits can work with private capital and governmental agencies to create spaces now of inclusion, equity, sustainability, and beauty.

What does it take to persist in these catalytic efforts? Let us return to the wisdom shared by Patricia Hill Collins. The "ability to persist" in work for social justice requires three things. First, an awareness that focusing on critique "leaves us perpetually responding to the agenda of other people." Second, knowing that success in the present does not mean that there will not be challenges as great or even greater in the future. And, third, the meaning of this generation's long struggle is found in the soul-expanding joy of deep connections in the present.

For our activism to endure we need much more than e-mail blasts, financial donations, signing petitions, writing letters, and showing up for episodic protests. What sustains us and what motivates us is ongoing deep connection with people we value, people we support, and people who support, challenge, and value us.

We can avoid the sixth and seventh Windigos, the illusion of linear and assured progress, or the dual danger of either denouncing or settling for partial reforms. The key lesson here is related to the second Windigo of excessive individualism. We are not seeking an expansion of economic prosperity and political rights only for ourselves as individuals, or even only for our particular social and cultural group. A society that truly values all is genuinely better for all: it overcomes the isolation and arrogance of class- and race-based social systems; it embodies the joy and creativity of plentitude, reciprocity, and generative interdependence.

Conclusion

The Soul of Democracy

In this book we have explored what happens when we take up the third wave of progressive social action. The first wave is the denunciation of systems of injustice, the second is the inclusion of the voices and experiences of all people, especially those marginalized and excluded by the dominant culture, and the third is moving from denouncing what is wrong to building what may be right. Furthermore, it is my wager that there is a fourth wave of catalytic social engagement. To engage in the tasks of denouncing, including, and building with genuine accountability and the utmost creativity requires that we see, name, and contain our Windigos, our constitutive and intrinsic forms of evil.

Our better ideas are straightforward: a commitment to generative interdependence, practices of respect, reciprocity, and gratitude that are shaping our civic, professional, personal, and economic lives. These ideas are long-standing, deeply grounded in indigenous wisdom and the basic African American and European American ideals of democracy, and can be nurtured, cultivated, and expanded.

It is easier to live out this version of generative democracy if we do so in light of the compelling analysis of Karen Stenner who, as we saw earlier, provides both a stark depiction of the threats to democracy and calls us to address those threats by living out "the science and not the religion of democracy." I concur with Stenner's turn to the science of democracy, yet find in my reading of contemporary analyses by political scientists of conservatism and liberalism opportunities for the maintenance and expansion of a pluralistic democracy not envisioned by those same scholars. Sinn and Hayes, for example, provide a compelling account of the competing visions of conservatism and liberalism. Their research is heartening for it demonstrates that there is a commitment to generative interdependence that can be nurtured, expanded, and expressed more fully in our economic, political, professional, and personal lives. It is highly significant that Sinn and Hayes point to where their current research on liberalism is limited, and what needs to be explored further. Where it is lacking is crucial—what are the intrinsic challenges of generative interdependence? What are our fundamental flaws?

We must become as aware of our particular failings as we are of the constitutive dangers of conservatism. Without this awareness we, too, end up reinforcing systems of injustice. For every social group, the challenge of indigenous wisdom is to recognize that none of us are immune from constitutive forms of destructiveness and imbalance, and that we are far more likely to contain and limit these dangers if we are first aware that they exist.

Here the role of parents and of the education of children and youth is clear. We can begin these lessons in age-appropriate ways. What Kimmerer and Sanchez invoke and share is not a logic of moralistic shaming but an empowering mentality of honesty and accountability. Leslie Marmon Silko, who, like Sanchez, is from the Laguna Pueblo, describes the process of responding to mistakes with the gift of Laguna storytelling, an oral tradition that recounts "disturbing or provocative" events in the presence of all members of the family, even, and especially, children:

> The effect of these inter-family or inter-clan exchanges is the reassurance of each person that she or he will never be separated or apart from the clan. . . . Neither the worst blunders or disasters nor the greatest financial prosperity and joy will ever be permitted to isolate anyone from the rest of the group. . . . You are never the first to suffer a grave loss or profound humiliation. You are never the first, and you understand that you will probably not be the last to commit or be victimized by a repugnant act.[1]

We are not the first to suffer and fail, and we will not be the last. We are not the first to also embody a measure of justice, and we will not be the last. As workers, professionals, and citizens, how do we continuously remind ourselves of this past and name it when we see it emerging? How do we create institutional practices that activate our expansive best and contain our defensive and insular worst?

An example of the latter can be seen in the evocative use of the statement of the Lutheran pastor Martin Niemöller. Although Niemöller did oppose the Nazis and spent seven years in a concentration camp, he was honest in his admission that his opposition, and his resistance, came too late.[2]

> First they came for the Socialists, and I did not speak out—Because I was not a Socialist.
> Then they came for the Trade Unionists, and I did not speak out—Because I was not a Trade Unionist.
> Then they came for the Jews, and I did not speak out—Because I was not a Jew.
> Then they came for me—and there was no one left to speak for me.[3]

In response to blatant calls for a ban on Muslim immigrants and refugees, and for the deportation of Latinx immigrants, and in response to the failure of members of the Republican Party to challenge the fundamental immorality of those discriminatory policies, many activists turned to the words of Niemöller for inspiration: "At first they came for the Muslims, and we said no way!"[4]

These statements are powerful for three reasons. First, they are concise and memorable. Second, they expose the evil of the oppressor who is unjustly targeting specific populations. Third, they also name our own evil, the patterns of inertia, fear, or ignorance that keeps us from speaking in time, that allow us to wait on others to act, or hope that things will change of their own accord.

There is a catalytic power in that kind of exposure and warning. We are now challenged to create more warnings of just this sort in light of the rising power of authoritarian racism and hatred throughout the world.

We have explored seven of our Windigos and there may well be others. Recall the seven that we have identified:

1. Extractive capitalism and excessive consumerism.
2. Excessive individualism.
3. Paralyzing infighting over strategies and tactics.

4. Ignorance of the possibility of unintended consequences and our ongoing capacity for partiality and error.
5. Inattentiveness to implicit bias, structural racism, and resurging white violence against people who are African American, Native American, Muslim, and Latinx.
6. Expectation of linear and assured progress.
7. Falling prey to the complacency of reformism or the delusions of revolutionary victory.

What does it mean to confront these Windigos and become catalysts of justice in our daily lives as parents, citizens, neighbors, consumers, workers, managers, owners, professionals, and investors? For those with a measure of economic, political, and cultural power, it is disingenuous to merely "Speak Truth to Power." Rather, for many of us, we are the ones in power who are being spoken to! We are the ones being challenged to confront and rectify fundamental inequities. This is a multifaceted task. First, it requires becoming aware of the complex histories and ongoing structures of systemic disparities in power. Second, it entails using the power that we do have to rectify the damage of injustice and to expand networks of empowerment to include all people. Third, in this work of both reparations and transformation, we must be in ongoing accountable partnerships with those who have been, and are, excluded from full participation in civic, economic, and political life.

How do we set about accomplishing these lofty goals? Along with Lynda Sutherland, I have created a guidebook for doing just that, a "Just Living Passport: Journey of Discovery." It is a discussion guide for group and self-reflection on ongoing forms of catalytic social and civic engagement. The full guide is found in the appendix. Below is a glimpse, outlining some of what we can do to change our habits so that our lives reflect our commitment to live mindfully and responsibly within this complex and beautiful interdependent web of life. Key elements include the following:

- Identifying resources, allies, and support systems;
- Noticing the ways in which our everyday decisions already create more justice;
- Engaging in a process of continuous innovation, adaptation, and learning.

As activists for social justice, we are familiar with protests, petitions, and similar means of putting pressure on public officials to change systems of injustice. Yet many of us are just beginning to learn how to build systems of justice into our civic, corporate, and personal lives. And these systems of justice must be developed in full cognizance of the history and ongoing impact of systemic injustice. To that end, the journey begins with these questions:

What is the history of the indigenous peoples who now live or who once lived in my community? What are their practices of engagement and respect? How did practices of cultural and physical genocide oppress or displace them? Where are the spaces in which they are able to engage the community with genuine equity and respect?[5]

How is the wealth of this part of the country dependent upon slavery? How is it dependent upon the ongoing exploitation of workers? What are current structures of racial discrimination and economic inequality?[6]

Once aware of this history, we can consider where we have power or influence, in our everyday lives, to affect the people and institutions around us and to rectify that injustice and to create just institutions. We can explore where we may have the potential to use our power, as workers, managers, investors, business owners, consumers, parents, citizens, or neighbors, to strive for environmental sustainability, economic equity, and racial justice. For example, with regard to the businesses that we support, work for, own, or in which we invest, we can ask:

Are the basic principles of economic responsibility being fulfilled? Are these social enterprises that pay attention to the triple bottom line of people, planet, and profit?

For this business, what are the metrics of social equity in terms of the populations served? What racial and cultural groups benefit from the daily operations of the business?

What are the metrics of social inclusion and equity in how the business is operated?

Do the leadership and processes of decision making reflect the racial and cultural demographics of the surrounding area?

Does the organization pay a living wage with an equitable ratio between highest and lowest paid workers?

What are the environmental impacts of the daily operation of the organization? How is energy conserved and the environment sustained?

What are the Windigos at work in this operation? What stories are told to help us to see and contain those constitutive dangers?

Similarly, as we take up the responsibility of direct political action, we can ask ourselves:

What are the forms of rising authoritarianism, racism, and bigotry in my local and national context? How do I move from being a bystander to one who creatively calls out hatred and bigotry and resolutely calls others to a more expansive and just community?

What forms of political engagement do I find most engaging, and where can I have the most impact as a citizen and as an activist? Are my efforts best spent on exposing and dismantling systems of injustice? If so, what forms of nonviolent direct action are best suited to my talents and forms of power and influence?

Are my efforts best spent on including others and shaping existing political institutions?

How do I assure that my actions benefit all, and not only my racial or economic class? With which groups am I in relationships of ongoing accountability in both the decisions about how to act and in evaluation of actions taken?

How do I support those who are involved in different forms of political action, finding resonance between our respective efforts?

What are the Windigos at work in these political activities? What stories are told to help us to see and contain those constitutive dangers?

In the full Passport guide, we explore more deeply the specific challenges of creating community economies and sustainable and resilient political resistance.

Effective social action not only exposes what is wrong, but it empowers us to be agents of what may be right. We can create an alternative, more just social order through

(a) blocking and denouncing injustice through protests, strikes, and civil disobedience;
(b) healing the wounds of centuries of exploitation and the new wounds of hatred and violence through alliance, support, and collaboration and through communal rituals of truth-telling, vulnerability, and accountability;
(c) building alternative educational and economic institutions;
(d) participating in the governing process as voters or elected officials.

Each of these endeavors is characterized by different emotional energies, as well as by different actions. While one individual may not be able to tackle all of these tasks, as activists we can acknowledge and respect the equal necessity of each type of work. We can support the emotional power of each and nurture the expansive imagination that leads to an ability to respect and value the creativity of others, rather than trying to impose our own form of creativity, our own way of living out our gifts with responsibility, as the only way for others. Again, the indigenous wisdom shared by Kimmerer is essential. There are multiple gifts, all needed, all to be nurtured and valued.

Finally, we can ask, what are the ethical and spiritual challenges of this ongoing work? What are the spiritual and ethical resources of communal practices, of aesthetic, spiritual, and physical disciplines that can sustain us as we live justly? To address these questions moves us to a fundamental revision of the ethical imagination.

An Altermodern Existentialism

What is the form of ethical imagination that can sustain and evoke a forthright reckoning with the undeniable reality of lesser evils in service of a possibly greater good? What form of the ethical imagination can free us from the illusion of lasting victory? Why would we think that the struggle of living justly would ever be ended? Recall the powerful statement by Anthony Pinn: "Struggle centered approaches recognize we may never destroy systems of injustice in ways that can constitute what we mean typically by 'freedom,' 'liberation' or 'justice.' . . . We should understand 'liberation' not as an outcome but rather as a process, a process of perpetual rebellion against injustice." I would add that we can also understand liberation as a process of the soul-satisfying embrace of love and responsibility.

Along with Pinn's African American humanist theology, I offer a joyful and ironic existentialism. We can be stewards, and we can be destroyers. We can fully acknowledge both possibilities, and create ongoing individual and collective practices that nurture the former and check the latter. At the core of checking the latter is deliberate immersion in webs of reciprocity, acknowledging all that gives us life, the bounty of nature and the web of human connections. As the philosopher Grace Jantzen wrote, we are natals: alive only because other humans nurtured us, alive because of a natural world that also nourishes us.[7] Our task is to honor that sustenance, and one of the greatest forms of evil is to defile this sustenance: exploiting the work of other people that provide our shelter and food, despoiling and exploiting the natural world as an object solely for our use. We can be stewards, not of the natural world, but of the human world, limiting and shaping our human reliance on the natural world in ways that are sustaining, rather than exploitative, extractive, and fundamentally destructive.

To be this type of steward requires a recognition that there is nothing in the natural world that needs us to survive. Our bodies and our waste may be used as fertilizer for other beings, but all beings could find other forms of sustenance if we were extinct. In contrast to philosophers and theologians who make humanity central to the world, this approach is just the opposite. Our existence is absolutely inessential. There are no beings (other than other humans) dependent upon us for their survival, and yet all beings are threatened by our capacity for destruction. We routinely despoil habitats in our economic practices and could literally destroy all life with the use of nuclear weapons.[8]

The meaning of our existence, then, is quite literally, only what we make of it. We can make meaning out of reciprocity and gratitude, humility, and wonder. We can choose to live, see, connect, and flourish in harmony with the natural world. Our creativity, however, is intrinsically amoral. It can be used for expansive, interdependent flourishing, or for self-centered, exploitative survival.

How do we live out of this dual understanding—our inessential existence and our dependence on the natural world, our capacity for devastating forms of evil, and our capacity for generative interdependence? How do we learn to live in a way in which we do not harm the social and natural worlds that give us life? Once again, the challenge of Robin Wall Kimmerer:

> We do indeed stand at the crossroads. Scientific evidence tells us we are close to the tipping point of climate change. . . . Ecologists estimate that we would need seven planets to sustain the lifeways we have created. And yet those lifeways, lacking balance, justice, and peace, have not brought us contentment. They have brought us the loss of our relatives in a great wave of extinction.[9]

This awareness calls us to ongoing, multifaceted practices of just living—exposing and resisting injustice, including all people and building just structures, containing our worst and sustaining our best.

The theologian Michael Hogue describes the multiple elements of such a living justice "as sacred work":

> The work of living justice depends on the embrace of the creative potential of uncertainty, empathic response to the creatural vulnerabilities that we all share, and the prophetic critique and dismantling of the contingent vulnerabilities that disproportionately afflict some of us. A theopolitics of resilient democracy understands these tasks of living justice as sacred work, as an expression of reverence for the nature of reality-in-process, humility in face of the finitude of human being and knowing, and deep respect for the perishability of all things.[10]

It is my conviction that life does not make sense, but when there is a modicum of justice, life can be exhilarating, joyful, and full of deep wonder and delight. Does anyone give more joy than the children we nurture? Is there any greater beauty than the natural world that surrounds us, or greater satisfaction than celebrating that world in sustainable gardening and appreciative art?

I have a paradoxical wager—what may lead to real progress is giving up our expectation of such progress! We can embrace the tasks of just living with the wisdom expressed by the midwife Ina Mae Gaskins. No matter how many births she has seen, no matter how many times she has given birth herself, each time is fraught with peril and possibility, each time requires all of her attention and effort to the complex process of giving life.[11] The same may be true of our efforts to live justly and well. We will always have the possibility of living with respect and reciprocity, and always have the threat of our worst—of isolation, exploitation, and exclusion of the many for the benefit of a few.

For activists, this awareness calls us away from moral narcissism, the assumption that we have acted with moral integrity when we voice our most stringent critiques of what is unjust and share our heartfelt visions of what might be, yet fail to take up the equally difficult task of the design, implementation, evaluation, and revision of alternative economic and social policies. Critique and vision are the impetus to further action—the hard work of immersion in problems that we can only address collectively. Furthermore, as we create constructive policies to redress common needs and aspirations, there are no perfect solutions. Every action has risks, trade-offs, foreseen and unforeseeable consequences. The recognition of this latter factor reminds us that there is no moral safe harbor, no course of action guaranteed to be free of risk, loss, and negative side effects.

I became aware of the concept of moral narcissism through conversations with Major Mark Schimmelpfenning (U.S. Army, retired), who used it to describe what I have also criticized as a weakness in the peace movement. Too often activists such as myself have stopped with the critique of military action without taking up ourselves the risk of designing and implementing nonviolent responses to deadly conflict and crimes against humanity.[12]

Here, then, is the twofold ethical challenge—forgoing the delusion of moral narcissism and forthrightly reckoning with likely trade-offs and finding ways, as professionals, of bearing ourselves the costs of losses too often borne only by the most vulnerable and marginalized.

What is essential in checking these mistakes is the realization that they cannot be corrected by changes in individual attitudes. We need each other to be moral. We need social structures to embody our highest ideals and hold us to our best insights. Taking this need seriously leads to a fundamental shift in the moral imagination and our understanding of the social contract required for an equitable, expansive, and self-critical democracy. William Schulz describes it well. He states that what we have at this juncture in society is "almost the reverse of the title of the great theologian Reinhold Niebuhr's famous work, for what we see today is Immoral Humans and Moral Society."[13] As we move from *Moral Man and Immoral Society* to the converse, we take up the challenge of creating institutions that are systematically designed to check not only greed and ill will, but the deleterious effects of well-intentioned delusion.

Let me pose with you a wager—the challenge of giving sustainable material shape to revolutionary aspirations is not served by the isolating rhetoric of righteous indignation, but by deep grief at the costs of injustice and a forthright recognition of the failures and limits of even the revolutionary vanguard. We can tell ourselves a new individual and national story, one that forgoes, even for peacemakers and social activists, the assumption of moral exceptionalism.

What is the import of all of these strategies, of creating new honor worlds, of ending physical violence and expanding human rights, of checking implicit bias, of exposing and checking the masks of innocence that sanction moral atrocities? Let us return to the claim of Gustavo Gutiérrez: the theology of liberation frees the oppressed from their exploitation and the oppressor from their isolation, arrogance, and alienation. As we who are the heirs of oppression and who are complicit in ongoing structural injustice see that legacy of injustice, name its consequences, and work together to transform it, we may join the process that Ta-Nehisi Coates describes as "freeing ourselves from the Dream" and becoming instead "conscious citizens of this beautiful and terrible world."[14]

For whites, our challenge is to see the ways in which our adherence to the Dream is intrinsic to the historical and ongoing exploitation of both African Americans and the natural world. Many of us who are white have long denied how our wealth as a nation was created and how our own relative prosperity is sustained. Coates is clear. This Dream is deadly for millions in the present and for all of us in the future.

The Dreamers will have to learn to struggle themselves, to understand that the field for their Dream, the stage where they have painted themselves white, is the deathbed of us all. The Dream is the same habit that endangers the planet, the same habit that sees our bodies stowed away in prisons and ghettos.[15]

There are two dimensions of the Dream that are crucial—the pretense of innocence and the denial of our fundamental frailty and vulnerability as human beings.[16] Coates is not optimistic about the ability of whites to free themselves from the Dream. In spite of my immersion in the work of whites and people of color who are reckoning with our frailty and intrinsic limits, who are trying to find ways of living out a new honor code of resolute commitment to social and economic justice for all and for sustainable environmental practices, I, too, am not an optimist about the long-term success of this movement. I am, however, deeply grateful that it exists, profoundly humbled by the courage and persistence of those who embody it, and resolutely committed to doing all that I can to help keep it alive. It will always be difficult to exercise power collaboratively, creatively, and sustainably. It is, however, possible to take up this task with honesty and self-awareness.

As we began this exploration of constructive social and civic engagement with a test of faith, let us conclude with a prayer, a prayer for hearts and minds and wills open to the genuine plenitude that graces our world, and equally open to growing threats and danger. May our grounding in the former give us the catalytic power to confront the latter.

JUST LIVING PASSPORT

A Journey of Discovery

WITH LYNDA J. SUTHERLAND

Name_____

INTRODUCTION

How do we incorporate social justice into our everyday lives?

How do we change our habits so that our lives reflect our commitment to live mindfully and responsibly within this complex and beautiful interdependent web of life?

You are invited to join in a soul journey, as we explore ways to deepen and broaden our ability to live justly.

This booklet can be used as a guide, and as a record of your spiritual journey into what Just Living means to you, in your life, within the context of your circumstances and your community.

Prompts are provided as suggestions for reflecting on your experiences in learning ever more sustainable and effective ways to practice Just Living.

PREPARING FOR THE JOURNEY

Which areas of Just Living am I already engaged with?

Which area calls me to do more?

My biggest question about Just Living is:

LOCATING AREAS OF STRENGTH AND OPPORTUNITY

What is Just Living? It is a grassroots phenomenon, not a master plan. Key elements in living more justly include:

- Identifying resources, allies, and support systems;
- Noticing the ways in which our everyday decisions already create more justice;
- Engaging in a process of continuous innovation, adaptation, and learning.

As activists for social justice, we are familiar with protests, petitions, and similar means of putting pressure on public officials to change systems of injustice. Yet we are just beginning to learn how to build systems of justice into our civic, corporate, and personal lives. And, these systems of justice must be developed in full cognizance of the history and ongoing impact of systemic injustice. To that end, the journey begins with these questions.

Questions:
What is the history of the indigenous peoples who now live or who once lived in my community? What are their practices of engagement and respect? How did practices of cultural and physical genocide oppress or displace them? Where are the spaces in which they are able to engage the community with genuine equity and respect?

For histories of the culture of indigenous peoples in the United States prior to the European conquest, and examinations of that conquest, its ongoing impact, and past and present resistance to it, the following works are a valuable place to begin: James Wilson, *The Earth Shall Weep: A History of Native America* (New York: Grove Press, 1998); Roxanne Dunbar-Ortiz, *An Indigenous Peoples' History of the United States* (Boston: Beacon Press, 2014).

How is the wealth of this part of the country dependent upon slavery? How is it dependent upon the ongoing exploitation of workers? What are current structures of racial discrimination and economic inequality?

Begin this exploration with the pivotal essay by Ta-Nehesi Coates on the importance of learning and responding to this history, "The Case for Reparations," in *We Were Eight Years in Power: An American Tragedy* (New York: One World Publishing, 2017), 163–210. For histories of racial domination, see Carol Anderson, *White Rage: The Unspoken Truth of Our Racial Divide* (New York: Bloomsbury, 2016); Ibram X. Kendi, *Stamped from the Beginning: The Definitive History of Racist Ideas in America* (New York: Nation Books, 2016); David F. Krugler, *1919, the Year of Racial Violence: How African Americans Fought Back* (New York: Cambridge University Press, 2015); Nicholas Lemann, *Redemption: The Last Battle of the Civil War* (New York: Farrar, Straus and Giroux, 2006). For an example of a detailed study of the history and ongoing impact of slavery and racial discrimination and exploitation, see Tiya Miles, *The Dawn of Detroit: A Chronicle of Slavery and Freedom in the City of the Straits* (New York: New Press, 2017).

What power or influence do I have, in my everyday life, to affect the people and institutions around me and to rectify that injustice and create more just institutions?

Where am I already using my power as worker, manager, investor, business owner, consumer, parent, etc. to live for environmental sustainability, economic equity, and racial justice?

How do I assure that my actions benefit all, and not only my racial or economic class? With which groups am I in relationships of ongoing accountability in both the decisions about how to act and in evaluation of actions taken?

What emotional, social, ethical, or spiritual challenges do I encounter as I engage in these practices? What are the resources of communal connections, and of aesthetic, spiritual, and physical disciplines that sustain me in this work?

LOCATING AREAS OF STRENGTH AND OPPORTUNITY IN OUR ECONOMIC LIVES

In our lives as consumers, workers, managers, owners, and investors we can reject the practices of extractive capitalism and live out a community economy of plenitude, respect, and flourishing.

Questions:

In the businesses that I support, work for, own, or in which I invest, are the basic principles of economic responsibility being fulfilled? Are these social enterprises, whether large or small, that pay attention to the triple bottom line of people, planet, and profit?

For this business, what are the metrics of social equity in terms of the populations served? What racial and cultural groups benefit from the daily operations of the business?

What are the metrics of social inclusion and equity in how the business is operated? Does the leadership and processes of decision making reflect the racial and cultural demographics of the surrounding area?

Does the organization pay a living wage with an equitable ratio between highest and lowest paid workers?

What are the environmental impacts of the daily operation of the organization? How is energy conserved and the environment sustained?

What are the Windigos at work in this operation? What stories are told to help see and contain those constitutive dangers?

LOCATING AREAS OF STRENGTH AND OPPORTUNITY IN THE WORK OF NONPROFITS

The nonprofits in which I work, either as a staff or volunteer, or to which I donate, can be "impact driven," paying as much attention to long-lasting and multifaceted effects as to driving goals.

Questions:

What is the mission of the organization? Which racial and cultural groups are enhanced by the work of the organization?

Does the organization work with, rather than for, select populations? How are all voices regularly reflected in governance, goal setting, decision-making, and assessment?

What are the relevant metrics of success? What is the appropriate time scale for measuring success?

What are the Windigos at work in this operation? What stories are told to help see and contain those constitutive dangers?

LOCATING AREAS OF STRENGTH AND OPPORTUNITY IN DIRECT
POLITICAL ACTION

Effective social action not only exposes what is wrong, but it empowers us to be agents of what may be right. We can create an alternative, more just social order through

(a) blocking and denouncing injustice through protests, strikes, and civil disobedience;
(b) healing the wounds of centuries of exploitation and the new wounds of hatred and violence through alliance, support, and collaboration and through communal rituals of truth-telling, vulnerability, and accountability;
(c) building alternative education and economic institutions;
(d) participating in the governing process as voters or elected officials;
(e) working on the reform of our electoral system by ending gerrymandering and voter suppression, removing the dysfunctional role of money in politics, and changing the Electoral College system;
(f) honoring our governmental system of checks and balances and finding ways to deliberate across differences in service of the larger common good.

I doubt that the same people can do all of these tasks. Each is characterized by different emotional energies, as well as different actions. As activists we can acknowledge and respect the equal necessity of each type of work. As religious and spiritual leaders we can support the emotional power of each and nurture the expansive imagination that leads to an ability to respect and value the creativity of others, rather than trying to impose our own form of creativity, our own way of living our gifts with responsibility, as the only way for others. Again, the indigenous wisdom shared by Kimmerer is essential. There are multiple gifts, all needed, all to be nurtured and valued.

Questions:

What are the forms of rising authoritarianism, racism, and bigotry in my local and national context? How do I move from being a bystander to one who creatively calls out hatred and bigotry and resolutely calls others to a more expansive and just community?

What forms of political engagement do I find most engaging, and where can I have the most impact as citizen and as activist? Are my efforts best spent on exposing and dismantling systems of injustice? If so, what forms of nonviolent direct action are best suited to my talents and forms of power and influence?

Are my efforts best spent on including others and shaping existing political institutions?

How do I maintain self-critical accountability and solidarity with others in my political work? How do I support those who are involved in different forms of political action, finding resonance between our respective efforts?

What are the Windigos at work in these political activities? What stories are told to help see and contain those constitutive dangers?

ACKNOWLEDGMENTS

I am deeply grateful to my parents and grandparents who taught me what it meant to be builders of community. From them, I learned that the greatest joy can be found in working with others to honestly confront the dire threats that face us, and in working with the same people to nurture the opportunities we have to live in relationships of belonging, reciprocity, and gratitude. My daughters, Zoë and Hannah, continue this legacy in their professions and personal lives, and are an ongoing source of inspiration.

I am sustained by friends and colleagues who live forthrightly for justice—working together and laughing together in doing all that we can to embody a measure of justice in our collective lives—HK Hall, Meg Riley, Lisa Davis, Roxsand King, Mark Schimmelpfennig, Ron Reed, Karen Debord, Karen Touzeau, Luanne Sullivan, Neil Winston, the Chicago chapter of the League of Women Voters, the members of the Cook County Commission on Social Innovation and the Chicago Social Enterprise Alliance, and all the members of the Workgroup on Constructive Theology, especially Peter Heltzel, Shannon Craigo-Snell, Johnny B. Hill, Stephen Ray, Stephanie Mitchem, Anthony B. Pinn, and Mary McClintock Fulkerson.

I would like to thank Meadville Lombard Theological School for funding the sabbatical leaves that allowed time for research and reflection. I am also grateful to my faculty colleagues at MLTS (Michael Hogue, John Crestwell, Nato Hollister, Mark Hicks, Nicole Kirk, Darrick Jackson, John Tolley, Arvid Straube, Mark Morrison-Reed, Leslie Takahashi, Lee Barker, William Sinkford, and William Schulz), as well as the students at MLTS, for their support, critique, and inspiration.

It was a privilege to work with Reverend Lynda Sutherland on the interviews with people who are "living justly" in their professions. Her gifts as a storyteller are essential in honoring those stories and bringing them to life. I am also indebted to the wisdom and critical insights of

Jennifer Hammer and the outside reviewers of the book. Their critiques were spot-on and essential in making the arguments of the book clearer and stronger.

Finally, I am also deeply grateful for all those who stand and live for justice, who find ways of embodying their commitments to justice, equity, and compassion in their personal, professional, and civic lives.

NOTES

INTRODUCTION

1 Michael Eric Dyson, *Tears We Cannot Stop: A Sermon to White America* (New York: St. Martin's Press, 2017), 3.

2 Iris Marion Young, *Justice and the Politics of Difference*, with a new introduction by Danielle S. Allen (Princeton: Princeton University Press, 2011), 207–227, 41.

3 Ibid., chapter 2.

4 Sharon D. Welch, *A Feminist Ethic of Risk* (Minneapolis, MN: Fortress Press, 1990 and 2000).

5 Carol Lee Sanchez, "Animal, Vegetable, Mineral: The Sacred Connection," in *Ecofeminism and the Sacred*, ed. Carol J. Adams (New York: Continuum, 1993).

6 Robin Wall Kimmerer, *Braiding Sweetgrass: Indigenous Wisdom, Scientific Knowledge, and the Teachings of Plants* (Minneapolis, MN: Milkweed Editions, 2013), 7.

7 Ibid., 377.

8 Ibid.

9 Ibid., 375.

10 Ibid., 308.

11 Thomas E. Mann and Norman J. Ornstein, *It's Even Worse That It Was: How the American Constitutional System Collided with the New Politics of Extremism. New and Expanded Edition* (New York: Basic Books, 2016); E. J. Dionne Jr., Thomas E. Mann, and Norman J. Ornstein, *One Nation after Trump: A Guide for the Perplexed, the Disillusioned, the Desperate, and the Not-Yet-Deported* (New York: St. Martin's Press, 2017).

12 Dionne, Mann and Ornstein, *One Nation after Trump*, 288.

CHAPTER 1. A DECLARATION OF INTERDEPENDENCE

1 According to Marc J. Hetherington and Jonathan Weiler, "there are . . . fewer Americans at the nonauthoritarian pole than at the authoritarian pole and the center of gravity of the distribution remains on the authoritarian side of the scale" (*Authoritarianism and Polarization in American Politics* [New York: Cambridge University Press], 2009), 62. In their 2006 study, only about 25% of the population was solidly nonauthoritarian (51).

2 In "The Rise of American Authoritarianism," Amanda Taub, writing for *Vox*, March 1, 2016, provides a summary of the conclusions drawn by Hetherington and Weiler in their 2009 study, *Authoritarianism and Polarization in American*

Politics: "Their book concluded that the GOP, by positioning itself as the party of traditional values and law and order, had unknowingly attracted what would turn out to be a vast and previously bipartisan population of Americans with authoritarian tendencies. This trend had been accelerated in recent years by demographic and economic changes such as immigration, which 'activated' authoritarian tendencies, leading many Americans to seek out a strongman leader who would preserve a status quo they feel is under threat and impose order on a world they perceive as increasingly alien. . . . Trump embodies the classic authoritarian leadership style: simple, powerful and punitive" (4).

3 Hetherington and Weiler, (33–34). Can authoritarians be leftist, or are they always conservative? Hetherington and Weiler, along with Karen Stenner, make a distinction between authoritarianism and conservatism. Stenner makes a distinction between authoritarianism and "status quo conservatism," "an enduring inclination to favor stability and preservation of the status quo over social change" and "laissez-faire conservatism—a persistent preference for a free market and limited government intervention in the economy" (Stenner, *The Authoritarian Dynamic* [Cambridge: Cambridge University Press, 2005], 86—see also chapters five and six). Hetherington and Weiler claim that while there may well have been an authoritarianism of the left, when "Stalinism and Maoism were major forces in world politics, with nontrivial followings in Western liberal democracies," this authoritarianism no longer exists in a politically relevant way: "Those movements, animated by rigidity, varying degrees of ethnocentrism, political intolerance, and intolerance of ambiguity, could fairly be said to share many of the characteristics associated with authoritarianism of the right. However, Stalinism and Maoism, outside of North Korea, are long dead" (42).

4 "We find that authoritarianism can provide the most complete account of intolerance, explaining around 32 percent of the variance in intolerance of difference expressed across three decades of U.S. history. That is to say, fundamental orientations toward oneness and sameness, reflected by nothing more than preferences on whether children should be obedient, neat, and well-mannered, account for almost a third of the variance in contemporary opinion on such issues as interracial marriage and residential segregation; civil rights, censorship, and freedom of speech and assembly; pornography, homosexuality, and compulsory school prayer; gun ownership, aggressive policing, and capital punishment" (Stenner, *Authoritarian Dynamic*, 194).

5 For a further exploration of these issues, see the works of Carol Anderson, *White Rage: The Unspoken Truth of Our Racial Divide* (New York: Bloomsbury, 2016); Ibram X. Kendi, *Stamped from the Beginning: The Definitive History of Racist Ideas in America* (New York: Nation Books, 2016); Anthony Pinn, *When Colorblindness Isn't the Answer: Humanism and the Challenge of Race* (Durham, NC: Pitchstone Publishing, 2017); Sharon D. Welch, "Now. Next: Confronting the Past and Shaping the Future," in *Religion in the Age of Obama*, ed. Anthony Pinn and Juan Floyd-Thomas (forthcoming).

6 Stenner, *Authoritarian Dynamic*, 13, 7–8, 18.

7 Ibid., 14–15.

8 Ibid., 330.

9 Ibid., 335.

10 Taub, 21.

11 For Stenner, another way of measuring the same dynamic is not to ask about child-rearing values per se, but "by subject's choices of the word that 'appeals to you more' . . . predispositions toward authoritarianism were indicated here simply by their varying inclinations to prefer the words 'obey,' 'rules,' and 'obedience,' over 'question,' 'progress,' and 'curiosity'" (Stenner, *Authoritarian Dynamic*, 53).

12 This is the four-term authoritarianism index introduced by the NES (National Election Study) in 1992. Hetherington and Weiler (*Authoritarianism and Polarization*, 48–49) correlated responses to this scale with Feldman's 2003 Social Conformity-Autonomy Scale and the RWA (Right-Wing Authoritarianism) scale.

13 For a rich description of the ethical challenges and political power of cohesive communities based on interdependence and collective problem-solving, see Miguel De La Torre, *Latina/o Social Ethics: Moving beyond Eurocentric Moral Thinking* (Waco, TX: Baylor University Press, 2010); Patricia Hill Collins, *Fighting Words: Black Women and the Search for Justice* (Minneapolis: University of Minnesota Press, 1998); Monica A. Coleman, *Making a Way Out of No Way: A Womanist Theology* (Minneapolis, MN: Fortress Press, 2008); Karen Baker-Fletcher and Garth Kasimu Baker-Fletcher, *My Sister, My Brother: Womanist and Xodus God-Talk* (Maryknoll, NY: Orbis Books, 1997); Thomas King, *The Truth about Stories: A Native Narrative* (Minneapolis: University of Minnesota Press, 2003); Kimmerer, *Braiding Sweetgrass*.

14 Stenner, *Authoritarian Dynamic*, 229–231.

15 Ibid., 198–238.

16 Jeffrey S. Sinn and Matthew W. Hayes, "Replacing the Moral Foundations: An Evolutionary-Coalitional Theory of Liberal-Conservative Differences," *International Society of Political Psychology* 20, no. 20 (2016): 1.

17 Ibid., 8, 10.

18 Ibid., 11–12.

19 Ibid., 16.

20 Ibid., 5.

21 Ibid., 4.

22 Ibid., 17.

23 We will take up this challenge directly in chapter seven.

24 Van Jones, *The Green Collar Economy: How One Solution Can Fix Our Two Biggest Problems* (New York: Harper One, 2008), 22.

25 Ibid., 22–23.

26 Ta-Nehisi Coates, *Between the World and Me* (New York: Spiegel and Grau, 2015), 98–99.

27 Ibid., 143, 146.

28 Ibid., 108.
29 Ibid., 151.
30 Anthony B. Pinn, "On Struggle in Our Historical Moment," *Huffington Post*, July 12, 2016. www.huffingtonpost.com.
31 Miguel De La Torre, *Embracing Hopelessness* (Minneapolis, MN: Fortress Press, 2017), 155.
32 "I initially estimated a total of 30,000 environmental organizations around the globe; when I added social justice and indigenous peoples' rights organizations, the number exceeded 100,000. . . . I now believe there are over one—and maybe even two—million organizations working toward ecological sustainability and social justice." Paul Hawken, *Blessed Unrest: How the Largest Social Movement in History Is Restoring Grace, Justice and Beauty to the World* (New York: Penguin Books, 2007), 2, 1–26.
33 Ibid., 12.
34 For a thorough discussion of the genesis of the Occupy movement and an exploration of its implications for ongoing political activism, see the book by Micah White, one of the founders of the Occupy movement, *The End of Protest: A New Playbook for Revolution* (Toronto: Alfred A. Knopf, 2016), 1, 22.
35 Charles M. Blow, "Occupy Wall Street Legacy," *New York Times*, September 13, 2013.
36 Chicago Council on Global Affairs, "Cities Drive the World: What Drives the World's Cities?," May 27–29, 2015, www.chicagoforum.org. Accessed May 27, 2015. The panel brought together expertise from both the world of business and the academy: Richard Burdett, professor, Urban Studies and director of LSE Cities and the Urban Age Programme, London School of Economics; Jeanne Gang, founder and principal, Studio Gang Architects; Francisco Gonzalez-Pulido, president and chief of design, JAHN; William Reilly, senior advisor, TPG Capital.
37 Ibid.
38 Theaster Gates, https://rebuild-foundation.org; Ben Austen, "The Opportunity Artist," *New York Times Magazine*, December 22, 2013, 31.
39 This issue of social equity and inclusion was explicitly addressed as well in a panel on "Inclusive Cities: Poverty, Youth, and Immigration." Here the questions were compelling and clear: "What policies have cities adopted to encourage a culture of inclusion so that their populations are free from discrimination based on age, gender, race, ethnicity, socioeconomic status, disabilities, or special needs? How are global cities managing the challenges and opportunities presented by such a socially and economically diverse population? What is the economic benefit to the city to invest in inclusive policies?" See more at Chicago Council on Global Affairs, "Cities Drive the World: What Drives the World's Cities?," May 27–29, 2015, www.chicagoforum.org. Accessed May 27, 2015.
40 Ibid.
41 "This year's IDEAS CITY Festival will take place May 28–30 and centers on the theme of The Invisible City. Dozens of artists, one hundred organizations, and

tens of thousands of visitors will come together to explore questions of transparency and surveillance, citizenship and representation, expression and suppression, participation and dissent, and the enduring quest for visibility in the city. The Festival will kick off with a series of talks, panels, discussions, and short films at the Great Hall at Cooper Union. Speakers will include some of the world's most forward-thinking visionaries, who will discuss key civic issues and formulate action for the city of tomorrow." New Museum, "The Ideas City Festival, May 28–30, 2015," www.ideas-city.org, accessed May 28, 2015.

42 Ibid.

43 J. K. Gibson-Graham, *A Post-Capitalist Politics* (Minneapolis: University of Minnesota Press, 2006), 80–81.

44 Ibid., 88.

45 Ibid., 159.

46 J. Gregory Dees, "The Meaning of 'Social Entrepreneurship,'" original draft: October 31, 1998; reformatted and revised: May 30, 2001. Paper funded by the Kaufman Foundation.

47 Schumpeter, "Gregory Dees: Social Capitalist," *Economist*, December 2, 2013. www.economist.com.

48 Social Enterprise Alliance, "The Case for Social Enterprise Alliance," https://se-alliance.org. Accessed December 26, 2013.

49 B Impact Assessment, "Measure What Matters: Your Company's Social and Environmental Impact," https://bimpactassessment.net. Accessed January 23, 2018.

50 Benefit Corporation, "Benefit Corporation and Certified B Corps," http://benefit-cor.net, accessed January 23, 2018; and Jonathan Storper, "What's the Difference between a B Corp and a Benefit Corporation?" https://consciouscompanymideal.com.

51 Storper, "What's the Difference between a B Corp and a Benefit Corporation?"

52 Certified B Corp, "The B Corp Declaration: The Declaration of Interdependence." https://www.bcorporation.net/what-are-b-corps/the-b-corp-declaration. Accessed May 1, 2018.

53 William F. Schulz and Chuck Spence, *Engagement, Innovation, and Impact: UUSC 2012 Annual Report* (Cambridge, MA: Unitarian Universalist Service Committee, 2012), 2.

54 Hawken, *Blessed Unrest*, 15.

55 Ibid.

56 Michel Bachmann, "How the Hub Found Its Center," *Stanford Social Innovation Review* 12, no. 1 (Winter 2014): 22–27.

57 Impact Hub, "Our Global Network," https://islington.impacthub.net. Accessed January 23, 2018.

58 William F. Schulz, syllabus for "Problems in Public Ethics," Meadville Lombard Theological School. Chicago, Illinois: July 2016.

59 In *Social Ethics in the Making*, his comprehensive study of the history and contemporary trajectory of social ethics, Gary Dorrien describes the way in

which social ethics weaves together religiously based moral convictions and the best social science of the time: "To learn patiently what *is*—and to promote diligently what *should* be—this is the double duty of all of the social sciences. The founders of social ethics believed in that double duty. The crucial thing was to hold together the *is* and the *ought*. On the other hand, social scientists had very little social agency besides writing books. To make real impact on American society, the social sciences and Christian ethics had to be fused together, mobilizing the churches to promote progressive social change" (18). This book is grounded in that tradition, yet, as mentioned earlier, in moving from "is to ought to how," and in the exploration of how to live out the mandates of social justice, it draws as much on the social sciences as the founders of the discipline did in their delineations of the "is" and "ought." Gary Dorrien, *Social Ethics in the Making: Interpreting an American Tradition* (Oxford: Wiley-Blackwell, 2011), 18 and chapter one.

60 Johnny Bernard Hill, *Prophetic Rage: A Postcolonial Theology of Liberation* (Grand Rapids, MI: William B. Eerdmans, 2013), 151.

61 Ibid., 155.

62 Peter Heltzel and Alexia Salvatierra, *Faith-Rooted Organizing: Mobilizing the Church in Service to the World* (Downers Grove, IL: Intervarsity Press, 2014), 33.

63 Ibid., 30.

64 Ibid., 65.

65 Ibid., 106–122.

66 Van Jones, with Ariane Conrad, *Rebuild the Dream* (New York: Nation Books, 2012), xvi–xvii.

CHAPTER 2. "THE LIGHTNING OF POSSIBLE STORMS"

1 Michel Foucault, in an interview for *Le Monde* conducted on April 6–7, 1980 by Christian Delacampagne. Foucault opted to interview under anonymity, going by "The Masked Philosopher." Interview reprinted in *Michel Foucault, Ethics: Subjectivity and Truth, Essential Works of Foucault (1954–1984), vol.1,* ed. Paul Rabinow (New York: New Press, 1997), 323.

2 Abhijit V. Banerjee and Esther Duflo, *Poor Economics: A Radical Rethinking of the Way to Fight Global Poverty* (New York: Public Affairs, 2011), 1–16, 267–273.

3 Maria J. Stephan directs the Program on Nonviolent Action at the U.S. Institute of Peace and holds an MA and PhD from the Fletcher School of Law and Diplomacy. Erica Chenoweth is professor and associate dean for research at the Josef Korbel School of International Studies at the University of Denver, and associate senior researcher at the Peace Research Institute in Oslo. She holds an MA and PhD in political science from the University of Colorado.

4 Erica Chenoweth and Maria J. Stephan, *Why Civil Resistance Works: The Strategic Logic of Nonviolent Conflict* (New York: Columbia University Press, 2011), 6.

5 Ibid., 69, 7.

6 Ibid., 233–236.

7 Kimmerer, *Braiding Sweetgrass*, 7.
8 Ackerman wrote his dissertation with Gene Sharp, and Ackerman was the dissertation advisor for Stephan. Chenoweth works with Ackerman and DuVall at the International Center on Nonviolent Conflict (Chenoweth and Stephan, *Why Civil Resistance Works*, xv, xiii).
9 Although the uprisings of the Arab Spring may have seemed spontaneous, they emerged from intensive and disciplined study of the techniques of nonviolence. Young activists in Tunisia and Egypt became aware of the strategies of nonviolence through the work of other young activists in Serbia, who themselves had studied and utilized the work of Gene Sharp. The campaigns in Serbia were far more effective than those in the Arab Spring, and studies are still going on about what led to the success of the former and the stalemate, if not complete failure, of the latter.

   On February 17, 2011, Sheryl Gay Stolberg reported the assessment of the importance of Sharp's ideas by Dalia Ziada, an Egyptian blogger and activist who attended trainings led by the International Center on Nonviolent Conflict. Sharp's claim that "advancing freedom takes careful strategy and meticulous planning" is advice that Ms. Ziada said resonated among youth leaders in Egypt. Peaceful protest is best, says Sharp, not for any moral reasons, but because violence provokes autocrats to crack down. "If you fight with violence," Sharp said, "you are fighting with your enemy's best weapon, and you may be a brave but dead hero." Sheryl Gay Stolberg, "Shy U.S. Intellectual Created Playbook Used in a Revolution," *New York Times*, February 17, 2011, A1, A11.
10 Gene Sharp, Albert Einstein Institute: Research. Publications and Consultations on Nonviolent Struggle, www.aeinstein.org.
11 Chenoweth and Stephan, *Why Civil Resistance Works*, 220–221.
12 Ibid., 11, 91.
13 Ibid., 197.
14 Ibid., 43.
15 Ibid., 59–60.
16 Ibid., 213–214.
17 Ibid., 207.
18 Schulz's 2011 address was also published as William F. Schulz, "The Virtuous Circle: Making Justice Happen," in *What Torture Taught Me: And Other Reflections on Justice and Theology* (Boston: Skinner House Books, 2013), 29.
19 Ibid., 30.
20 Ibid., 31.
21 Ibid. 40.
22 Ibid., 42.
23 Gustavo Gutiérrez, *A Theology of Liberation: History, Politics and Salvation*, trans. and ed. Sister Caridad Inda and John Eagleson (Maryknoll, NY: Orbis Books, 1973), 275.
24 Eldar Shafir, ed., *The Behavioral Foundations of Public Policy* (Princeton, NJ: Princeton University Press, 2013), 325–326.

25 Kwame Anthony Appiah, *The Honor Code: How Moral Revolutions Happen* (New York: W. W. Norton and Company, 2010).

26 Ibid., xii.

27 Ibid., xii, 170.

28 Ibid., 161–162.

29 Ibid., 109. "To understand the abolitionist movement we need first to grasp that it required more than the conviction that slavery was morally wrong. What we have to explain here, as with foot binding, is why, in the political life of the nation, people came to act on the conviction. For anti-slavery sentiments were widely diffused well before the abolitionist movement really took off" (ibid., 108).

30 Ibid., 111.

31 Ibid., 112.

32 Ibid., 170–171.

33 Ibid., 105.

34 William F. Schulz, *In Our Own Best Interests: How Defending Human Rights Benefits Us All* (Boston: Beacon Press, 2001).

35 Steven Pinker, *The Better Angels of Our Nature: Why Violence Has Declined* (New York: Viking, 2011), xv.

36 Ibid., xxv–xxvi, 680–681.

37 Ibid., 692.

38 Ibid., 671. Italics mine.

39 Steven Pinker, *Enlightenment Now: The Case for Reason, Science, Humanism, and Progress* (New York: Viking Press, 2018), 344–345.

40 Pinker seems certain that the negative trends of 2016–2017 are temporary setbacks (344). Yet he fails to take on the use of new media to directly counter two core forces of the Enlightenment, the expansion of the circle of sympathy and the escalator of reason (349). He also assumes that authoritarian populism worldwide is limited to older populations and does not address ongoing attempts to actively recruit young people by those who explicitly advocate white nationalism and American exceptionalism. For a cogent study of the latter as expressed in the work of Turning Point USA, see Jane Mayer, "A Conservative Nonprofit That Seeks to Transform College Campuses Faces Allegations of Racial Bias and Illegal Campaign Activity," *New Yorker*, December 21, 2017. Equally troubling is that Pinker seemingly succumbs to one of the drivers of authoritarian populism and rising racism, sexism and homophobia: the idea that genuine equality is a "zero-sum game" (31). In mistakenly saying that the left wants "a forced egalitarianism," he misses the real goal of achieving generative interdependence and mutual flourishing (357).

41 Pinker, *Better Angels of Our Nature*, 123.

42 Patrisse Khan-Cullors and Asha Bandele, *When They Call Me a Terrorist: A Black Lives Matter Memoir* (New York: St. Martin's Press, 2017); Christopher J. Lebron, *The Making of Black Lives Matter: A Brief History of an Idea* (Oxford: Oxford University Press, 2017).

43 Carl Hulse, "Unlikely Cause Unites the Left and the Right: Justice Reform," *New York Times*, February 18, 2015.

44 Jon Swaine, Paul Lewis, and Dan Roberts, "Grand Jury Declines to Charge Darren Wilson for Killing Michael Brown," *Guardian*, November 25, 2014, www.theguardian.com. For a full discussion of the protests and organizing following the killing of Michael Brown, see Leah Gunning Francis, *Ferguson and Faith: Sparking Leadership and Awakening Community* (St. Louis, MO: Chalice Press, 2015).

45 Juan Gonzalez and Amy Goodman, interview with Michelle Alexander, *Democracy Now*, March 4, 2015. www.democracynow.

46 "One Year Later, Still Seeing Wrongs," *New York Times*, August 10, 2015, A11.

47 Vern Redekop and Shirley Paré, *Beyond Control: A Mutual Respect Approach to Protest-Crowd Relations* (New York: Bloomsbury Academic, 2010).

48 Ibid., 139.

49 Curtis D. Hardin and Mahzarin R. Banaji, "The Nature of Implicit Prejudice: Implications for Personal and Public Policy," in *The Behavioral Foundations of Public Policy*, ed. Eldar Shafir, 17 (Princeton, NJ: Princeton University Press, 2013).

50 Kevin Fagan, "With Body Camera's Rolling, Police Use Less Force," *San Francisco Chronicle*, May 10, 2015.

51 For an in-depth study of what is entailed in criminal justice reform, see Barack Obama, "The President's Role in Advancing Criminal Justice Reform," *Harvard Law Review*, January 5, 2017; Final Report of the President's Task Force on 21st Century Policing, May 2015; Gerhardstein and Branch Co. LPA, Police Reform Toolkit, www.gbfirm.com.

52 Redekop and Paré, *Beyond Control*, 11–16.

53 Ibid., 96–102.

54 Ibid.

55 Theophus H. Smith, *Conjuring Culture: Biblical Formations of Black America* (New York: Oxford University Press, 1994), 145.

56 Redekop and Paré, *Beyond Control*, 140–153.

57 Pinker, *Better Angels of Our Nature*, 671.

58 Ibid., 175.

59 Ibid., 590.

60 Ibid., 689–690.

61 Ibid, 691.

62 Ibid., xxvi.

63 Ibid., 683.

64 Ibid., 123.

65 Ibid., 688.

66 Charles M. Blow, "In Defense of the Truth," *New York Times*, September 4, 2017, A 21.

67 Pinker, *Better Angels of Our Nature*, xxvi.

68 Daniel Kahneman, *Thinking, Fast and Slow* (New York: Farrar, Straus and Giroux, 2011), 3, 417.

69 Ibid., 418.
70 Ibid., 3–4.
71 Ibid., 10, 8, 411, 418.
72 Daniel Kahneman, foreword to *The Behavioral Foundations of Public Policy*, ed. Eldar Shafir (Princeton: Princeton University Press, 2013), vii.
73 Ibid., ix.
74 Guy B. Adams and Danny L. Balfour, *Unmasking Administrative Evil*, rev. ed. (London: M. E. Sharpe, 2004), 9 and 4.
75 Ibid., 10.
76 Ibid., 151.
77 Ibid., xxii.
78 Matthew Bishop and Michael Green, *Philanthrocapitalism: How Giving Can Save the World* (New York: Bloomsbury Press, 2009).
79 Ibid., 67.
80 Ibid., 73.
81 Ibid., 204.
82 From the toolkit entitled "Learning Community on Taking Action to Stop Racist Policing in Our Cities and Towns": "Led by [Unitarian Universalist] leading civil rights attorneys Al and Adam Gerhardstein and community advocates, your team will receive hands-on, practical mentoring on how to keep your community safer by eliminating racial profiling and reducing arrests and police violence. Locally-based teams will learn how to address racially-biased policing." For a description of the range of Alphonse Gerhardstein's work for criminal justice reform, see www.uua.org.

CHAPTER 3. "GO SOCIAL, GO GREEN"

1 In this book my focus is on the ethical challenges and opportunities for consumers, investors, workers, managers, and owners to live out an economy of equity and environmental responsibility. For a thorough exploration of the ethical challenges and opportunities for professional economists, see the groundbreaking work of George F. De Martino. In his 2011 book, *The Economist's Oath*, he lays out the case for economists to forthrightly name core ethical imperatives of challenging "oppression, inequality and injustice." He also calls economists to remain "alert to the dangers of economic experimentation . . . and to . . . anticipate and prepare for unintended consequences" (George F. DeMartino, *The Economist's Oath: On the Need for and Content of Professional Economic Ethics* [Oxford: Oxford University Press, 2011]), 232) This work has been fundamentally expanded in the influential volume that he edited with Deirdre N. McCloskey, *The Oxford Handbook of Professional Economic Ethics*. In that book, over 40 professional economists take up just this challenge. George F. DeMartino and Deirdre N. McCloskey, *The Oxford Handbook of Professional Economic Ethics* (Oxford: Oxford University Press, 2016).
2 William D. Eggers and Paul MacMillan, *The Solution Revolution: How Business, Government, and Social Enterprises Are Teaming Up to Solve Society's Toughest Problems* (Boston: Harvard Business Review Press, 2013), 3.

3   Bishop and Green, *Philanthrocapitalism*, 175.

4   Andrew Kassoy, Bart Houlahan, and Jay Coen Gilbert, the founders of B Lab, posted "An Open Letter to Business Leaders" on February 6, 2017. https:// bthechange.com. Accessed May 1, 2018.

5   Ibid.

6   Roger L. Martin and Sally R. Osberg, *Getting beyond Better: How Social Entrepreneurship Works* (Boston: Harvard Business Review, 2015), 7–11.

7   Ibid., 8–9.

8   Ibid., 7–8.

9   Ibid., 9–11.

10 Interview conducted and vignette written by Lynda Sutherland.

11 Interview conducted by Lynda Sutherland and Sharon Welch, and vignette written by Lynda Sutherland.

12 Joseph B. Glackin, "What Exactly Is a L3C?" Boston College Legal Services Lab, March 21, 2017. http://bclawlab.org/eicblog/2017/3/21/what-exactly-is-a-l3c. Accessed April 30, 2018.

13 Marc J. Lane, *The Mission-Driven Venture: Business Solutions to the World's Most Vexing Social Problems* (Hoboken, NJ: Jossey-Bass, 2015), 46–47.

14 One source of such third party certification is the B Lab (www.bcorporation. net), a nonprofit that provides "B(Beneficial) Cor[poration] certification. B Lab's certification process requires that the enterprise be specifically organized, through inclusion of applicable language in its governance documents, of the promotion of a social purpose" (13). While the B Lab is one of the largest organizations providing independent certification, Lane names others that provide the same service: "Global Reporting Initiative (GRI), Ceres Roadmap to Sustainability, Greenseal, Underwriters Laboratories (UL), ISO2600, Green America Business Network." Ibid., 48.

15 Ibid., 97.

16 For a further discussion of Mondragon, see Gibson-Graham, *Post-Capitalist Politics*, chapter five, 101–126.

17 Ibid.

18 Rachel Abrams, "Companies See Benefits in Publicizing Pay Ratios," August 5, 2015, *New York Times*.

19 Lane, *Mission-Driven Venture*, 54.

20 J. Gregory Dees, "The Meaning of 'Social Entrepreneurship,'" original draft: October 31, 1998; reformatted and revised: May 30, 2001. Paper funded by the Kaufman Foundation.

21 Social Enterprise Alliance, "About Social Enterprise Alliance," https://socialenterprise.us, accessed January 1, 2014.

22 Certified B Corporation, "What Are B Corps?," www.bcorporation.net, accessed January 24, 2018.

23 Ibid.

24 B Corporation, "Open Letter to Business Leaders," August 1, 2013, www.bcorporation.net.

25 Ibid.
26 Ibid.
27 Editorial Team, "Organization in the Social Innovation and Sustainable Development Arena: An Overview," in *Solving Problems That Matter and Getting Paid for It: STEM Careers in Social Innovation and Global Sustainable Development*, ed. Khanjan Mehta (State College, PA: Khanjan Mehta, 2015), 35–36.
28 Gibson-Graham, *Post-Capitalist Politics*, chapter four, 79–100.
29 Ibid., xvi.
30 ibid., 80.
31 Ibid., xxxv.
32 Ibid., 2.
33 Ibid., 3.
34 Ibid., xxxv.
35 Ibid., xxxv.
36 Ibid., 98.
37 Ibid., 139–140.
38 Ibid., 140–141.
39 Ibid., 143–144, 159–160.
40 Ibid., 6.
41 Ibid., 7.
42 Lane, *Mission-Driven Venture*, 22.
43 Ibid.
44 Eric Nee, "Learning from Failure," *Stanford Social Innovation Review* (Spring 2015): 4.
45 Michael Cobb, Caitlin Rosser, Andreas Vailakis, with Robert Tomasko, "Case Study: Cause for Reflection," *Stanford Social Innovation Review* 13, no. 2 (Spring 2015): 22.
46 Ibid., 24.
47 Ibid., 23.
48 Ibid., 22–23.
49 Ibid., 23.
50 Banerjee, and Duflo, *Poor Economics*, 14.
51 Ibid., 16.
52 Ibid., 272.
53 Ibid., vii–viii.
54 Ibid., 35.
55 Ibid., 258.
56 Ibid., 259.
57 John Paul Lederach, *The Moral Imagination: The Art and Soul of Building Peace* (Oxford: Oxford University Press, 2010), 58.
58 Interview conducted and vignette written by Lynda Sutherland.
59 Kwok Pui Lan and Joerg Rieger, *Occupy Religion: Theology of the Multitude* (New York: Rowman and Littlefield, 2012), 78–79.

60 Barbara Ehrenreich and John Ehrenreich, "The Professional Managerial Class," in *Radical America* 11, no. 2 (March/April 1977): 13–15, 17–18, 22–26.
61 Ravi Kanbur, "Exposure and Dialogue Programs in the Training of Development Analysts and Practitioners," in *The Oxford Handbook of Professional Economic Ethics*, ed. George F. DeMartino and Deirdre N. McCloskey (New York: Oxford University Press, 2016), 697–713.
62 Eggers and MacMillan, *Solution Revolution*, 33.
63 Ibid., 226.
64 Ibid., 224.
65 Ibid., 224–225.
66 Ibid., 225.
67 Ibid., 228.
68 Marc Lane, *Mission-Driven Venture*, 232.
69 Juliet B. Schor, *Plenitude: The New Economics of True Wealth* (New York: Penguin Press, 2010).

CHAPTER 4. "BELONGING, NOT BELONGINGS"
1 Sanchez, "Animal, Vegetable, Mineral," 215–218.
2 Ibid., 221–227.
3 Kimmerer, *Braiding Sweetgrass*, 304.
4 Ibid., 304–306.
5 Ibid., 307.
6 Ibid.
7 Ibid., 336.
8 Ibid., 382.
9 "We are deluged by information regarding our destruction of the world and hear almost nothing about how to nurture it. It is no surprise then that environmentalism becomes synonymous with dire predictions and powerless feelings. Our natural inclination to do right by the world is stifled, breeding despair when it should be insuring action. . . .
"When my students learn about the latest environmental threat, they are quick to spread the word. They say, 'If only people knew that snow leopards are going extinct,' 'If people only knew that rivers are dying.' If people only knew . . . then they would, what? Stop? I honor their faith in people, but so far the if-then formula isn't working. People do know the consequences of our collective damage, they do know the wages of an extractive economy, but they don't stop. They get very sad, they get very quiet. . . .
"Despair is paralysis. It robs us of agency. It blinds us to our own power and the power of the earth. Environmental despair is a poison every bit as destructive as the methylated mercury in the bottom of Onondaga Lake. . . . Restoration is a powerful antidote to despair. Restoration offers concrete means by which humans can once again enter into positive, creative relationship with the more-than-human world, meeting responsibilities that are simultaneously ma-

terial and spiritual. It's not enough to grieve. It's not enough to just stop doing bad things" (Kimmerer, *Braiding Sweetgrass*, 327–328).

10 Ibid., 371.

11 Ibid., 384.

12 Ibid., 336.

13 Michael Pollan, "Why Bother?," in *Drawdown: The Most Comprehensive Plan Ever Proposed to Reverse Global Warming*, ed. Paul Hawken (New York: Penguin Books, 2017), 52.

14 Hawken, *Drawdown*, 3.

15 Ibid.

16 Ibid., 7.

17 Ibid., vii.

18 Kimmerer, *Braiding Sweetgrass*, 336.

19 Hawken, *Drawdown*, 216.

20 Ibid., x.

21 Ibid., 217.

22 Jones, *Green Collar Economy*, 2.

23 Ibid., 10.

24 Ibid., 22–23.

25 Hawken, *Drawdown*, 217.

26 Ibid., 217.

27 Janine Benyus, "Reciprocity," in *Drawdown*, 215.

28 Hawken, *Drawdown*, 15.

29 Ibid., 22.

30 Mark Hertsgaard, "The Man Who Stopped the Desert," in *Drawdown*, 118–119.

31 Ibid., 118, 120.

32 Hawken, *Drawdown*, 170.

33 Ibid., 188.

34 Ibid., 189.

35 Ibid., xi.

36 Interview conducted by Sharon Welch and Lynda Sutherland. Vignette written by Lynda Sutherland.

37 Juliet B. Schor, *Plenitude: The New Economics of True Wealth* (New York: Penguin Press, 2010), 1.

38 Ibid., 4–7.

39 Ronald Heiftetz, Alexander Grashow, and Marty Linsky, *The Practice of Adaptive Leadership: Tools and Tactics for Changing Your Organization and the World* (Cambridge: Harvard Business Press, 2009).

40 Schor, *Plenitude*, 13.

41 For further exploration of specific examples of the technical means by which the values of reciprocity can be expressed, see the book edited by Juliet B. Schor and Craig J. Thompson, *Sustainable Lifestyles and the Quest for Plentitude: Case Studies of the New Economy* (New Haven: Yale University Press, 2014).

42 Judith Ramalay, "Plenary Session," Engagement Scholarship Conference, Texas Tech University, Lubbock, Texas, October 9, 2013.

CHAPTER 5. GLOBAL CONNECTIONS AND CULTURAL HUMILITY
1 Andrew Swinard, "Corporate Social Responsibility Is the Millennials' New Religion," *Crain's Business Weekly*, March 25, 2014.
2 Deloitte Millennial Survey 2017, www2.deloitte.com.
3 Engagement Scholarship Consortium, https://engagementscholarship.org.
4 Valerie Paton, "Assessing Engagement and Outreach: Lessons Learned," Engagement Scholarship Conference, Texas Tech University, Lubbock, Texas, October 9, 2013.
5 Peter McPherson, 14th Annual Conference of the Engagement Scholarship Consortium, Awards Presentation, Texas Tech University, October 8, 2013.
6 Valerie Paton, "Assessing Engagement and Outreach."
7 Fourteenth Annual Conference of the Engagement Scholarship Consortium, Awards Presentation, Texas Tech University, October 8, 2013, 2, 4.
8 Ibid., 5.
9 "Welcome to the Dedman College Center for Academic-Community Engagement (ACE)," http:www.smu.edu.
10 Dwight Hopkins, introduction to *Disrupting White Supremacy from Within*, ed. Jennifer Harvey, Karin A. Case, and Robin Hawley Gorsline (Cleveland, OH: Pilgrim Press, 2004), xvii.
11 Ibid., viii.
12 Ibid.
13 Peter Butler, "What Is STEM Anyways?," in *Solving Problems That Matter and Getting Paid for It: STEM Careers in Social Innovation and Global Sustainable Development*, ed. Khanjan Mehta (State College, PA: Khanjan Mehta, 2015).
14 B. L. Ramakrishna, "Changing the Conversation about Engineering in K-12," in Mehta, *Solving Problems That Matter*, 11–12.
15 Mehta, introduction, *Solving Problems That Matter*, xvi.
16 Interview conducted by Sharon Welch and Lynda Sutherland. Vignette written by Lynda Sutherland.
17 Khanjan Mehta, *The Kochia Chronicles: Systemic Challenges and the Foundations of Social Innovation* (State College, PA: Khanjan Mehta, 2013).
18 Phil Weilerstein, "Science and Technology for Societal Impact," in Mehta, *Solving Problems That Matter*, 4.
19 Ibid., 4.
20 Butler, "What Is STEM Anyway?," in Mehta, *Solving Problems That Matter*, 6.
21 Weilerstein, "Science and Technology for Societal Impact," in Mehta, *Solving Problems That Matter*, 5.
22 Stephanie Brown and Virginia Cope, "Global Citizenship for the Non-traditional Student," *Journal of Community Engagement and Scholarship* 6, no. 1 (September 2013), 29.

23 Ibid., 30.
24 Ibid., 31.
25 Ibid.
26 Ibid., 33.
27 Ibid., 30.
28 Eldar Shafir, ed., *The Behavioral Foundations of Public Policy* (Princeton: Princeton University Press, 2013), 3.
29 Ibid.
30 Hardin and Banaji, "Nature of Implicit Prejudice," 14.
31 Ibid., 23.
32 Ibid., 13.
33 Ibid.
34 Ibid., 14–15.
35 Ibid., 17. Italics mine.
36 Ibid.
37 Ibid., 18.
38 Ibid., 13.
39 Ibid., 24.
40 Shafir, introduction to *Behavioral Foundations of Public Policy*, 3.
41 J. Nicole Shelton, Jennifer A. Richeson, and John F. Dovidio, "Biases in Interracial Interactions: Implications for Social Policy," in *Behavioral Foundations of Public Policy*, 32–33.
42 Ibid., 36, 37, 46.
43 Ibid., 38–39.
44 Ibid., 46.
45 Susan T. Fiske and Linda H. Krieger, "Implications of Unexamined Discrimination: Gender Bias in Employment as a Case Study," in *Behavioral Foundations of Public Policy*, 59, 55.
46 Ibid., 62–63.
47 Ibid., 66.
48 Kendi, *Stamped from the Beginning*, 9.
49 Ibid., 9, 10.
50 Ibid., 10.
51 Ibid., 6.
52 For a further exploration of these dynamics, see my essay "Now. Next: Confronting the Past and Shaping the Future," in *Religion in the Age of Obama*, ed. Anthony Pinn and Juan Floyd-Thomas (forthcoming).
53 Lawrence Kirmeyer, response to Paul Farmer, "An Anthology of Structural Violence: Sidney W. Mintz Lecture for 2001," *Current Anthropology* 45, no 3 (June 2004): 321.
54 Ibid.
55 Ibid.

56 Marc Ellis, *Practicing Exile: The Religious Odyssey of an American Jew* (Minneapolis, MN: Fortress Press, 2002), 260.

57 "Photos Allege Abuse of Iraqis by British Troops," *CNN*, May 1, 2004; http://edition.cnn.com.

58 William F. Schulz, "The Way We Live Now: Security Is a Human Right, Too," *New York Times Sunday Magazine*, April 18, 2004, 1–3. www.nytimes.com.

59 Albert Bandura, "Moral Disengagement in the Perpetration of Inhumanities," *Personality and Social Psychology Review* 3, no. 3 (July 1, 1999): 193–0209.

60 Ibid., 195.

61 Ibid.

62 Ibid., 196–197.

63 The quote by Gonzales occurred after the Bandura article, and can be found in a transcript of the Amy Goodman show of July 1, 2005, www.democracynow.org.

64 Bandura, 197–199.

65 In May 2005, Amnesty International asked for an independent investigation of "the atrocious human rights violations at Abu Ghraib and other detention centers." Alan Crowell, "U.S. Thumbs Its Nose at Rights, Amnesty Says," *New York Times*, May 26, 2005, A8. In June 2005, some Republican members of the Senate, including Lindsey Graham, John McCain, and John Warner, also asked for such an independent investigation. Douglas Jehl, "Some Republicans Seek Prison Abuse Panel," *New York Times*, June 22, 2005, A14. While a few subordinate soldiers were convicted of abuse, no thorough independent investigation has been conducted, nor have charges been brought against those most responsible for such abuses: President George W. Bush, Vice President Dick Cheney, and Secretary of Defense Donald Rumsfeld.

66 Bandura, 199–200.

67 Ibid., 200.

68 Bandura has expanded this argument to address processes of moral disengagement in the entertainment industry, the gun industry, the corporate world, capital punishment, terrorism and counterterrorism, and environmental sustainability. Albert Bandura, *Moral Disengagement: How People Do Harm and Live with Themselves* (New York: Worth Publishers, 2016).

69 Sharon Welch, Nicole Kirk, Mark Hicks, and Amber Dion, Engagement Scholarship Workshop, Edmonton, Canada, October 6, 2014.

70 Paul Fitzgerald, "Doing Theology in the City," *Cross Currents* (Spring 2001), p. 89. Michael Hogue, "From Resistance to Resurrection: Meadville Lombard's Touch-Point Model of Theological Education," *Theological Education* 48, no 2 (2014): 39, 33–41.

71 Khanjan Mehta, Ruth Mendum, and Careen Yarnal, "Development of an 'Engagement Review Board' for Appropriate and Ethical Community Engagement." Workshop, Engagement Scholarship Consortium, Edmonton, Canada, October 8, 2014. This material is also developed in an article by Eric Obeysekare, Irena Gorski, Khanjan Mehta, and Careen Yarnal, "Equitable Engagement: Building a

Culture of Concern," special conference issue of the *Journal of Community Engagement and Scholarship* (2014).

72 Irena Gorski, Eric Obeysekare, Careen Yarnal, and Khanjan Mehta, "Responsible Engagement: Building a Culture of Concern," *Journal of Community Engagement and Scholarship* 8, no. 2 (2015): 16–25.

73 Ibid.

74 Nicholas Lemann, *Redemption: The Last Battle of the Civil War* (New York: Farrar, Straus and Giroux, 2006); David F. Krugler, *1919, the Year of Racial Violence: How African Americans Fought Back* (New York: Cambridge University Press, 2015); Ta-Nehisi Coates, *We Were Eight Years in Power: An American Tragedy* (New York: One World Publishing, 2017), 186; Anderson, *White Rage*, 42–43.

CHAPTER 6. JUST LIVING

1 Patricia Hill Collins, *Fighting Words: Black Women and the Search for Justice* (Minneapolis: University of Minnesota Press, 1998), 190.

2 Ibid., 187.

3 Ibid., 189–190.

4 Ibid., 190, 191.

5 Ibid., 191.

6 Ibid., 194.

7 Ibid., 200.

8 Barbara A. Holmes, *Liberation and the Cosmos: Conversations with the Elders* (Minneapolis, MN: Fortress Press, 2008), 187, 190–191.

9 Coleman, *Making a Way Out of No Way*, 76.

10 Victor Anderson, *Creative Exchange: A Constructive Theology of African-American Religious Experience* (Minneapolis, MN: Fortress Press, 2008) 132. These authors are explored further in Sharon D. Welch, "Aesthetic Pragmatism and a Third Wave of Radical Politics," in Monica Coleman, *Ain't I a Womanist, Too? Third-Wave Womanist Religious Thought* (Minneapolis, MN: Fortress Press, 2013), 175–186.

11 Niccolò Machiavelli, *The Prince*, trans. W. K. Marriott (1513; reprint, St. Petersburg, FL: Red and Black Publications, 2008), 11.

12 Anna Peterson, *Being Human: Ethics, Environment, and Our Place in the World* (Berkeley: University of California Press, 2001); Wes Jackson, "Toward an Ignorance-Based World View." LR81. Salina, KS: Land Institute, 2011. www.landinstitute.org.

13 Nelson Mandela, *Long Walk to Freedom* (Boston: Little, Brown and Company, 1994), 593.

14 For a fuller exploration of using the logic of jazz as a model for constructive social engagement, see Sharon D. Welch, *Sweet Dreams in America: Making Ethics and Spirituality Work* (New York: Routledge, 1999).

15 Patrick Chamoiseau, *Texaco*, trans. Rose-Myriam Rejois and Val Vinokurove (New York: Pantheon Books, 1997), 119.

16 Dan Olweus and Susan Limber, "Bullying in School: Evaluation and Dissemination of the Olweus Bullying Prevention Program," *American Journal of Orthopsychiatry* 80, no. 1 (2010): 124–134.

17 Maria M. Ttofi and David Farrington, "Effectiveness of School-Based Programs to Reduce Bullying: A Systematic and Meta-analytic Review," *Journal of Experimental Criminology* 7 (2011): 27–56; Joshua R. Polanin, Dorothy L. Espelage, and Therese D. Pigott, "A Meta-Analysis of School-Based Bullying Prevention Programs' Effects on Bystander Intervention Behavior," *Social Psychology Review* 41, no. 1 (2012): 47–65.

18 David Remnick, "Obama Reckons with a Trump Presidency," *New Yorker*, November 28, 2016.

19 Ibid., 7–11. "The new media ecosystem 'means everything is true and nothing is true,'" Obama told me later. "'An explanation of climate change from a Nobel Prize-winning physicist looks exactly the same on your Facebook page as the denial of climate change by somebody on the Koch brothers' payroll. And the capacity to disseminate misinformation, wild conspiracy theories, to paint the opposition in wildly negative light without any rebuttal—that has accelerated in ways that much more sharply polarize the electorate'" (8).

20 Patricia Williams, *The Alchemy of Race and Rights: Diary of a Law Professor* (Cambridge: Harvard University Press, 1991), 163.

21 Ibid., 165.

22 Paul Krugman, "In Defense of Obama," *Rolling Stone*, October 8, 2014. www.rollingstone.com.

23 While proofreading the manuscript I discovered that Perkins' success with the work week was not repeated with Social Security. "Agricultural and domestic workers were exempted, against Frances's wishes. . . . Therefore, blacks and Hispanics, who were more likely to be farm workers or domestic servants were disproportionately excluded. . . ." Kristen Downey, *The Woman behind the New Deal: The Life and Legacy of Frances Perkins—Social Security, Unemployment Insurance, and the Minimum Wage* (New York: Anchor Books, 2009), 41–45, 241.

24 Solutions Journalism Network, "What Is Solutions Journalism?" www.solutionsjournalism.org. Accessed April 20, 2015.

25 In "Solutions Journalism Imposters," the Solutions Journalism Network has some suggestions for reporters: In addition to 'What are the results?," ask "Which measurements matter most and what are they?"
    Organizations can throw metrics your way all day, but if they don't represent the most critical measurement of change, you can get distracted.
    In addition to "What do the experts think?," ask "What do the people directly affected by this model think?"
    Whenever possible, have real conversations with folks on the ground in addition to some of the usual suspects (think-tank wonks, professors, thought leaders).

Replace "Is it working?" with "In what ways is it succeeding and in what ways is it failing?"
Social change is complex. Our reporting should reflect that complexity. Solutions Journalism Network, "Solutions Journalism Imposters," http://solutionsjournalism.org, accessed April 20, 2015.

26 Ibid.

27 Richard Pérez-Peña and Timothy Williams, "Through a Lens, Views of Police Forces in Flux," *New York Times*, July 31, 2015, A15.

28 Nicolas Bourriaud, *The Radicant* (New York: Lucas and Sternberg, 2009), 17.

29 Ibid., 40, 22.

30 Claire Bishop, "Antagonism and Relational Aesthetics," *October* 110 (Autumn 2004): 51–79.

31 Leslie Kaufman, "In Kansas, Climate Skeptics Embrace Cleaner Energy," *New York Times*, October 18, 2010.

32 Nicolas Bourriaud, *Postproduction: Culture as Screenplay: How Art Reprograms the World* (New York: Lukas and Sternberg, 2002), 69.

33 Nicholas Bourriaud, *Relational Aesthetics* (Dijon: Les Presses du Reel, 2002), 103.

34 Ibid.

35 Ibid., 52.

36 Nikil Saval, "Three Artists Who Think Outside the Box," *New York Times*, December 6, 2015.

37 Ben Austen, "The Opportunity Artist," *New York Times Magazine*, December 22, 2013, 28.

38 Ibid., 31.

39 Ibid., 28.

40 Ibid., 29; Susie Allen, "Theaster Gates Takes New Leap as Arts Pioneer," October 25, 2011, www.uchicago.edu.

41 Ibid.

42 Cassie Walker Burke, "The 100 Most Powerful People in Chicago," *Chicago: The Power Issue*, March 2014, 82.

43 Allen, "Theaster Gates Takes New Leap as Arts Pioneer."

44 Burke, "100 Most Powerful People in Chicago," 82.

45 Interview conducted by Sharon Welch and Lynda Sutherland. Vignette written by Lynda Sutherland.

CONCLUSION

1 Leslie Marmon Silko, "Landscape, History and the Pueblo Imagination," in *The Woman That I Am: The Literature and Culture of Contemporary Women of Color*, ed. D. Soyini Madison (New York: St. Martin's Press, 1994).

2 U.S. Holocaust Museum, "Martin Niemöller: 'First They Came for the Socialists,'" www.ushmm.org, accessed January 24, 2018.

3 Ibid.

4   Megan Garber, "'First They Came': The Poem of the Protests," *Atlantic*, January 29, 2017, https://www.theatlantic.com.

5   For histories of the culture of indigenous peoples in the United States prior to the European conquest, and examinations of that conquest, its ongoing impact, and past and present resistance to it, the following works are a valuable place to begin: James Wilson, *The Earth Shall Weep: A History of Native America* (New York: Grove Press, 1998); Roxanne Dunbar-Ortiz, *An Indigenous Peoples' History of the United States* (Boston: Beacon Press, 2014).

6   Begin this exploration with the pivotal essay by Ta-Nehesi Coates on the importance of learning and responding to this history, "The Case for Reparations," in *We Were Eight Years in Power: An American Tragedy* (New York: One World Publishing 2017), 163–210. For histories of racial domination, see Anderson, *White Rage*; Kendi, *Stamped from the Beginning*; David F. Krugler, *1919, the Year of Racial Violence: How African Americans Fought Back* (New York: Cambridge University Press, 2015); Nicholas Lemann, *Redemption: The Last Battle of the Civil War* (New York: Farrar, Straus and Giroux, 2006). For an example of a detailed study of the history and ongoing impact of slavery and racial discrimination and exploitation, see Tiya Miles, *The Dawn of Detroit: A Chronicle of Slavery and Freedom in the City of the Straits* (New York: New Press, 2017).

7   Grace M. Jantzen, *Becoming Divine: Towards a Feminist Philosophy of Religion* (Bloomington: Indiana University Press, 1999).

8   Jonathan Schell's *The Fate of the Earth* (New York: Alfred A. Knopf, 1982), a detailed account of the devastating impact of a nuclear war on not just human society but on all of life, is as timely now as it was when it was published in 1982. See also the recent exploration of the increasing threat of nuclear war by Elaine Scarry, *Thermonuclear Monarchy: Choosing between Democracy and Doom* (New York: W. W. Norton and Company, 2014).

9   Kimmerer, *Braiding Sweetgrass*, 368.

10 Michael Hogue, *American Immanence: Democracy for an Uncertain World* (New York: Columbia University Press, 2018), 194.

11 Ina Mae Gaskin, *Spiritual Midwifery* (Summertown, TN: Brook Publishing, 1975).

12 For those who are taking up such work, see the work of the Alliance for Peacebuilding, www.allianceforpeacebuilding.org.

13 William F. Schulz, *What Torture Taught Me and Other Reflections on Justice and Theology* (Boston: Skinner House Books, 2013), xvi.

14 Coates, *Between the World and Me*, 108.

15 Ibid., 151.

16 Ibid., 146.

BIBLIOGRAPHY

Ackerman, Peter, and Jack DuVall. *A Force More Powerful: A Century of Nonviolent Conflict*. New York: Palgrave, 2000.

Ackermann, Peter, and Christopher Kruegler. *Strategic Nonviolent Conflict: The Dynamics of People Power in the Twentieth Century*. Westport, CT: Praeger, 1994.

Adams, Guy B., and Danny L. Balfour. *Unmasking Administrative Evil*. Rev. ed. London: M. E. Sharpe, 2004.

Alexander, Michelle. *The New Jim Crow: Mass Incarceration in the Age of Colorblindness*. New York: New Press, 2011.

Allen, Susie, "Theaster Gates Takes New Leap as Arts Pioneer." October 25, 2011. www.uchicago.edu.

Anderson, Carol. *White Rage: The Unspoken Truth of Our Racial Divide*. New York: Bloomsbury, 2016.

Anderson, Victor. *Creative Exchange: A Constructive Theology of African American Religious Experience*. Minneapolis, MN: Fortress Press, 2008.

Appiah, Kwame Anthony. *The Honor Code: How Moral Revolutions Happen*. New York: W. W. Norton, 2010.

Bachmann, Michel. "How the Hub Found Its Center." *Stanford Social Innovation Review* 12, no. 1 (Winter 2014): 22–27.

Baker-Fletcher, Karen, and Garth Kasimu Baker-Fletcher. *My Sister, My Brother: Womanist and Xodus God-Talk*. Maryknoll, NY: Orbis Books, 1997.

Bandura, Albert. *Moral Disengagement: How People Do Harm and Live with Themselves*. New York: Worth Publishers, 2016.

———. "Moral Disengagement in the Perpetration of Inhumanities." *Personality and Social Psychology Review* 3, no. 3 (July 1, 1999): 8662–8683.

Banerjee, Abhijit V., and Esther Duflo. *Poor Economics: A Radical Rethinking of the Way to Fight Global Poverty*. New York: Public Affairs, 2011.

Bishop, Claire. "Antagonism and Relational Aesthetics." *October* 110 (Autumn 2004): 51–79.

Bishop, Matthew, and Michael Green. *Philanthrocapitalism: How Giving Can Save the World*. New York: Bloomsbury Press, 2009.

Bourriaud, Nicolas. *Postproduction: Culture as Screenplay: How Art Reprograms the World*. New York: Lukas and Sternberg, 2002.

———. *The Radicant*. New York: Lukas and Sternberg, 2009.

———. *Relational Aesthetics*. Dijon: Les Presses du Reel, 2002.

Brown, Stephanie, and Virginia Cope. "Global Citizenship for the Non-traditional Student." *Journal of Community Engagement and Scholarship* 6, no. 1 (September 2013): 28–36.

Cannon, Katie G. *Black Womanist Ethics*. Atlanta, GA: Scholars Press, 1988.

Chamoiseau, Patrick. *Texaco*. Translated by Rose-Myriam Rejouis and Val Vinokur. New York: Pantheon Books, 1997.

Chenoweth, Erica, and Maria J. Stephan. *Why Civil Resistance Works: The Strategic Logic of Nonviolent Conflict*. New York: Columbia University Press, 2011.

Chicago Council on Global Affairs. "Cities Drive the World: What Drives the World's Cities?" May 27–29, 2015. www.chicagoforum.org. Accessed May 27, 2015.

Coates, Ta-Nehisi. *Between the World and Me*. New York: Spiegel and Grau, 2015.

Cobb, Michael, Caitlin Rosser, Andreas Vailakis, with Robert Tomasko. "Case Study: Cause for Reflection." *Stanford Innovation Review* 13, no. 2 (Spring 2015).

Coleman, Monica A. *Making a Way Out of No Way: A Womanist Theology*. Minneapolis, MN: Fortress Press, 2008.

Collins, Patricia Hill. *Fighting Words: Black Women and the Search for Justice*. Minneapolis: University of Minnesota Press, 1998.

Dees, Gregory J., Jed Emerson, and Peter Economy. *Enterprising Nonprofits: A Toolkit for Social Entrepreneurs*. New York: John Wiley and Sons, 2001.

Delacampagne, Christian. "The Masked Philosopher." In *Michel Foucault, Ethics: Subjectivity and Truth, Essential Works of Foucault (1954–1984), vol.1*, edited by Paul Rabinow. New York: New Press, 1997.

De La Torre, Miguel. *Embracing Hopelessness*. Minneapolis, MN: Fortress Press, 2017.

———. *Latina/o Social Ethics: Moving beyond Eurocentric Moral Thinking*. Waco, TX: Baylor University Press, 2010.

DeMartino, George F. *The Economist's Oath: On the Need for and Content of Professional Economic Ethics*. Oxford: Oxford University Press, 2011.

DeMartino, George F., and Deirdre N. McCloskey. *The Oxford Handbook of Professional Economic Ethics*. New York: Oxford University Press, 2016.

Dionne, Jr., E. J, Norman J. Ornstein, and Thomas E. Mann. *One Nation after Trump*. New York: St. Martin's Press, 2017.

Dorrien, Gary. *Economy, Difference, Empire: Social Ethics for Social Justice*. New York: Columbia University Press, 2010.

———. *Social Ethics in the Making: Interpreting an American Tradition*. Oxford: Wiley-Blackwell, 2011.

Downey, Kristen. *The Woman behind the New Deal: The Life and Legacy of Frances Perkins—Social Security, Unemployment Insurance, and the Minimum Wage*. New York: Anchor Books, 2009.

Dyson, Michael Eric. *Tears We Cannot Stop: A Sermon to White America*. New York: St. Martin's Press, 2017.

Eggers, William D., and Paul MacMillan. *The Solution Revolution: How Business, Government, and Social Enterprises Are Teaming Up to Solve Society's Toughest Problems*. Boston: Harvard Business Review Press, 2013.

Ehrenreich, Barbara, and John Ehrenreich. "The Professional Managerial Class." *Radical America* 11, no. 2 (March/April 1977): 13–15, 17–18, 22–26.

Ellis, Marc. *Practicing Exile: The Religious Odyssey of an American Jew.* Minneapolis, MN: Fortress Press, 2002.

Farmer, Paul. "An Anthology of Structural Violence: Sidney W. Mintz Lecture for 2001." *Current Anthropology* 45, no. 3 (June 2004): 305–325.

Fiske, Susan T., and Linda H. Krieger. "Implications of Unexamined Discrimination: Gender Bias in Employment as a Case Study." In *The Behavioral Foundations of Public Policy*, edited by Eldar Shafir, 52–76. Princeton, NJ: Princeton University Press, 2013.

Frances, Leah Gunning. *Ferguson and Faith: Sparking Leadership and Awakening Community.* St. Louis, MO: Chalice Press, 2015.

Gaskin, Ida Mae. *Spiritual Midwifery.* Tennessee: Brook Publishing, 1975.

Gibson-Graham, J. K. *A Postcapitalist Politics.* Minneapolis: University of Minnesota Press, 2006.

Gorski, I., E. Obeysekare, C. Yarnal, and K. Mehta. "Responsible Engagement: Building a Culture of Concern." *Journal of Community Engagement and Scholarship* 8, no. 2 (2015): 16–25.

Gutiérrez, Gustavo. *A Theology of Liberation: History, Politics and Salvation.* Translated and edited by Caridad Inda and John Eagleson. Maryknoll, NY: Orbis Books, 1973.

Hardin, Curtis D., and Mahzarin R. Banaji. "The Nature of Implicit Prejudice: Implications for Personal and Public Policy." In *The Behavioral Foundations of Public Policy*, edited by Eldar Shafir, 13–31. Princeton, NJ: Princeton University Press, 2013.

Hawken, Paul. *Blessed Unrest: How the Largest Social Movement in History Is Restoring Grace, Justice, and Beauty to the World.* New York: Penguin Books 2007.

———. *Drawdown: The Most Comprehensive Plan Ever Proposed to Reverse Global Warming.* New York: Penguin Books, 2017.

Heifetz, Ronald, Alexander Grashow, and Marty Linsky. *The Practice of Adaptive Leadership: Tools and Tactics for Changing Your Organization and the World.* Cambridge, MA: Harvard Business Press, 2009.

Heltzel, Peter, and Alexia Salvatierra. *Faith-Rooted Organizing: Mobilizing the Church in Service to the World.* Downers Grove, IL: Intervarsity Press, 2014.

Hetherington, Marc J., and Jonathan Weiler. *Authoritarianism and Polarization in American Politics.* New York: Cambridge University Press, 2009.

Hill, Johnny Bernard. *Prophetic Rage: A Postcolonial Theology of Liberation.* Grand Rapids, MI: William B. Eerdmans, 2013.

Hogue, Michael. *American Immanence: Democracy for an Uncertain World.* New York: Columbia University Press, 2018.

———. "From Resistance to Resurrection: Meadville Lombard's TouchPoint Model of Theological Education." *Theological Education* 48, no. 2 (2014): 33–41.

Holmes, Barbara A. *Liberation and the Cosmos: Conversations with the Elders.* Minneapolis, MN: Fortress Press, 2008.

Hopkins, Dwight. "Introduction." In *Disrupting White Supremacy from Within*, edited by Jennifer Harvey, Karin A. Case, and Robin Hawley Gorsline. Cleveland, OH: Pilgrim Press. 2004.

Jackson, Wes. "Toward an Ignorance-Based World View." LR81. Salina, KS: Land Institute, 2011. www.landinstitute.org.

Jantzen, Grace. *Becoming Divine: Towards a Feminist Philosophy of Religion*. Bloomington: Indiana University Press, 1999.

Jones, Van. *The Green Collar Economy: How One Solution Can Fix Our Two Biggest Problems*. New York: HarperOne, 2008.

Jones, Van, and Ariane Conrad. *Rebuild the Dream*. New York: Nation Books, 2012.

Kahneman, Daniel. "Foreword." In *The Behavioral Foundations of Public Policy*. Princeton, NJ: Princeton University Press, 2013.

———. *Thinking, Fast and Slow*. New York: Farrar, Straus and Giroux, 2011.

Kanbur, Ravi. "Exposure and Dialogue Programs in the Training of Development Analysts and Practitioners." In *The Oxford Handbook of Professional Economic Ethics*, edited by George F. DeMartino and Deirdre N. McCloskey, 697–713. New York: Oxford University Press, 2016.

Kaufman, Leslie. "Global Warming? Kansans Scoff, but Conserve." *New York Times*, October 19, 2010, A4. www.nytimes.com.

Kendi, Ibram X. *Stamped from the Beginning: The Definitive History of Racist Ideas in America*. New York: Nation Books, 2016.

Khan-Cullors, Patrisse, and Asha Bandele. *When They Call Me a Terrorist: A Black Lives Matter Memoir*. New York: St. Martin's Press. 2017.

King, Thomas. *The Truth about Stories: A Native Narrative*. Minneapolis: University of Minnesota Press, 2003.

Kimmerer, Robin Wall. *Braiding Sweetgrass: Indigenous Wisdom, Scientific Knowledge, and the Teachings of Plants*. Minneapolis, MN: Milkweed Editions, 2013.

Krugler, David. *1919, the Year of Racial Violence: How African Americans Fought Back*. New York: Cambridge University Press, 2015.

Krugman, Paul. "In Defense of Obama." *Rolling Stone*, October 8, 2014. www.rollingstone.com.

Lane, Marc J. *The Mission-Driven Venture: Business Solutions to the World's Most Vexing Social Problems*. Hoboken, NJ: Jossey-Bass, 2015.

Lebron, Christopher J. *The Making of Black Lives Matter: A Brief History of an Idea*. Oxford: Oxford University Press. 2017.

Lederach, John Paul. *The Moral Imagination: The Art and Soul of Building Peace*. Oxford: Oxford University Press, 2010.

Lemann, Nicholas. *Redemption: The Last Battle of the Civil War*. New York: Farrar, Straus and Giroux, 2006.

Machiavelli, Niccolò. *The Prince*. Translated by W. K. Marriott. 1513; reprint, St. Petersburg, FL: Red and Black Publications, 2008.

Mandela, Nelson. *Long Walk To Freedom: The Autobiography of Nelson Mandela*. Boston: Little, Brown and Company, 1994.

Martin, Roger L., and Sally R. Osberg. *Getting beyond Better: How Social Entrepreneurship Works*. Cambridge: Harvard Business Review Press, 2015.

Mayer, Jane. "A Conservative Nonprofit That Seeks to Transform College Campuses Faces Allegations of Racial Bias and Illegal Campaign Activity." *New Yorker*, December 21, 2017.

Mehta, Khanjan. *The Kochia Chronicles: Systemic Challenges and the Foundations of Social Innovation*. State College, PA: Khanjan Mehta, 2013.

———. "Organization in the Social Innovation and Sustainable Development Arena: An Overview." In *Solving Problems That Matter and Getting Paid for It: STEM Careers in Social Innovation and Global Sustainable Development*, edited by Khanjan Mehta. State College, PA: Khanjan Mehta, 2015.

Nee, Eric. "Learning from Failure." *Stanford Innovation Review* (Spring 2015).

Niebuhr, Reinhold. *Moral Man and Immoral Society: A Study in Ethics and Politics*. Louisville: Westminster Knox Press, 2001.

Obeysekare, Eric, Irena Gorski, Khanjan Mehta, and Careen Yarnal. "Equitable Engagement: Building a Culture of Concern." Special conference issue of *Journal of Community Engagement and Scholarship* (2014).

Olweus, Dan, and Susan B. Limber. "Bullying in School: Evaluation and Dissemination of the Olweus Bullying Prevention Program." *American Journal of Orthopsychiatry* 80, no. 1 (2010): 124–134.

Pinker, Steven. *The Better Angels of Our Nature: Why Violence Has Declined*. New York: Viking, 2011.

Pinker, Steven. *Enlightenment Now: The Case for Reason, Science, Humanism, and Progress*. New York: Viking, 2018.

Pinn, Anthony B. "On Struggle in Our Historical Moment." *Huffington Post*, July 21, 2016. www.huffingtonpost.com.

———. *When Colorblindness Isn't the Answer: Humanism and the Challenge of Race*. Durham, NC: Pitchstone Publishing, 2017.

Polanin, Joshua R., Dorothy L. Espelage, and Therese D. Pigott. "A Meta-analysis of School-Based Bullying Prevention Programs' Effects on Bystander Intervention Behavior." *School Psychology Review* 41, no. 1 (2012): 47–65.

Redekop, Vern, and Shirley Paré. *Beyond Control: A Mutual Respect Approach to Protest-Crowd Relations*. New York: Bloomsbury Academic, 2010.

Rieger, Joerg, and Kwok Pui-Lan. *Occupy Religion: Theology of the Multitude*. New York: Rowman and Littlefield, 2012.

Rosenberg, Paul. "The Moral Foundations of Fascism: Warring Psychological Theories Struggle to Make Sense of Hitler, Mussolini and You-Know-Who." *Salon*, December 4, 2016. www.salon.com.

Sanchez, Carol Lee. "Animal, Vegetable, Mineral: The Sacred Connection." In *Ecofeminism and the Sacred*, edited by Carol J. Adams. New York: Continuum, 1993.

Scarry, Elaine. *Thermonuclear Monarchy: Choosing between Democracy and Doom*. New York: W. W. Norton and Company, 2014.

Schell, Jonathan. *The Fate of the Earth*. New York: Knopf. 1982.

Schor, Juliet B. *Plenitude: The New Economics of True Wealth*. New York: Penguin Press, 2010.

Schor, Juliet B., and Craig J. Thompson. *Sustainable Lifestyles and the Quest for Plenitude: Case Studies of the New Economy*. New Haven, CT: Yale University Press, 2014.

Schulz, William F. *In Our Own Best Interests: How Defending Human Rights Benefits Us All*. Boston: Beacon Press, 2001.

———. "The Way We Live Now: Security Is a Human Right, Too." *New York Times Sunday Magazine*, April 18, 2004, 1–3. www.nytimes.com.

———. *What Torture Taught Me and Other Reflections on Justice and Theology*. Boston: Skinner House Books, 2013.

Schulz, William F., and Chuck Spence. *Engagement, Innovation, and Impact: UUSC 2012 Annual Report*. Cambridge, MA: Unitarian Universalist Service Committee, 2012.

Shafir, Eldar, ed. *The Behavioral Foundations of Public Policy*. Princeton, NJ: Princeton University Press, 2013.

———. "Introduction" to *The Behavioral Foundations of Public Policy*. Princeton, NJ: Princeton University Press, 2013.

Shelton, J. Nicole, Jennifer A. Richeson, and John F. Dovidio. "Biases in Interracial Interactions: Implications for Social Policy." In *The Behavioral Foundations of Public Policy*, edited by Eldar Shafir, 32–51. Princeton, NJ: Princeton University Press, 2013.

Silko, Leslie Marmon. *Yellow Woman and a Beauty of the Spirit: Essays on Native American Life Today*. New York: Touchstone, 1996.

Sinn, Jeffrey S., and Matthew W. Hayes. "Replacing the Moral Foundations: An Evolutionary-Coalitional Theory of Liberal-Conservative Differences." *International Society of Political Psychology* 20, no. 20 (2016).

Smith, Theophus H. *Conjuring Culture: Biblical Formations of Black America*. New York: Oxford University Press, 1994.

Stenner, Karen. *The Authoritarian Dynamic*. Cambridge: Cambridge University Press, 2005.

Taub, Amanda. "The Rise of American Authoritarianism." *Vox*, March 1, 2016. www.vox.com.

Ttofi, Maria M., and David P. Farrington. "Effectiveness of School-Based Programs to Reduce Bullying: A Systematic and Meta-analytic Review." *Journal of Experimental Criminology* 7 (2011): 27–56.

Weaver, Jace. *Other Words: American Indian Literature, Law, and Culture*. Norman: University of Oklahoma Press, 2001.

Welch, Sharon D. *A Feminist Ethic of Risk*. Minneapolis, MN: Fortress Press, 1990.

———. *A Feminist Ethic of Risk, Revised Edition*. Minneapolis, MN: Fortress Press, 2000.

Welch, Sharon D. *Sweet Dreams in America: Making Ethics and Spirituality Work*. New York: Routledge. 1999.

White, Micah. *The End of Protest: A New Playbook for Revolution*. Toronto: Alfred A. Knopf, 2016.

Williams, Patricia J. *The Alchemy of Race and Rights: Diary of a Law Professor*. Cambridge, MA: Harvard University Press, 1991.

Young, Iris Marion. *Justice and the Politics of Difference*. Princeton, NJ: Princeton University Press, 2011.

INDEX

Abu Ghraib prison, 158–60

abundance: "living buildings" and, 127; understanding of, 117

Ackerman, Peter, 44

Adams, Guy, 73–74

Advocacy Investing, 88–89

agriculture, regenerative, 125–26

The Alchemy of Race and Rights (Williams), 175–76

Alexander, Michelle: on Brown, M., shooting, 60; *The New Jim Crow: Mass Incarceration in an Age of Colorblindness*, 58–59

altermodern: defined, 181; ethics, 182; existentialism, 199–204

altermodernity, challenges of, 181–85, 190

American Dream, 20–21, 203–4; honesty and, 21–22

Anderson, Carol, 155–56

Anderson, Elijah, 147

Anderson, Victor, 170

antiglobalization, 35

Appiah, Kwame Anthony, 71; *The Honor Code: How Moral Revolutions Happen*, 52–56, 77

applied behavioral science, 71–75; cultural change and, 72; decision making and, 73

authoritarianism, 9; characteristics of, 13–14; childbearing values and, 15–16; racial injustice and, 156; rise of, 3, 13, 15; social change followed by increased, 1–2, 14–15; violence and, 13–14

Balfour, Danny, 73–74

Banaji, Mahzarin, 62, 148–51

Bandura, Albert, 159–60

Banerjee, Abhijit, 42; on economic policy, 103–5

B corporations, 32–33, 77; certification, 93–94, 96–97; honor codes, 95; legislation, 96

Beauty Way, 117

The Behavioral Foundations of Public Policy (Kahneman), 73

Behavioral Public Policy (Shafir), 147–48

Benyus, Janine, 125

The Better Angels of Our Nature: Why Violence Has Declined (Pinker), 56–58

Between the World and Me (Coates), 21–22

Beyond Control: A Mutual Respect Approach to Protest-Crowd Relations (Paré, Redekop), 60–61

biases, 72; explicit, 148. *See also* implicit bias

bigotry, 69

biomimicry, 125

Bishop, Matthew, 74

#BlackLivesMatter, 58

Black Lives Matter movement, 15, 58, 59

Blessed Unrest (Hawken), 24, 34–35, 178

Blow, Charles M., 70

Booker, Cory, 17

Bornstein, David, 178–81

Bourriaud, Nicolas, 181–82

Braiding Sweetgrass (Kimmerer), 44

Brown, Michael, 59–60, 62

Brown, Stephanie, 145–47

extractive capitalism, 195; combating, 44, 87, 111, 166

failure, 112; learning from, 101–2, 173, 177–78; of nonviolent campaigns, 46; partial, 177; of strategic nonviolence, 46–47
fallibility-based worldview, 171
fascism, 13
feminist theory, 31, 100
feminization process, 69
Fiske, Susan, 153
Foucault, Michel, 42

Garcia, Jesus 'Chuy,' 91–92
Garner, Eric, 62
Garret, Laurie, 74
Gaskins, Ina Mae, 201–2
Gates, Bill, 78, 80
Gates, Theaster, 28; ecology of opportunity, 181–85; work of, 183–85
Gates Foundation, 74–75
generative interdependence, 16–17; challenges, 194; commitment to, 193; embodying, 43; limitations and risks of, 19–20; paradoxes, 40
geothermal energy, 122
Gibson-Graham, J. K., 30–31, 97–98, 178; on community economies, 98–99
global citizenship, developing, 165
globalization: antiglobalization, 35; indigenous resistance to, 24, 116
Graham, Julie. See Gibson-Graham, J. K.
gratitude: economy of, 116–33; for indigenous peoples, 116–17; Kimmerer on, 117–19
greed, 118
Green, Michael, 74
The Green Collar Economy: How One Solution Can Fix Our Two Biggest Problems (Jones), 124
green economy, 20; structural racism and, 124

Guattari, Felix, 182
Gurría, Angel, 26, 77
Gutiérrez, Gustavo, 51, 203

Haidt, Jonathan, 18
halo effect, 72
Hardin, Curtis, 62, 148–51
Hawken, Paul, 116, 125; Blessed Unrest, 24, 34–35, 178; Drawdown: The Most Comprehensive Plan Ever Proposed to Reverse Global Warming, 120–23, 126–28, 132
Hayes, Matthew W., 18–19, 193–94
Heltzel, Peter, 38–39
Hetherington, Marc, 15–16
Hill, Johnny Bernard, 38–39
historical amnesia, 136–37, 189
Hogue, Michael, 201
Holmes, Barbara, 170
Holocaust, 69
honesty, 21–22
The Honor Code: How Moral Revolutions Happen (Appiah), 52–56, 77
honor codes: abolition of slavery and, 53–55; pay equity and, 95; shifts in, 53; social change and, 42–56; success and, measuring, 75
Hopkins, Dwight, 136–37
humanitarian engineering: community partnerships and, 143; social entrepreneurship and, 138–44; technology and, 144; wind energy and, 139–40
Humanitarian Engineering and Social Entrepreneurship program, Penn State, 138–44
human rights, 4–5; extending, 175–76; respect for, 10; support for, 65–71; violations, 159; violence and, 65–71

identity politics, 4
ideologies, 42–43; rigidity, 47
impact-driven nonprofits, 34–35

struggle centered approaches, 23, 199–200
success, 190; economic, 115, 117; honor
codes and, 75; of nonviolent campaigns, 43–46, 48–49; partial, 177;
social entrepreneurship, 102; social
movement, 49, 55–56; of violent campaigns, 49
sustainable energy, 128–32; geothermal
energy, 122; solar energy, 130; wind
energy, 121–22, 130, 139–40
Sutherland, Lynda J., 196, 205–10
sympathy, circle of, 67, 70–71, 76
systemic racism: impact of, 185; police
violence and, 59–60; scholarship, 60

tactical rigidity, 47
theology of liberation, 38, 51, 110, 136, 203
Thinking, Fast and Slow (Kahneman),
72–73
Thompson, Aaron, 60–62
Tomasko, Robert, 101–3
torture, 158–60
transformative learning, 146
Trump, Donald, 2, 70

unemployed, 99–100
unintended consequences, 196
unjust social structures, economics and,
98–99
urban planning, 27–30; relational aesthetics and, 183–84; social inclusion and, 29

Vailakis, Andreas, 101–3
violence: authoritarianism and, 13–14;
containing physical and structural,
65–71; decline of, 56–58, 66–67; human
rights and, 65–71; physical, 65–71;
police, 65; protests, 64–65; radical

violent fringe, 48–49; reducing, 68;
social change followed by increased,
1–2, 56–58; structural, 65–71, 156–57.
See also police violence, racialized;
white violence
violent campaigns, 43–45; success of, 49
violent racism, 9; resurgence of, 148
visionary pragmatism, 168–70, 190

wage inequality, 94–95, 187–88
Weiler, Jonathan, 15–16
Weilerstein, Phil, 143–44
We Were Eight Years in Power (Coates),
166
white rage, 155–56
*White Rage: The Unspoken Truth of Our
Racial Divide* (Anderson, C.), 155–56
white supremacy, 136; racial justice and,
154; Trump campaign and, 2
white violence, 2, 3; history of, 166; inattentiveness to, 196; moral disengagement and, 166–67
*Why Civil Resistance Works: The Strategic
Logic of Nonviolent Conflict* (Chenoweth, Stephan), 43–46, 48–49
"wicked problems," 143
Williams, Patricia, 175–76
wind energy, 121–22, 130; humanitarian
engineering and, 139–40
Windigos, 7–8, 33, 156; complacency and
delusions, 75; extractive capitalism, 87,
111; failure, 112; infighting, 47, 75; Kimmerer on, 117–18; progress, 191; seven,
195–96; strategy, tactics and basic
principles, 75, 100
Wolf, Martin, 25–26

Young, Iris Marion, 2

ABOUT THE AUTHOR

Sharon D. Welch is Senior Fellow of the Institute for Humanist Studies, a member of the League of Women Voters, and a member of the Unitarian Universalist Peace Ministry Network. She is Affiliate Faculty and served as Provost and Professor of Religion and Society at Meadville Lombard for 10 years. She has held positions as Professor and Chair of Religious Studies, Professor of Women's and Gender Studies, and Adjunct Professor of Educational Leadership and Policy Analysis at the University of Missouri from 1991 to 2007. She was Assistant and then Associate Professor of Theology and Religion and Society at Harvard Divinity School from 1982 to 1991. While at the University of Missouri, Welch was a Senior Fellow in the Center for Religion, the Professions, and the Public, a project leader of the Ford-sponsored Difficult Dialogues Program, and cochair of the MU Committee for the Scholarship of Multicultural Teaching and Learning. Welch is the author of five books: *Real Peace, Real Security: The Challenges of Global Citizenship*; *After Empire: The Art and Ethos of Enduring Peace*; *A Feminist Ethic of Risk*; *Sweet Dreams in America: Making Ethics and Spirituality Work*; and *Communities of Resistance and Solidarity*.

Lightning Source UK Ltd.
Milton Keynes UK
UKHW010425300820
368968UK00015B/387